R0128414606   MARCH 1999

	DATE DUE		

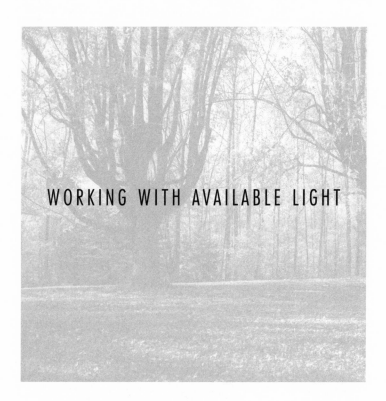

WORKING WITH AVAILABLE LIGHT

WORKING
WITH
AVAILABLE
LIGHT

A FAMILY'S WORLD AFTER VIOLENCE

JAMIE KALVEN

W. W. NORTON & COMPANY / NEW YORK · LONDON

First Edition

The author gratefully acknowledges the support of the Sophia Fund, Margaret Schink, the Open Society Institute, and Sunny Fischer, who is present on every page.

The text of this book is composed in Bembo with the display set in Futura Condensed
Composition by Julia Druskin
Manufacturing by The Haddon Craftsmen, Inc.
Book design by JAM Design
Photograph by Patricia Evans

Library of Congress Cataloging-in-Publication Data

Kalven, Jamie.
Working with available light : a family's world
after violence / Jamie Kalven.
p. cm.
ISBN 0-393-04690-7
1. Evans, Patricia (Patricia Burdick), 1943–
2. Kalven, Jamie. 3. Rape victims—Illinois—Chicago—
Biography. 4. Rape victims—Illinois—Chicago—
Family relationships. 5. Violent crimes—Illinois—
Chicago—Psychological aspects. I. Title.
HV6568.C4K35 1999
362.883'092—dc21
[b]   98-20500
CIP

W. W. Norton & Company, Inc., 500 Fifth Avenue, New York, NY 10110
http://www.wwnorton.com

W. W. Norton & Company Ltd., 10 Coptic Street, London WC1A 1PU

1 2 3 4 5 6 7 8 9 0

For Josh and Betsy

CONTENTS

PART

———

I

1988–89

O N E

———

I T's AS if a deep wound, long buried, has been laid open. Lying beside my wife, I'm confused by my maleness—so hard, so insistent—and feel somehow implicated in her wounding. Every caress feels coercive. Yet there is another kind of touching she welcomes. In the past, I often gave her massages; sometimes as a prelude to lovemaking. Now massage has become a lifeline between us. I imagine my fingers are drawing out the tension and fear that have invaded her body. And for the moment at least, it seems to be so.

She lies on our bed on her stomach. I straddle her from behind, lean forward, and work my fingers through her hair, massaging her scalp. I rub her neck and shoulders, then work down her back. How fragile she seems, this woman who runs marathons, climbs mountains, skis the most demanding trails. Her shoulders and neck, her wrists and fingers seem impossibly delicate. This is a perception I have often had of the children but never before of her: how *breakable* a human being is.

I move down to her buttocks. Years ago she taught me how to make bread. Now I am the baker in the family—a better bread maker than breadwinner, we used to joke—and the children have grown up eating what they call "Daddy's bread." As I massage her there, I am invariably, helplessly, reminded of kneading dough. And vice versa. This is one of the surprises life has held: this ripening of sexual passion over time— the way it deepens and ramifies, embracing not only children but also garden and kitchen in the sexuality of the household.

Looking down at Patsy's backside, I am shadowed by the knowledge that there was a moment when he was in much the same position I am in now. After smashing her in the face with his fists, he dragged her off the lakefront running path, his hands around her neck, choking her. In the middle of a small grove of trees he forced her to the ground and straddled her from behind. With one hand, he yanked her head back by the hair, blood streaming from her face, as he forced his other hand inside her. The perception is hard to absorb: tenderness and cruelty inhabit the same space in the world. All it takes is two bodies.

I massage her strong runner's legs: thighs, calves, and—her favorite moment—feet. She relaxes completely, gives herself over to pleasure. Her feet are endearingly ugly. Misshapen and calloused, they testify to all the miles she has run and skied. Bunions protrude. Her toes are a tangle. Some toenails are blackened or missing altogether. Yet these abused extremities are the sites of such feeling. Thousands of nerve ends converge in the feet. Hence the sensations that radiate through the body when they are rubbed. (And hence the widespread torture tech- nique of beating the soles of the feet: the torturer, like the lover, is drawn to concentrations of nerve ends.) When I have finished—this is part of the ritual—Patsy asks, "Are you sure you did *both* feet?"

Heavy with relaxation, she turns over and lies on her back. A love- ly sight. Amid all my confused feelings of desire and frustration and grief, I feel much simple affection for her body. I stroke the area defined by hips and pelvis—a loose and fleshy drum, as soft as an infant's skin. No number of sit-ups, thank God, will completely elim- inate the hint of a pouch across her abdomen—the residue childbear- ing has left on her body.

We had been together close to ten years before we had our first child. The pregnancy was a revelation for me. After a lifetime of being excited by women's bodies, I found that they finally made sense. Patsy's round belly seemed not a distortion but the missing piece that com- pletes the female form. It was as if she had always been slightly off-bal- ance, then in pregnancy had found her center of gravity.

Bearing a child was, for her, an immersion in her animal nature. Soon after she learned she was pregnant, she stood before a supermar- ket meat counter and sized up an eight-pound turkey, taking the measure of the thing inside her. As the pregnancy advanced, she grew ever closer to the presence within her. A photographer by vocation, she compared the process to the focusing of a lens. Toward the end, she interacted with the fetus constantly—feeling it hiccup and change positions, making out its limbs, head, buttocks. When she was by herself, she was not alone.

I remember being awakened by an August thunderstorm several weeks before the birth and seeing her naked by the shuttered bedroom window, in full pregnant profile, inhaling the night. It was as if the natural world were reclaiming her. No longer simply an individual in the environment, she was herself an environment for another. I came to think of her as a watery sort of ecosystem—a bog or a marsh or a tide pool.

When she felt the first stirrings of life, she laughed.

"It feels like a little fish," she said, "like a fish's tail slapping against the side of the bowl."

For me, it was different. I put hand and cheek on her belly, felt the kicks, made out the shape of foot and buttock. Yet the child was not *there* for me in the same way. Early in the pregnancy, Patsy had a funny, punning dream: she was in the ninth month, awaiting the birth, when she received a phone call. The voice on the other end informed her, "Your baby has been delivered in Buffalo. You must come and pick it up." My experience was more like that—as if the baby were en route toward us, traveling across a great distance, getting closer day by day. One day we would go to the hospital as if to the train station and pick it up.

The second pregnancy was in some ways different. No longer pioneers pushing back the frontiers of the unknown, we knew the shape of the process, knew where it led. We didn't joke, as we had the first time, about the fetus as a blind date. Also, this time there was another male looking on, one deeply implicated in the sexuality of the household: our son Josh, then three years old.

It was Josh who named the fetus. Given a doll for Christmas, he christened it "Tummy" as in "the-baby-in-Mommy's-tummy." We followed his lead and throughout the pregnancy referred to—and addressed—the fetus as "Tummy." After the birth, it took us all a few days to break the habit and get used to calling her Betsy Rose. Today she is wholly Betsy. What the name "Tummy" evokes for me now is how my feelings for my children began as an extension of my love for their mother, how loving her body I felt within me the first gentle fish-tail slaps of love for the life it contained.

For some minutes during the attack, Patsy lived with the thought that it was up to him whether she lived or died, that she would only live if he let her. Overpowered physically, utterly alone, she sought in him something she could appeal to. Prepared to concede the rape, she pleaded for her life.

"You can't kill me," she sobbed. "I have a baby at home."

This falsehood was not calculated. It issued from her deepest sense of what a human being is. He was unmoved.

I massage her breasts, trace the line of her collarbone with my fingers, stroke her cheeks and forehead. It's astonishing how quickly the physical wounds, the visible signs of suffering, healed. The effects of the attack are intensely physical, but they are on the inside. That's how she talks about it. The knowledge, the fear—it's something she carries within her. Harrowing images seize her in the night, and she cries out. I hold her and feel the terror inside her—a shudder in the hollow where she carried our children.

When I arrived at the emergency room, I was met at the door by a woman doctor.

"Your wife has been assaulted and badly beaten," she told me. "She's hysterical. She needs you to be calm. Can you do that?"

I nodded, and she led me to the curtained enclosure where Patsy was being attended by nurses. The police were in attendance, too, at a discreet distance. Patsy was half upright on the bed. She was dressed in a hospital smock. Her running shorts and T-shirt, blood-soaked, lay on the floor. Her face was impossibly swollen; her eyes almost sealed shut by the swelling. A nurse was cleaning caked blood from her face. I took her hand and tried to comfort her. She released a sob and began, in discontinuous fragments, to tell me what had happened.

I didn't know what she was feeling, only that it was overwhelmingly powerful. At one point, there in the emergency room, she spoke of a conversation we'd had the week before about endings, about last things—the last time we'd go out for a walk, the last time we'd awaken to dawn light, and so on. She recalled that I had said, "There'll be a last time we make love."

"Last night," she said, "might have been it."

Our children were born in this hospital. As Patsy labored, her face swollen with effort and pain, I stood by the bed and held her hand: a man, looking on, filled with awed recognition of what it means to be a woman. I find myself saying now words I said then. "Breathe deeply." "Try to stay relaxed." "I love you." Flooded by feelings I haven't the words to speak, I stand by her savaged body and hold her hand. A man, looking on.

T W O

___

$\mathbf{W}$HERE'S MOMMY?"

Betsy was surprised to see me; usually Patsy picks up the children at school. I told her and Josh to get their lunch boxes and come with me. We sat on the curb outside the school: a forty-year-old man in jeans and a work shirt, speaking softly to his four-year-old daughter and eight-year-old son, who listen with startled attention, as if they had suddenly found themselves falling through the air.

"An angry, crazy man hurt Mommy. It happened while she was running. She's in the hospital. She won't be home when we get there."

Betsy's tears were immediate. She leaned against me. I put my arm around her. Josh was very quiet.

As we drove home, I tried to reassure them.

"Mommy was very brave," I said. "She got away. She's going to be okay."

"Why was the man so angry?" Betsy asked.

"I don't know, sweetie. He wasn't angry at Mommy. He didn't know her. She was just in the wrong place at the wrong time."

I parked illegally in the alley. Our co-op apartment building is located at the edge of the University of Chicago campus, across the street from the library and athletic facilities, on a block that includes several fraternities. Parking is a problem. I left the emergency lights on our rust-pocked 1980 Honda blinking on and off.

We entered the building through the backyard. A full city lot, much of it devoted to a flower garden, this is Patsy's domain. Since we had returned two weeks earlier from our annual August visit to her parents in Vermont, she had been addressing herself to the weeds that had thrived in her absence.

Before I left the emergency room, Patsy had asked me to do several things. To call our friend Vera Mihailovic and ask her to come to the hospital. To bring fresh clothes for her to wear home when she was released. And to drop off photos at one client's house, a note at another's. I had been surprised she had the presence of mind to focus on such details.

I went into our bedroom and gathered jeans, a shirt (one with buttons, so she wouldn't have to pull it over her battered head), and underwear. Inhaling the fragrance that emanated from her closet, I felt a sob begin to rise but didn't allow it to surface. There wasn't time.

Our cat—a spirited young calico named Casey—had been inside all day. Frantic to get out into the world, she brushed her body insistently against my ankles. I opened the kitchen door, and she bolted into the backyard.

I made arrangements with friends in the building, Rick and Cindy Chrisman, to watch the children while I was at the hospital, and took Betsy up to their apartment.

Josh went out into the backyard with his baseball glove and ball. As I drove away, he remained in the yard. A solitary figure throwing a ball in the air and catching it, throwing a ball in the air and catching it.

En route to the hospital, I delivered Patsy's photographs. As I walked back to the car, I encountered our friend Martha Friedberg, out for a walk. Growing up, I had known her as the mother of a high school friend, a high-spirited jock. Years later, I discovered she was a poet who wrote with unsentimental lucidity of domestic life. The ardors and griefs that animate her lines are also inscribed in her face, giving her in her seventies a fierce sort of beauty. She greeted me warmly and asked after Patsy. I told her, in a few sentences, what had happened. Her expression reflected back at me the gravity of my words. I hurried on to the hospital.

Patsy now had a broad bandage across her nose. She seemed calmer. Vera was at her side.

When I had asked if she wanted someone to come to the hospital,

Patsy had not hesitated; she had asked for Vera. Born and raised in Yugoslavia—her father was Montenegrin, her mother Serbian—Vera had as a teenager been imprisoned in a Croatian concentration camp during World War II. In 1956 she came to this country, newly married to a Serbian doctor. Soon they divorced, and she was left with two small children. For many years, she had worked at the university as curator of slides in the art department. A fascinating woman—her beauty somehow enhanced and complicated by the plastic eye that replaced the eye she had lost several years earlier to cancer—Vera is passionate, moody, unrestrained in her affections and disaffections, full of emotional color and drama.

Commenting on her own emotional reticence, Patsy once observed that she has always been drawn to women like Vera who give strong, full-throated expression to their feelings. She herself is pitched differently. Her manner can seem distant and diffident; the flow of her feelings into expression subterranean. As a result, others sometimes misread her. It takes a while to discern the passionate turbulence beneath her seemingly calm self-command. Several lifetimes ago, when we were first getting to know each other, this reserved Vermont Yankee with her no-nonsense air of competence and self-control told me that she fantasized about being a torch singer belting out songs. And over the years, she has had a special fondness for rough-voiced singers like Janis Joplin and Joe Cocker who give the impression of risking everything on the song they are singing, holding nothing back. She, by contrast, holds a great deal back. Yet when unimpeded, she is wonderfully eloquent, expressing herself with clarity and force, making her own soulful music. I savor these moments, even when her eloquence is animated, as is often the case, by anger toward me.

A nurse came with a fresh cold compress. For my benefit, she described the damage to Patsy's face: broken nose, broken eye socket, a gash in her nose apparently left by his ring. Before releasing her, the nurse said, the doctors wanted to run some tests to check for possible damage to her eyes and nervous system.

While I was gone, a doctor had stitched up her nose.

"I told him to be sure to do a good job," Vera said. "We don't want our beautiful Patsy to have any scars."

The nurse asked one of us to leave. Emergency-room policy was that only one person at a time could stay with the patient. I walked Vera out to the waiting room. Once past the emergency-room doors, we embraced. The last time we had been in this hospital together had been the day Betsy was born. Patsy used to joke that Vera was responsible for our having children. Once, as we lingered over one of her wonderful meals, Vera had announced, "What we need around here are some little babies." The line had become part of our household vernacular. We repeated it, imitating Vera's accent, as we edged up, after years together, on the decision to have children.

Now Vera spoke of her love for us, of Patsy's strength, of the quality of our marriage. I only half heard her. What struck me was that she didn't seem surprised. Composed and grave, she seemed to be encountering something familiar, something she recognized.

I returned to the emergency room. Patsy was reclining, with her head tilted back. A still point amid the activity around her. Her swollen face was a mask I couldn't see behind. She took my hand. She seemed at once immediately present and very far away.

The call from the emergency room had been alarming not because the person on the other end of the line told me what had happened but because she didn't. She had refused to answer my questions, and her reticence had conveyed what it was meant to withhold: Patsy had been sexually assaulted. I didn't know how badly hurt she was. Running across campus to the hospital, I knew only that she was alive. Everything hung on a verb tense. When I saw her, touched her, heard her voice, my senses were flooded by her physical presence. Something terrible had happened—I knew that—but the first and dominant emotion I felt was relief that something worse had not.

Hours passed. We were waiting for X-rays to be taken. Vera returned and sat with Patsy, while I filled out insurance forms at the desk. When I finished, I paced the halls. The emergency room reflected the population of Chicago's South Side: overwhelmingly black and poor. For the most part, people sat near the television set in the waiting area. They sat with the patience of those whom experience has taught not to expect much from institutions. Police officers came and went, accompanying crime victims and suspects in need of treatment; often the cops too would stand around for long periods, waiting to question someone. The emergency room was a world unto itself. A peculiar floating world that confounded one's sense of time. Perhaps that was its true function—to convert emergencies into bureaucratic ordeals, desperation into boredom.

WE MET in the mountains. The year was 1971. Patsy was teaching French and skiing at the Colorado Rocky Mountain School, a private school on the west slope of the Rockies. I was hired to teach anthropology.

Just out of college, I had grown up in the Hyde Park–Kenwood neighborhood on the South Side of Chicago near the university, where my father was a law professor, and had attended Wesleyan University in Connecticut during the political and cultural turbulence of the late 1960s. Five years older, Patsy had grown up in Burlington, Vermont— the family business was the ferry company that provided service across Lake Champlain—and had attended Skidmore College in upstate New York during the early 1960s. In some respects, we almost belonged to different generations. She seemed at once vastly experienced and somehow naïve.

Tall and graceful, she had long tawny hair and watchful eyes. Poised and reserved, she didn't impose herself on others. I loved the way she moved. Her body was beautiful. It was also strong and autonomous; it had other uses than to please men. What, I wondered, would it be like to make love with such a woman?

I soon knew.

The basis of our deepening friendship was a shared appetite for travel and physical adventure. Patsy had spent years abroad. Studying in France and Germany. Working on a kibbutz in Israel. Traveling overland from Europe to India. Working on development projects in Morocco and Tunisia. And on whatever continent, at every opportunity, heading for the mountains to ski or climb—mountains anywhere being a sovereign realm in which she was at home.

My life, too, had been full of movement during those years. Backpacking and mountaineering out west—in the Sierra Nevada, the Sawtooth Mountains, the Wind River Range. An expedition on Mount Logan in the Yukon. A motorcycle journey from Paris to New Delhi. A year spent living in a village in the foothills of the Himalayas.

Until I met Patsy, it had never occurred to me that a beautiful woman might want to share such experiences—to be a companion rather than a fantasy one carried as part of one's gear. I had never known anyone like her. I loved the way she inhabited her body, and through her body the world. Her beauty was illuminated by her vitality. During our early days together, I felt like a boy in the presence of a woman—amazed that she was in my life and had admitted me to hers.

After spending a summer together in a primitive cabin in the Rockies, we traveled in 1970–71 to South Asia for six months during which, by chance, we witnessed the Indo-Pakistani war over Bangladesh from several perspectives. We were in Lahore on the eve of the war; in Delhi the night it erupted; and afterward were among the first Westerners to enter the bereaved city of Dacca.

We returned to the States unsettled by what we had seen. It no longer seemed possible to knock around South Asia, to travel and climb, without performing some useful function. In my case, vague aspirations to be a writer—I had published a few small pieces—began to harden into a sense of vocation. I set out to become the sort of journalist who combines an appetite for firsthand experience of distant realities with the craft to make his explorations immediate to readers back home.

Patsy shared this vision. She had always traveled with a camera. Now she decided to make photography her profession. A novelist friend once asked her how she became a photographer. She understood, the friend said, how writers are made—"They're born with pencils in their hands"—but photography, perhaps because of the technical apparatus involved, seemed different to her. Patsy was unsure how to respond, but it occurred to me later that she has always been a looker, someone who takes the world in through her eyes. Early in our relationship, I used to get irritated when we were out walking together and she would drift out of the conversation as her eyes became engaged by something in the environment we were passing through. "You're not listening to me," I would snap, a creature of the word who didn't yet recognize that for her the eye had priority.

We spent two years in San Francisco. Full of plans to return to India as journalists, we lived and worked with the sense that life was elsewhere. Patsy studied photography, and I submitted to writing as a daily discipline. We thought of ourselves as apprentices, learning our crafts. I felt the need to withdraw from friends and family, to exile myself, in order to become a writer. Storms of grandiosity and self-doubt blew through the rooms where I spent my solitary days—rooms located in various houses and apartments throughout the Bay Area in which, to minimize our expenses, we stayed as house-sitters. Groping to locate the real issues in our lives and work, we lived among other people's things and slept in other people's beds.

Our lives revolved, in tight orbits, around one another. A note that had been present but muffled while we were on the road became stronger. Being out in the world was a kind of refuge for Patsy; on unfamiliar terrain, she was bold and resourceful. It was at home, on intimate ground, that she sometimes seemed oppressed by unnamed sorrows. At such times she would become distant and wordless. Guilty and confused, I was confounded by her silences. Her reserve had been part of what had drawn me to her; it promised much. More and more, though, it felt like a withholding of herself. We began to talk about her "problem."

When we first became lovers, I had been thrilled by the idea of Patsy and bewildered by the reality. Something was missing. Some range of movement and expression was denied her. She seemed half-formed, like a bird with stunted wings, a dolphin whose flippers had not fully developed. At first I didn't recognize her sexual unhappiness. For a time, her willingness to do what I wanted to do when I wanted to do it had been enough. As we grew closer, though, her sexual fluency began to give way to stuttering distress. When we made love, a strange dislocation occurred. Her effort was not to enter the experience but to absent herself. It was as if she had to numb herself before she could bear to be touched. To my alarm, the lovely body I embraced in the night came to seem uninhabited.

Nothing in my experience had prepared me for this. I talked and talked, as if there were some misunderstanding I could clear up, some argument I could make that would persuade her. She listened and said little. Often we arrived at impasses where I waited for her to respond and she stared back at me in mute distress. Her pain seemed to lie beyond the reach of language. She just stared at me. I didn't know what she was feeling. I didn't know what she saw. At moments of deepest distress, her face became puffy and swollen, as if bruises from some injury deep inside were ripening outward.

As we were about to return to Asia, the trajectory of our lives changed. My father died. He had been working on a book about the American tradition of freedom of speech. He left an unfinished first draft of more than a thousand pages. This manuscript posed a painful dilemma: on one hand, it was unpublishable in the form he left it; on the other, it was too good to put aside, too precious to cede to death. The solution, insofar as there was one, was for me to edit and, where necessary, to rewrite and supplement the manuscript.

I returned to Chicago and set to work. Patsy followed. Isolated by my absorption in the book and oppressed in my parents' house, she became increasingly depressed and restless. When an opportunity to reenter the world came in the form of a Fulbright fellowship, she took it and spent nine months in Paris doing a photo study of Gypsies. Distance proved clarifying for us. Soon after her return, in a ceremony held in the garden of her parents' home in Vermont, on the side of Mount Mansfield, we were married.

THREE

Doctors came and went. They probed Patsy's wounds and did tests to evaluate the damage to her nose and eyes. She didn't tell them in any detail what had happened; they didn't ask. Unlike the police, whose questions had been directed toward determining the specifics of the crime and developing a description of the criminal, they sought through their questions to locate the sites of injury in her body. One doctor, a woman, asked if she had been raped, in order to determine whether certain antibiotics should be administered. No, she replied, she had gotten away before he could penetrate her with his penis.

Sitting beside her, I experienced emotions as questions. *Anger? Guilt? I-told-you-so?* I had often felt uneasy when she went out running alone or when she went off on a photo project in a tough area of the city. I had curbed the impulse to restrain her. It had seemed like an issue between us, a matter of *me* trying to impose restrictions on *her*, rather than a question of her freedom and safety in the world. And now?

A policewoman entered the curtained cubicle. She said they had apprehended a suspect who matched the description Patsy had given them: a black male, wearing a dark baseball cap and a red jacket. They wanted to bring him into the emergency room to see if she could identify him. He would be handcuffed, she assured Patsy, and wouldn't be able to hurt her. Patsy's grip on my hand tightened.

Several minutes later, the policewoman returned with another officer and the suspect. A black teenager. Just a boy, I thought. He looked
frightened.

I sensed something emanating from the police officers. It wasn't so
much overt pressure to identify him as a sort of wishfulness, almost a
yearning that he would prove to be the one.

Patsy was certain he was not.

As I worked on my father's book, life quietly, almost stealthily, closed
in on me. We moved into an apartment in a building I used to pass
daily en route to and from high school track practice. Our marriage
ripened into a family: first Josh, then Betsy. As the children grew and
our apartment shrank, I rented an office on the fourth floor of the
Chicago Theological Seminary, next door to the nursery school I had
attended as a child.

The work on my father's book went on and on. The aim was to
advance the process of composition while keeping it *his* book, while
keeping faith with his intentions. The editorial process this gave rise to
was at once compelling and perplexing: a matter of trying to follow
the direction of his thoughts while restraining the impulse to change
his mind by way of his prose. I found myself inside a vast, intricate puzzle, from which friends feared I might never emerge.

Held in place by my circumstances, I rediscovered Hyde
Park–Kenwood. When I first returned, I had felt isolated by my grief
and my task. I had found the neighborhood claustrophobic as only the
place where one grew up can be, but over time that changed, and I
recovered a powerful, almost primitive, sense of place.

Bounded by the Lake to the east and by all-black neighborhoods to
the south, west, and north, Hyde Park–Kenwood has sharp definition.
It is an integrated, middle-class enclave, surrounded by the largest con-
tiguous African-American settlement in the country. It assumed its
present form during the 1950s and 1960s—shaped by an "urban
renewal" process that was driven by the interests of the university. Years
ago Mike Nichols, who attended the U of C and got his start in local
clubs on Fifty-fifth Street (torn down as part of the "renewal"), joked
of racial integration in Hyde Park: "Whites and blacks, shoulder to
shoulder, united against the poor."

The area of Kenwood where I grew up was a place of tree-lined
streets and grand houses. It was a middle-class white neighborhood,

with academic families living, sometimes beyond their means, in the mansions of a bygone era. And it was an elite black neighborhood—the preferred address of prominent African-American businessmen and professionals, politicians and entertainers, who had the means but didn't have a wide range of neighborhoods to choose from. It made for a singular mix.

My father had grown up on the North Side, then had come, as a freshman, to the U of C in 1932. Thereafter he left the South Side for an extended period only once: during the war he was stationed in Alberta in western Canada, where he met my mother. He was at home in Hyde Park. We often took long walks together. We would walk through the neighborhood to the Lake, along the lakefront, sometimes stopping to skip stones, then walk home again—talking all the way. Once I had lost interest in playing catch (he never did), that was the primary thing we *did* together: walked and talked. Our conversations were, for me, a domain of freedom and delight; I loved talking with him. When my mother phoned me in San Francisco, her voice girlish with amazement, to tell me that he had died, my first thought was, But who will I *talk* with now?

As it turned out, the conversation didn't end with his death. It not only continued but in some respects deepened and intensified. Dwelling within his manuscript, brooding on the intellectual and emotional riddles it posed, I became a fierce walker. Each day, sometimes more than once, I would leave my desk and roam the streets. Sometimes, unable to sleep, I would walk the neighborhood in the middle of the night.

I found the streets of my childhood largely intact. A maze of memories and associations. To move through them was to move through my history, to retrace the map of my identity. I walked with hungry eyes, trying to unlock the significance of sights seen countless times before, looking for clues.

Full of longing to explore the world, Patsy had cast her lot with a man whose great adventure was coming home. She made the best of it. Chicago was no more home to her than Paris or Delhi. She approached it as a foreign place. On journalistic assignments and while working on her own projects, she wandered the city with her cameras. Soon she knew her way around better than I did. She did photo studies of various neighborhoods, documented life along the Chicago

River, did a series of photos of people waiting at bus stops, and pursued a project, begun years earlier, of photographing mothers and daughters of different ages and backgrounds.

Working primarily in black and white, she typically approached her subjects from a perspective in the middle distance, neither detached nor intrusive, at once respectful and inquiring. She rarely used a flash or artificial lighting; she preferred to work with available light. In the most varied settings, what drew her eye was human figures against richly textured backgrounds—individuals embedded in the weave of the world. Her work as a photographer was informed by the same qualities of honesty that sustained and confounded our marriage. An inability to say more than she knows. A refusal to force perceptions. A quality of sympathy edged by uncertainty. Every photo posed a question.

More interested in other people's lives than her own, she seemed to have found her calling. She was never happier than when out in the city, on the move, shooting. The small, quiet Leica cameras she used came to seem part of her—a natural extension of her way of moving through the world.

An adventurer in the midst of everyday life, she showed me my place in a different light, disclosing the strange in the familiar. Assigned to do a series of photos of the South Shore Country Club, she returned with pictures that could have been taken in Africa or Asia. When I was a boy, the South Shore neighborhood was predominantly white, and the club was a private institution. Today it is a public institution, renamed the South Shore Cultural Center, and serves a community almost completely African-American. In one photo, three black children sit under a canopy on what was once a private beach. Silhouetted against the sand, their bodies seem to emerge from the rectangle of shade in which they have taken refuge from the sun. In another, a black couple unpacks a picnic on the closely cropped lawn of the main country-club building. Grand and dilapidated, the building seems deserted. The man and woman have an air of unawed ease about them, as they prepare their afternoon on the grass, in the shadow of the imposing building. Unless one knew otherwise, one would assume these photos were taken in a Third World country emerging from colonialism. They helped me better understand why I had found postcolonial India strangely familiar.

On another assignment, Patsy photographed a huge public-works project known as the Deep Tunnel—a vast tunnel, 33 feet in diameter, being constructed beneath the Chicago River. (Its purpose: to divert and hold excess rainwater, produced when heavy storms exceed the capacity of the sewer system, and thereby to prevent the overflow of polluted water into rivers and the Lake.) This assignment yielded one of her most mysterious and affecting images. Taken from a catwalk high in the tunnel, it affords a commanding perspective on this strange space, opened by men and their machines, some 250 feet below the ground. In the foreground are several railroad cars and workers in hard hats; in the distance, the receding tunnel. Light has been brought down from the world above. Lamps illuminate, and make humanly habitable, this dark place in the interior of the earth. The lamps are powerful, yet the light from them is poignantly faint. It is resisted and absorbed by the masses of rock that bound the hollow of the tunnel. Light dances off puddles and hard hats. In the receding distance, it imparts softness to the ragged rock walls of the tunnel, making it a thing of soft folds, gentle turnings, and mud-slick surfaces. People often stare at the photograph for a while before they recognize how feminine the space is. Sometimes they laugh out loud or blush. Only then do we tell them that when she took the photo, Patsy—wearing a rain poncho to hide the fact from the city workers who shepherded her through the tunnel—was eight months pregnant.

A LARGE man with a thick mustache stepped through the curtain and introduced himself.

"Dorociak."

He was the detective handling the investigation. I had noticed him in the emergency-room waiting area hours earlier. He took Patsy through her account of the assault again. His manner was reassuring, but his words were unnerving.

"Did he fondle your vagina?" he asked.

"Yes," Patsy answered.

I said nothing but was startled that the same verb could be used to describe the hand that caresses and the hand that violates.

Dorociak left. A few minutes later, he returned with another policeman, who took a series of photos of Patsy's face with a Polaroid camera. This was a practice they had adopted, Dorociak explained, because when rape cases come to trial—long after the wounds of even a severely beaten victim have healed—the defendants often tell a story of consensual sex. The photos help counter that strategy. They keep the injury visible.

The officer took pictures of Patsy's face from several angles. Usually behind the camera and hence rarely photographed, she lay motionless: the photographer, her eyes swollen shut, as subject.

F O U R

_____

I T WAS only after we had been together for a number of years that Patsy began to allow herself to really *feel* what she experienced in my embrace. Although I didn't fully recognize it at the time, her willingness to suffer through the fear and pain that often overcame her during sex was a measure of deepening trust between us. Together we worked to clear a space for understanding, and she began to find words for things she had never talked about before.

As we talked, it became apparent that she had developed strategies for handling casual sexual relationships, as with men she had encountered while moving through the weightless dimension of travel. What was tortuously difficult for her was sex in a medium of deep feeling. It was as if the more she felt, the less she could express physically.

This pattern led us to wonder if she had been violated in some way as a child by someone she knew and trusted. There were other symptoms. At certain points when making love, she would be overcome by a need to rub her eyes. She said she felt as if someone had dropped a bag over her head. So visually alive to the world, she suffered from a kind of erotic sightlessness. She seemed to have no desire to look at me; she could scarcely bring herself to do so. It was as if she were blind. Or I were invisible.

I felt like a figure in a folktale living under a curse. In winning her love, I lost her sexually. The more she came to trust me, the more disabled she became. Sometimes, she reported, as I moved inside her, it was as if I had become a stranger.

PATSY WAS becoming agitated. The pain from the beating she had suffered, masked for a time by adrenaline and shock, had intensified. The doctors wouldn't give her any painkillers until her head had been X-rayed. The swelling was worsening. She could only open her eyes with great effort. I couldn't bear to entertain the possibility that the blows to her eyes had damaged her vision.

An orderly came to take her to the X-ray room. Vera and I were not permitted to accompany her. Later Patsy reported that she had been frightened. The orderly was a large black man. He rolled her through the corridors of the hospital to the X-ray room. He was behind her. She couldn't see him. Cheerful and talkative, he tried to make conversation.

"Your husband must have really popped you one," he said.

No, she explained, she had been attacked while running on the lakefront. It occurred to her that he probably saw lots of women who had been beaten by their husbands.

The orderly was sympathetic, but it bothered her that he referred to the incident as "a mugging."

"I thought to myself, *No*, that's not what it was."

After more than six hours in the emergency room, Patsy was finally released. She was enveloped by pain. She had taken pain medication, but it hadn't yet begun to work.

It was after ten when we got home. The first thing she wanted to do was take a shower to wash the dirt and dried blood out of her hair.

Before I went up to the Chrismans' to get Josh and Betsy, I helped her into bed. Concerned that the children would be alarmed by the sight of her face, we tried to soften the impact by covering the worst of her wounds with an ice pack and turning down the lights.

When I brought the children into the room, she was greatly moved.

"It was," she said later, "like hearing their voices on the phone when you've been away for a long, long time."

Betsy went directly to her mother, lifted the ice pack, and looked under.

"I want to see," she said, "I want to see."

Josh kept his distance. He stood at the foot of the bed, with tears in his eyes, looking on.

After putting the children to bed, I lay down beside Patsy. We couldn't easily embrace because of the condition of her face. I wasn't sure how to touch her, wasn't sure she wanted to be touched. She lay on her back, half sitting, her head propped up by pillows. I lay beside her, clothed, dozing and waking to check on her.

"Could it happen again?" she asked in the middle of the night. "Could the same guy attack me again? Is he after me?"

I rose at dawn and made coffee. I was moved by a strong nesting impulse, such as I had felt in the weeks before each child was born. An impulse to clean up, to wash the windows, to make various deferred repairs, to eliminate the threat of nuclear war, to fill the apartment with the smell of baking bread.

I brought a cup of coffee to Patsy in bed. The swelling had receded somewhat. Her eyes were visible. Her body was stiff and sore.

"I feel like I was in a car accident."

She hadn't slept all night.

"I was rigid. Like the trunk of a tree. I was afraid to close my eyes—afraid I'd be pulled back into that bubble."

Despite the weight of the swelling, she had kept her eyes open. "To make sure the world was still there."

When she closed her eyes, she said, the violence came rushing at her. What filled her mind was not so much the struggle, which seemed "dreamlike," as the moment he grabbed her. The moment of collision.

"I was still free, and at the same time I knew: this is it, this thing I have always feared."

She spoke in a tone of hushed amazement.

"I feel as if I looked into a black hole. He dragged me to the edge, and I looked in. I recognized it. It was the place where torture victims and people in concentration camps are thrown like pieces of garbage."

She didn't seem to be speaking metaphorically but to be describing an actual place.

"It was such a bright, sunny day, but it got very dark for a while."

FIVE

———

I SOMETIMES think one reason running is such an important part of our lives is that it's a way of playing out nomadic energies while living in one place. Patsy never seems more wholly herself than when she runs. Running is, for her, a form of expression; an exercise of autonomy and self-possession. It represents an essential freedom in her life—a freedom that became especially important to her after we settled in Chicago, so far from the nearest mountains.

Although intensely athletic, she was not a runner when we met. She learned to run; it didn't come easily to her. At first she bounded, landing high on the balls of her feet, jarring her body. Over time, she developed a strong, efficient stride and proved to be a gifted distance runner. As she got older, she continued to improve. She began to compete in road races, and soon our shelves were littered with trophies she had won in her age division.

Our opening to the natural world in Chicago is the lakefront. That is where we run. So large one can't see across it—at the horizon, water shades into sky—Lake Michigan gives this most inland of cities a coastal feel. Most of the lakefront remains undeveloped. To the far south, the steel mills of South Chicago and Gary block access to the water; and to the far north, on Sheridan Road, high-rises stand at the water's edge. But for a continuous stretch of more than twenty miles the lakefront is open and public. Parkland extends along most of its length, embracing beaches and boat harbors, playgrounds and athletic facilities. Lake Shore Drive, a major north-south artery, runs parallel to it. The most genteel of the city's highways—the speed limit is forty-five miles per hour and trucks are prohibited—the Drive presents drivers with ever-changing perspectives on Lake and skyline.

It's hard to imagine life in Chicago without the Lake. Yet I know there are those who live and work far to the west in the city for whom it is little more than a rumor or a place one visits occasionally as one might visit the Grand Tetons. And I once heard a community organizer say that there are children in the public housing developments on South State Street, less than a mile from the Lake, who have never seen it. For millions of Chicagoans, though—rich and poor, black and white, members of every urban tribe—the Lake is a touchstone. A necessary perspective.

I have been running on the lakefront for more than thirty years now. When I began at the age of twelve, long-distance runners were like members of some obscure monastic order. To strip down to shorts and run through the streets was seen as deviant rather than exemplary behavior. One provoked curiosity, jeering challenges to one's manhood, and an occasional beer can thrown from a passing car. I recall with particular clarity a woman sprawled on a park bench, drunk, her nylons bunched around her ankles, who shouted after me with robust good cheer, "To hell with the body!"

All that has changed. Today the ideal of fitness reigns. I'm uneasy about this. About the oppressiveness of the new physical ideal for those who simply would rather not. About the boring health-club-produced bodies-by-Nautilus, the packaged muscles that have never done a day of manual labor. About the hint of intolerance for physical and sexual variety conveyed by all those sculpted delts and pecs, lats and quads. About the extraordinary success of American capitalism in taking the simplest of activities—running!—and generating a vast market of commodities around it. I have come to feel over the years that perhaps the woman on the park bench had a point.

Yet the fitness movement has also had benign by-products. Chicago is rigidly segregated. The dominant pattern is fiercely defended ethnic autonomy. When I began running in the early 1960s, territorial boundaries were clear. The divisions of the city extended to the Lake. Efforts to erase those boundaries were met by violence. But in recent years a steady stream of runners and cyclists, hungry for distance, have quietly reshaped the social geography of the lakefront. A serious runner requires a large range; a cyclist, even larger. By degrees, segregated patterns in the use of the lakefront are yielding to the runners and cyclists ranging up and down its length.

The seven-mile stretch of lakefront that lies between our home and downtown runs parallel, on the other side of the Drive, to some of the poorest neighborhoods in the city. This is where the original "Black Belt" was located, and it's the only point at which the poor have direct access to the lakefront. During periods of peak use—weekends and holidays in seasonable weather—a continuous stream of people flows up and down the path. Men and women, young and old, black and white. Runners and walkers. Cyclists, like exotic birds in their brightly colored outfits, wing by. Occasional police cars, both marked and unmarked, patrol the path. A vaguely reassuring presence, but because I don't feel threatened, I don't see them as anything more than part of the passing parade.

Even on days when the lakefront is relatively deserted, we encounter familiar presences: the regulars. There is the art historian, an expert on the Renaissance, who rides by, prim and erect, on his three-speed bike. The literary scholar who sometimes bikes with a broom that he uses to sweep broken glass from the path. The powerful, white-bearded man—an aging Neptune—who once swam across the Lake and is today an avid windsurfer. The robust older man in hiking boots, often wearing a knapsack and binoculars, who would look as if he had just emerged from a month in the backcountry were it not for the fact that he is smoking a cigar and pushing a small child in a stroller.

There are also several mentally disturbed men, who seem to spend the day wandering the lakefront and talking to themselves. I think of them as clinging to the rocky shore—in danger of being swept away not by the Lake but by the city.

Whatever the time of day, one man in particular—tall, black, ill-coordinated—always seems to be there. Judging by the different points on the lakefront where we have seen him, he must cover twenty miles a day with his odd, disorganized stride. For him, as for us, the rhythms of movement and the sight of the Lake seem to steady the soul. He doesn't look like a homeless person.

"I imagine," Patsy observed one day as we ran by him, "that he has a mother somewhere preparing hot meals for him and washing his clothes."

Then there is the bearded, professorial-looking man who marches up the lakefront, tapping out his strides with a closed umbrella and holding a silk handkerchief unfurled before him like a flag. At the top of his lungs, he sings the theme music from the movie *The Bridge on the River Kwai*: "Dada da dada dat dat da." His manner is menacingly cheerful. He is said to have been, before the fall, an evolutionary biologist. Once quite dapper, he has become grimier and grimier. His shirt looks as if it had been marinated in oil, and his colorful handkerchief has been replaced by a tattered piece of cardboard crudely colored with red ink. When we pass him, he barks out—as if it's the refrain to his melody—"Hey, losers!" or "Cowards!" or "Cripples!" or "Masons!"

Finally, there are the runners. Among them are perhaps a dozen individuals I have saluted almost daily for years. In most instances, I don't know their names and we have never exchanged words. Yet we share a sense of fellowship. There is a special quality to the greetings runners exchange—the smiles and nods, waves and upraised fists. Across boundaries of age and gender and culture and race, despite great differences in ability, runners greeting one another are, in a way, intimates: each knows something of what the other feels.

IT WAS a Wednesday afternoon. Unusually warm for mid-September. Only the light—golden, slanting—was autumnal. Patsy had an hour free before picking up the children at school and so decided to go for a run. We were training for the Chicago Marathon, to be held at the end of October. So we were running more frequently and farther than usual. Often we ran together, but when we couldn't coordinate our schedules, we ran separately. Several times that month, on weekends, Patsy had run downtown and back alone.

Our minimum run, a distance of about seven miles, was to a point around Forty-third Street: a set of basketball courts just beyond a playground and a small building containing rest rooms. Beside the building there is a small hill and a grove of trees. An overpass bridges the Drive, connecting the lakefront to some of the poorest neighborhoods in the city.

When I was a boy, Forty-seventh Street marked the northern boundary of the area in which one felt secure on the lakefront. Beyond Forty-seventh Street was assumed to be hostile territory. But that boundary had dissolved years ago, and Patsy had made this run—with me and alone—many times. It was routine. She had noted the place where we turn around as a spot from which she might take a photograph of black youths playing basketball against the background of Lake and skyline.

Running alone, Patsy was always alert to possible dangers. If she saw someone on the path who looked suspicious, she would give him a wide berth and speed up. As she passed the rest rooms at Forty-third Street, she noticed a man standing by the men's-room entrance. She registered the information, moved to the other side of the path, and sped up a little. This maneuver, she reported later, was not driven by alarm. She compared it to the way one reflexively anticipates and avoids a collision in traffic.

About fifty yards beyond the rest rooms, as she approached the basketball courts, she heard footsteps behind her. She turned, saw a man in street clothes, and knew. He was upon her before she had time to react. He must have run on the grass beside the path, silently stalking her. He got his arm around her neck in a stranglehold, pulling her head back.

"My first thought was, Oh, God, this is it. This thing I've always feared is going to happen. I had an overwhelming sense of being sucked into this familiar bubble."

"Why," she cried, "why are you doing this?" She screamed for help. She screamed my name. She wasn't conscious of screaming. She only knew she was screaming because she heard her voice.

He stayed behind her. When he spoke, his voice was cold and flat.

"I'm going to kill you," he said.

She struggled to get free.

"I remember thinking, There must be some way to get out of this hold. I wish I knew what to do. I wish I knew some technique to get free."

She tried to kick him between the legs, but it was impossible.

He spun her around and struck her—one, two, three, four times—in the face with his fist.

"I was amazed. As he hit me, I remember thinking, My God, what's this? Never having been hit in the face by a man's fist, I just didn't know what it was."

The blows blinded her. She had the impression he aimed for her eyes, so she couldn't identify him. His violence was not measured, not graduated; it was absolute from the start.

"He wanted to see blood."

She continued to struggle, but the strength had drained out of her. "I kept thinking, I can't believe I'm not stronger. I didn't realize what a mess he'd made out of me."

He got behind her again. With both hands around her neck, choking her, he dragged her off the path and toward the Lake. He was trying to get her out of sight behind the hill. She could tell where they were going by the terrain. She was aware of the trees. She felt close to passing out.

"I couldn't breathe. I couldn't scream. I couldn't move. I couldn't do anything. I could only hear, 'I'm going to kill you.' That's all I heard. Right in my ear. 'I'm going to kill you.' I was so completely afraid. I thought I was going to die then. I had lost track of where I was. It was just me and him. I thought I was dead. There was only death."

She could see her body lying on the familiar ground she had run over so many times. The corpse of an unidentified woman. She could even see how the newspaper story would read. It was this outcome, this trajectory, that she struggled against.

He pushed her, facedown, to the ground and got on top of her. He had one arm around her neck. He pulled down her shorts and forced his hand inside her.

"I want to have sex with you," he said.

It was a relief when he forced her to the ground. She could breathe. Rape meant more time to live. She was amazed a man would want to have sex with a woman covered with blood. Able to breathe, to take in air, she became hysterical.

"You can't kill me," she sobbed. "I have a baby at home."

He said nothing.

Lying facedown on the ground, she somehow became aware of the diamond ring on the fourth finger of her right hand. Her mother's wedding ring. (Her mother had begun wearing the wedding ring of her own mother, who had recently died, and had given Patsy her ring.) When Patsy ran, she turned the diamond toward the inside of her hand so it wasn't visible.

"I'll make a deal with you," she said. "This ring is worth a lot of money. It's worth three thousand dollars."

"Take it off."

"How do I know you'll let me go?"

Straddling her bloodied body, he said, "You'll have to take my word."

The momentum of his violence, cruelty building on cruelty, was for a moment deflected. He hadn't attacked a woman running in shorts and a T-shirt expecting to carry off diamonds. He sat up, removed his hand from inside her, and grabbed her hand to examine the ring.

She isn't sure what happened next.

"Out of the corner of my eye I saw a bicycle go by, and I must have started screaming. The woman on the bike heard me scream, she didn't see me. I must have had a burst of strength. The woman remembers seeing me, covered with blood, running toward her."

When Patsy saw the cyclist on the path, she recovered "the idea that life was out there somewhere." She had a surge of power at a moment when he, confused by the ring possibility, had loosened his grip.

"I had gotten away from him. I was running toward the woman, and I have never ever been so happy in my life."

Having lived for a time with the expectation that she would never again see a kind human face, she recalls the horrified young woman, standing by her cycle, frozen with fear, as having the most beautiful face she had ever seen. "She looked like an angel."

He came after her. She ran to the young woman and got behind her bike.

"Help me, help me," she cried.

A male cyclist stopped and pushed the two women to the highway. They tried to wave down a car. For a few moments, her attacker remained on the bike path.

"That's him," she said. "That's him."

The male cyclist stepped toward the man but retreated when he reached inside his jacket and made a threatening gesture as if he had a weapon. Patsy saw him kick at a young boy riding by on a bicycle. He didn't flee. He walked back over the overpass and disappeared into the desolate streets on the other side of the Drive.

They waited for some time beside the highway before anyone stopped. Patsy was drenched in blood. Cars passed. Eventually, a doctor stopped, then a nurse. The police came. At the center of a widening group of people who were trying to determine what had happened and to give her aid, Patsy felt a great sense of elation. She later compared her escape to the experience of giving birth.

"It was," she said, "the happiest moment of my life."

SIX

———

WHEN WE woke the morning after, only a handful of people knew what had happened. In the course of the day, word spread quickly. I spent much of the day on the phone. I made calls to family and friends. I listened to the ringing at the other end, knowing the shock I would deliver—the depths that would open—when the receiver was picked up.

The most difficult call was to Patsy's parents, Dot and Lew, in Vermont. I worked up to it by making other calls, refining my account of what had happened. When I called, Lew answered.

"Oh my God," he said.

Dot came on the line. Telling them was different from telling even our closest friends. I felt I was informing them of a terrible injury inflicted not only on their daughter but on them. Their choked silence recalled the moment, sitting on the curb outside the school, when I told the children.

By midday, friends started to come by. Some brought gifts of food. Our refrigerator was soon full of dishes with special healing properties—several varieties of chicken soup and, in the same spirit, from Indian friends, chicken curry. The apartment filled with flowers from the gardens of neighbors and, via local florists, from far-flung friends and family. One friend gave Patsy a small scented pillow—a curious and somehow appropriate gift. There were many such consoling gestures. Small fortifications of the domestic.

Friends came and went throughout the day. They included people who are present in my earliest memories, like Flo and Herb Levy, owners of the house on Forty-eighth Street that my family had shared during the 1950s, and Hans Zeisel, my father's collaborator, still vital and prickly in his eighties. It was easy to see them as members of our extended family. Other friends, contemporaries, were harder to describe in kinship terms, yet were no less woven into our lives, and we into theirs: David Epstein, a childhood friend, and his wife Deborah, to whom we had introduced him in our backyard. And Bill Pinsof, a college friend whom I rediscovered when we returned to Chicago, and his wife Suzan, with whom Patsy had formed a sisterly bond.

There were also friends of more recent vintage: Rebecca Janowitz, a lawyer and gun-control activist, with whom I had collaborated on various community initiatives. Practical-minded and aware of how violent incidents disrupt households, she had Patsy dictate a grocery list over the phone and later arrived at our door pushing a shopping cart full of groceries. And Bernardine Dohrn and Bill Ayers, who had recently moved to Hyde Park from New York, trailing behind them clouds of celebrity and notoriety, not yet dissipated, from the days during the 1960s when they were leaders of the Weathermen faction of Students for a Democratic Society.

The atmosphere was quietly festive—a celebration of Patsy's survival—but there was also an undercurrent of helplessness. It was as if the attack provided an opening for others to acknowledge how frightened they were. Several women said, "If this can happen to *Patsy* . . ."—Patsy who is so strong and competent and experienced—then no one is safe. Again and again, in the faces of women friends I saw the same look of recognition: This thing I have always feared.

In our home, surrounded by the concern and generosity of friends, I felt displaced. Others were able to express outrage much more fluently; for me there was so much else to feel. I was aware, too, of a distance that had opened between women and men: a man had done this to Patsy. And I was a man.

Several male friends spoke of wanting to go out and catch the rapist, of what they would do to him if they caught him. I was impatient with such talk. It struck me as a retreat into fantasy. My impulse was to urge

people to go out and use the lakefront. Do so prudently, do so together, be mindful of the dangers, but refuse to surrender the common
ground. What is demanded, I wanted to say, is that we act together to
reclaim and enlarge the common ground. That was the form *my* fantasy took: hundreds of people—young and old, women and men, black
and white—running on the lakefront. Already, within twenty-four
hours of the assault, I realized, I was writing an op-ed piece in my
head—looking for a way to push back, in my fashion, with words.
Vaguely embarrassed that I wasn't moved by dreams of vigilante justice, I kept my vision to myself.

Usually uncomfortable being the center of attention, Patsy now
seemed beyond all that. It was as if everything nonessential had burned
away. Czesław Miłosz observes somewhere that when war or a com-
parable catastrophe strikes a human community, poetry becomes as
essential as bread. A catastrophe had struck our household, and I sensed
in Patsy a hunger for language equal to her experience. She listened
hard to the well-intentioned words of friends, as if weighing them
against the absolute measure of her experience.

Although she didn't challenge it, the therapeutic idiom in which
some expressed their concern—the attack described as "a traumatic
event"—sounded hollow in her presence. Nervous patter. Whistling in
the dark.

I noticed that others, upon learning the details of the assault, often
retold the story they had just heard back to Patsy, shaping the narrative
to underscore her heroism. I particularly recall Bernardine—vivid and
full of feeling—emphasizing the power and courage with which Patsy
had responded. It was a generous impulse: to tell the story in a way that
would help her heal. No more able to falsify her experience than to
fly, Patsy listened to the narratives urged on her with a polite, non-
committal air.

Amid all the talk, I was grateful for the words eloquently unspoken
by some—for the looks and embraces that said what could be said and
no more.

In the course of the day, I tried to insulate Patsy by fielding phone
calls and orchestrating visits. Periodically I checked in on her. She
remained in a peculiar heightened state: stunned, elated, amazed. She
reported her perceptions to me with economy and urgency. Like bul-
letins from the front.

During breaks between visits and phone calls, she returned to bed.

Late in the afternoon, I lay down beside her for a few minutes. She spoke of the man who attacked her, of how after she escaped, he had remained on the footpath for a few moments.

"I felt connected to him," she said. "I felt guilty, as if I hadn't held up my end of the deal."

I wasn't sure what she meant by her "end of the deal"—completion of the rape? giving him the ring? her death? I hated the idea that *he*— this faceless pronoun—was now a presence in our lives and that she, in some sense, remained in his grasp.

She couldn't shake the feeling, she said, that he had let her go rather than that she had escaped. It was as if, having lived for some moments with the thought that it was up to him whether she lived or died, her survival could only be due to his generosity.

"I still feel connected to him," she said. "Almost grateful to him for not killing me."

"I've got an idea for a photo project," Patsy said that night, as we got ready for bed. "A photo-collage on what happened." For the moment, she sees this as something she will do for herself; she isn't sure whether she will exhibit it or publish it. She isn't sure what it will be, but two elements in it are clear. It will include an image of her battered face. And it will include an image of Betsy.

I shudder when I think of his hands. He is faceless, a force, almost an abstraction, but his hands—grabbing Patsy, smashing her face, choking her, violating her—are immediate to me. They are reflected in her wounds. We say she "got away," we say she "wasn't raped," because he forced his hand, not his penis, inside her. Yet is that act any less monstrous, any less violently dehumanizing than penetration by his penis would be? The penis is blind. The hand is the instrument of the mind, the hand is aware, the hand chooses to inflict torment. The hand is wed to the eye.

All day Betsy had been full of questions for Patsy. "Why couldn't you run away?" she asked. "Why couldn't you hit back? How big was he? Did he have big muscles? Did he wear dark glasses? How did he grab you? What did he *want*?"

Trying to be helpful—and to reassure herself that this is a problem that has a solution—she suggested a countermeasure: when Patsy goes running, she should carry a hammer in a bag with a zipper. If some-one attacked her, she could unzip the bag and hit him on the head with the hammer.

As I checked the doors and turned out lights, Betsy called to me from her bed. I went to her. Josh was asleep in the upper bunk. She was frightened. She asked me whether the bad guys came *inside* people's houses and hurt them. I assured her that our doors were locked, that she was safe in the apartment. She then asked the question that, unasked, had played through most of the adult conversations I'd had that day.

"Daddy," she asked, "how *much* does what happened to Mommy happen in the world? Does it happen a lot or just a little?"

SEVEN

Looking out from our first-floor apartment on the garden in back and shrubbery in front, we sometimes almost forget the rest of the building and imagine that we live in a cottage. The illusion can't be sustained for long, though, for our apartment is one of twenty-four units in a four-story brick building. Constructed in 1927, the building comprises three tiers of eight apartments. The apartments are small. Ours, one of the largest, is nine hundred square feet; two bedrooms and a study radiating off a central living room–dining room. We live on the ground floor in the middle tier. The mass of the building bears down on all sides. Neighbors' heads regularly bob past our windows, coming and going by way of the back stairs.

It's like living in a village. The backyard functions as a sort of commons. Originally occupied by a fraternity, the lot was acquired by the co-op in the 1930s. The fraternity house was torn down. A structure at the back of the lot—the chapter house of the fraternity—was left standing. Known to several generations of children in the co-op as the Spooky House, it's used today as a storage shed. Grass and trees were planted on the lot. A flower bed now forms a border around the yard. Any co-op member who wants to garden is welcome to cultivate a section of this border. There is a patio with a picnic table and barbecue grills.

Different co-op members use the backyard in different ways. Patsy and a few others are passionate gardeners. Some barbecue regularly and entertain outside. For families with young children, the yard provides a domain where the children can roam freely, while allowing the parents easy surveillance of their activities. Some members of the co-op never come out into the garden. Yet they may partake of it in other ways. Several elderly residents sit by their windows for hours at a stretch, perhaps with a book or a drink close at hand, observing the small dramas that unfold in the garden.

The fact that twenty-four households share the yard gives rise to interactions more refined and nuanced than would be the case if all we held in common were the mailboxes and laundry facilities. If we are to enjoy this space as individuals, mutual consideration and tolerance, frequent accommodations and occasional interventions are required. This dynamic gives rise to a rich politics of everyday life. Patsy and I have come, over time, to play central roles in this dynamic—she as coordinator of the communal garden, I as chair of the co-op board. In view of our roles, a matter of some awkwardness for me was the issue of cats in the backyard—specifically, our cat. Patsy felt strongly that Casey should have her freedom, that she should have her full creaturely life. Some of our neighbors saw this as an abuse of the common space. I was prepared to yield to their objections, but Patsy was insistent. She couldn't bear the thought that Casey wouldn't have access to the physical world.

Looking to the west from the garden, across University Avenue, one sees Regenstein Library. The primary research library on campus, Regenstein ranges over the better part of a square block like a mountain range of books. Built in 1968, it occupies the site of what had been Stagg Field, the athletic stadium, where U of C teams had played Big Ten football until 1939, when Chancellor Robert Maynard Hutchins, to the horror of the alumni, abolished intercollegiate competition in the sport. It was under the west stands of Stagg Field that Enrico Fermi and his colleagues in 1942 conducted the first controlled nuclear chain reaction, releasing the power of the unbound atom into the suddenly fragile world of human affairs.

We moved into the building in 1977 after Patsy returned from her Fulbright year in Paris, but I had been aware of it many years earlier. As a high school runner, I had worked out almost daily at Stagg Field and, during the winter, in the neighboring field house. Emerging from the locker room into the evening air, the first thing I saw was the building at Fifty-sixth and University. Warm light emanating through the casement windows combined with the sensations in my spent body to generate a sense of well-being—a glow I associated with the building long before it became home.

The composition of the co-op is mixed: young and old; university and nonuniversity; and, in recent years, black and white (though for much of its history, whether by chance or design, it was all white). Narrative lines, crossing generations, intersect on this spot. The oldest resident, Gladys Campbell, approaching a hundred, was a charter member of the co-op. A poet and emeritus professor in the humanities, she taught my father freshman composition in the early 1930s. Another neighbor and friend, Lorraine Wallach, taught in the Lab School nursery school in the early 1950s when I toddled in to begin my undistinguished academic career. Jamie Redfield, a classics professor at the university, who grew up in the building, returned decades later to start a new family with his second wife. Dorothy Freedman, a friend of my parents to whom we had become close, had moved into the building, at our urging, after her marriage collapsed. The passage from the large Kenwood house in which she and her husband had raised five children to a small apartment in a cooperative had been difficult. It was only several years after she moved that the building became her home. Two developments seemed to make the difference: her deepening involvement in the garden and the ardent friendship she formed, across the decades, with Gladys Campbell. Ben Brown, a retired auto worker and union man, who lived on the second floor above us, had no such problems adapting to the co-op. As soon as he saw the building, he knew it was the place for his wife Abby and himself. An English teacher, Abby had grown up in Hyde Park; her mother had owned and operated a rooming house on Kenwood Avenue. What had attracted Ben, Abby once told me, was not only the location of the building and the spacious garden but the "modesty" of the apartments. The proportions— small private dwellings, large common space—fit well with his political values. As we worked together on building maintenance projects, Ben and I often talked politics. I was struck by the way his politics grew out of his neighborliness. His concern with the asbestos lining the pipes in the basement, the shenanigans of the Chicago City Council, and the threat of nuclear war were all of a piece.

Living in such a densely inhabited setting, one learns a lot—sometimes more than one wants to know—about one's neighbors. We are presences (however slight) in one another's lives, characters (however minor) in one another's stories. There are close friendships within the co-op, but even when the relationships are marginal, even when the dominant feeling is dislike, there is a sense in which we are, less by virtue of the depth of our contacts than by their dailiness, witnesses to each other's lives.

The day after Patsy was attacked, many of our neighbors looked in on us. The assault, we learned from a note slipped under our door by Dorothy Freedman, had occurred on Yom Kippur. She wrote:

> I've thought about you all night, brave, strong, beautiful Patsy. I feel so terrible that you were hurt. But I am so immensely grateful that you are still here, that in those awful moments you pulled upon your strength to live, and fought so valiantly for your life—for yourself and for Jamie and Josh and Betsy. On Yom Kippur we say God lays before us each a choice, life or death, and says to us—choose life. And you surely did. You must have found in yourself a strength you never could have known lay there—under all human doubts and frailties. I love you, dear Patsy, and am so glad you came through.

Throughout the day, neighbors brought food and offered help. One resident of the building, unaware of what had happened, came to our back door to complain about our cat. She said that Casey, on the outside looking in, was provoking her housebound cats through her screen door. She spoke with a sharp sense of injury and violation. I stared at her for a moment, uncomprehending, then went out and collected the cat.

Gladys Campbell, recovering from a broken leg, couldn't come by to see Patsy, but her companion and caretaker, Carrie Wagner, did. A former schoolteacher from Belize, Carrie had entered Gladys's life some eight years earlier, after Gladys had taken a fall and broken her hip. We had assumed the fall was the beginning of the end. Gladys, however, had rebounded. Her recovery was due, I came to believe, not only to her strong constitution but to the tonic effect of her friendship with Carrie. The two women lived to talk and were endlessly curious about each other's lives. Their laughter—Gladys's robust peal, Carrie's warm lilt—formed a single music.

Patsy once tried to catch some of this in a portrait of them sitting side by side, but the light refracted through the lens eclipsed the quality of their relationship by accentuating a detail we scarcely noticed in their presence: the fact that Gladys was very white and Carrie was very black.

Carrie and I spoke in the garden. She wanted to know about the man who had assaulted Patsy. She gestured toward her rich dark skin.

"Was he?" she asked.

I nodded. She looked back at me in silence. I don't have a word for the pain that showed in her face.

I ASKED Rick Chrisman how the children had behaved during our hours at the emergency room.

"They were very still," he said. "Like little sparrows under the shrubbery on a hot day."

That stillness stayed with Josh during the days that followed. He would often sit or lie on the bed beside his mother. He would read or work on some project. He didn't say much, but he was powerfully present—porous and watchful, absorbing everything.

He didn't speak of his own distress. It surfaced in other ways. There were moments when he cried a disproportionate amount about some small matter—as if it provided an opening for large feelings.

Three days after the attack, he got up from the dinner table and burst into tears. He said his stomach hurt.

"Do you have a stomachache?" Patsy asked.

"Not an ache, a *pain*."

"Are you sad about what happened?" she asked.

"No, it's not *that*," he replied emphatically. "It's not that."

Four days after the attack, he built a refuge in his room: a blanket draped over his desk and stool. He took a light, books, baseball cards, stuffed animals, and writing materials and retreated several times in the course of the day into this secure nest.

For the most part, though, he was quietly and attentively present, listening to the adult conversations swirling around him.

On the way to school, about a week after the assault, the children and I talked. One of the things we would have to struggle with, I said, is that the world which is so beautiful in so many ways also contains such ugliness—like the attack on Mommy, like gang violence, like war.

"And like *slime*," contributed Betsy.

Amused, Josh said gently, "No, he doesn't mean that kind of ugliness."

I encountered Dorothy Freedman in the garden. She asked how Josh was doing. I told her the story of Casey and the bird.

The previous year, on an autumn afternoon, Josh—then seven years old—had gone out in the backyard with his Instamatic camera and his pal Casey. I watched them for a while from the window. The little calico stalking windswept leaves. Josh behind the camera, his mother's son.

I went back to work. A few minutes later, Josh came into the study. He had a few grayish feathers in his hand.

"Dad, Casey almost got a bird."

He led me to Casey in the garden. She didn't have the bird. She was searching for it in the bushes. She was agitated. Her movements were abrupt. There was a rustling in the leaves. She pounced. Her prey was a small sparrow. Somehow, in that moment, it looked like something more exotic, like something rare.

The cat stepped back and the bird disappeared into a pile of leaves. I told Josh to get Casey. He grabbed her by the scruff of the neck. We stepped into the kitchen, and he put her down. Her first steps left a smear of blood on the floor, confirming what I already knew: the bird was beyond hope. I grabbed Casey and roughly washed off her paws. When I put her down, she resumed searching for the bird—in the same avid, herky-jerky manner—among the plants and under the sofa.

Josh wandered off to his room. A while later, I found him on the sofa reading a National Geographic book he had found on his bookshelf titled *Saving Our Animal Friends*. Then, later that afternoon, he showed me a picture he had drawn in pencil: a bird on the ground and a large black thing descending from the sky—the paw of his adored cat.

A week later, sitting in the car, en route home from school, he told Patsy, "I know the title for a story I'm going to write."

That night he wrote this story:

It was a wind fall day. I had let my cat out. A rattel in the leavs. A tubbel in the weeds. I looket behind me. I saw a littile brown and white creature that looket like a bird and a big brown and gray creature that looket like my CAT CHASEING A BIRD. I couldn't run becuase my leg was asleep but I limpet over to my cat. She was still chasing the bird but then she caught the bird. Blod on her teeth and blod on her paws. It was so sad. After my cat was in I went back outside. I saw the feathers that the bird lost. I picked one up. My hand started to beat and a tear out of my eye. It was just too sad to look at. Bird's were my best friend's.

The title of the story was "God Was Ther At the Wrong Time."

I told Dorothy that watching Josh move from bookshelf to drawing to narrative, I had felt as if I were witnessing the invention of culture in the face of the unacceptability of reality. This was, I said, a model for how I thought he would respond over time to the attack on Patsy.

We continued to talk about the children's reactions. I observed that one of the things that was unsettling for them was the realization that the parents they rely on for protection are themselves so vulnerable.

"Yes," she said. "The paw."

EIGHT

ONE OF the first phone calls I made the morning after the assault was to Quentin Young, our doctor, to request a prescription for sleeping pills for Patsy. His wife Ruth answered the phone. She was a good friend, a magazine editor with whom I had worked and on whose judgment, kindness, and tact I had come to rely. When I told her what had happened, she suggested we contact a woman named Barbara Engel. The organizer of a city-wide program for victims of sexual assault, Engel had recently stepped down as director of the program in order to spend more time at home with her young son, Ruth said. She lived in the neighborhood and had been helpful after an elderly relative of Ruth's had been mugged.

Later that day, Patsy spoke with Barbara Engel on the phone. Three days after the assault, she came by. She proved to be a woman in her late thirties with soulful eyes. She was pregnant. When she arrived, I was on my way out the door with the children so she and Patsy could be alone. We said hello in passing. Later Patsy reported the substance of their conversation.

When others had commented on her courage and resourcefulness, Patsy had been confused. She said she couldn't imagine responding other than she had. Barbara Engel seemed to have convinced her that women respond to such attacks in a wide variety of ways. Faced with the strength of the attacker, heightened by his rage and excitement, victims are often immobilized, Barbara said. Many are immediately overwhelmed; some even lose the capacity to scream. So it was not a foregone conclusion that Patsy would react, as she did, with sustained resistance. The key thing she did, according to Barbara, was to deflect the course of the attack by talking with him about the ring. He was like someone wearing earphones, she said, someone hearing only his own music. It was critical that Patsy managed to break through.

The following week Barbara came by again. This time I stayed and joined the conversation. She had a resonant way of talking I found consoling.

"Be gentle and patient with yourself," she urged Patsy. "This will take longer than you want it to. Much longer. You have to have faith in the healing process and not feel like there's something wrong if it takes a long time to feel like you did before the assault."

Some things, she added, may never be the same.

"There'll be things that will be different about how you put your life back together."

She warned that it was a process that would almost certainly get worse before it got better, that Patsy might feel worse six months or a year after the assault than she did now.

Patsy confided to Barbara that she was troubled by her feelings of connection to the man who had assaulted her. In the moments after she got away and for the first few days afterward, she said, she had felt "guilty," as if she owed him something.

This was perhaps, Barbara suggested, an instance of a phenomenon observed among hostages called the "Stockholm syndrome." Named after a six-day hostage-taking incident in Sweden in the course of which the hostages came to feel empathy and affection for those who had seized them, the Stockholm syndrome theory seeks to explain the tendency of hostages to speak well of and feel gratitude toward their captors. It's not, she emphasized, a matter of masochism or of slavish identification with the power of the aggressor. Rather, it arises from a natural survival instinct. At some primitive level, beyond conscious control or calculation, you experience the violent person who threatens your survival as life-giving. Caught in his absolute control, you search for and seize upon any evidence of his rationality and humanity. The upshot is that you may, for a time, feel gratitude toward your tormentor. Such a dynamic, she added, seems to operate as well with battered women who stay with and defend the men who abuse them.

I ventured a general observation. I was amazed, I said, by the degree to which a violent attack such as Patsy had suffered imposes an inexorable logic. The violence displaces the world, and the victim enters into the logic imposed by the violence.

"You can't know," Barbara said sharply, "unless you have experienced it directly, what it's like to be in the absolute control of such a person."

I wasn't sure how she intended this remark. I took it as a warning: Don't presume to understand too quickly.

Patsy said she wished she knew more about the man who attacked her, that she thought it might help her make sense of what had happened if she "knew his story." Barbara replied that it's possible to know quite a lot about him—not through particulars but through the larger pattern of which he is part. Among other things, he has, on the evidence of the character of the assault, done this many times before.

"If he saw me on the street," Patsy asked, "would he recognize me?"

"Probably not," replied Barbara.

TALK, TALK, talk. On the phone. With friends who came by. Telling the story again and again. Words and phrases recurred. The narrative took on a shape and began to harden. I spoke of the brutality of the assault, of the force of the hatred. It was like a lynching, I said, the lynching of a woman. I emphasized Patsy's resistance and resourcefulness. She got away, I said, but only after a terrifying struggle during which she was savagely beaten and choked.

I assumed the role of interpreting the event to others. A necessary role, I wonder now, or my own way of coping? I'm not sure. It wasn't that I had a secure sense of what had happened. It was more a matter of narrative self-defense—resisting the stories proposed by others, trying to keep the question of what happened open, and so preserving the possibility of future understanding.

"Do you think," Patsy asked several days after the attack, "that someone went home that night and said to his wife, 'I saw the most amazing thing today on Lake Shore Drive'?"

For her, this was a genuine question. Others seemed ready to assume that heartless or timid people drove by and saw the attack but didn't intervene. I wasn't so sure. What would one have seen passing by at fifty miles per hour, inside the perceptual tunnel that driving on a highway so often is? Did passing drivers witness the assault and drive on? Perhaps. There is no way of knowing. What we do know is that a number of people—the two cyclists, the doctor, the nurse—came to Patsy's aid.

Nor did I assume, as some of our friends seemed to, that the police were to blame, that they could have prevented the assault if they had been doing their job. Unless it's seen as a dereliction that the police were not present at the moment the crime was committed, it was hard to fault them. A police car, patrolling the lakefront, had come upon the scene within minutes of the attack.

Why did I resist such explanations? They were, after all, possible. Was I trying to protect Patsy? Was I concerned that if she embraced them, she would feel even more vulnerable and exposed than she did? Perhaps that was part of it. But more fundamentally, I felt that in the absence of evidence, such details would skew the story I was trying to bring into focus. They were distracting and, in a way, falsely consoling. They skirted the more difficult perception that one can be embedded in the world one moment and so hellishly alone the next.

Returning from an errand, I met our friend Aparna Dharwadker, an Indian graduate student in English, pushing her young daughter in a stroller. She had just come from visiting Patsy and had heard for the first time the story of the attack. With tears in her eyes, she recalled Auden's "Musée des Beaux Arts":

> About suffering they were never wrong,
> The Old Masters: how well they understood
> Its human position; how it takes place
> While someone else is eating or opening a window or
> just walking dully along. . . .

The human position of suffering. The recognition that evil occurs not in some other dimension but in the thick of life. Amid human busyness and distraction. Here.

Each week the *Hyde Park Herald* and the *University of Chicago Maroon* publish local crime information: a listing of reported crimes of different sorts during the week with the date, time of day, and location. There is also a map, showing where the crimes were committed. Meant to encourage realism and vigilance, this feature has a curious effect. It collaborates with denial by inviting one to locate evil elsewhere. "I look at the crime maps in the *Herald*," a friend remarked, "and because the crime was committed on the next block, not my block, I tell myself my family is safe." All my life, I realized, I had done this: placed evil elsewhere, if only a block away, in order to feel at home somewhere. A Palestinian friend, Mona Khalidi, who lived through the shelling of Beirut in the early 1980s, told me that she and her family managed to convince themselves that they lived in "a safe neighborhood." Shells were falling all around them, but they were landing elsewhere.

"The attack on Patsy could have happened anywhere," I wrote a friend several weeks after the assault. "That is one of the things that is so disturbing about it. What we are struggling to come to terms with is not some perception of Hyde Park as a uniquely dangerous place but rather the perception that men can hate women that much, and, even more fundamentally, that evil is not elsewhere."

"You say nothing of the criminal," she wrote back, "and yet I feel you have said everything when you remark that 'evil is not elsewhere.' A conclusion too frightening to live with; but you and Patsy are on the other side of that fright now, and do live with it. Civilization is a frail membrane, with raw brutality just on the other side."

She went on to offer a caution: "I fear you will let the anger go out of you. I beg you not to adopt a merciful attitude toward the cruel, and though it is true that 'evil is not elsewhere,' not to allow this cruelty to soar too quickly into the philosophical or the abstract or the general. I sense that Jacques Maritain is right when he says that 'evil is truly and substantially someone.' To which you add: a someone sometimes not elsewhere, but here."

I recognized this as good advice. For the first time in my life, I had used the word "evil," with its unfamiliar, acrid aftertaste. Yet even this strongest of words—by inviting, almost demanding, sweeping general-ity—was, in its way, a cheat, an evasion. *Evil is someone.* But how were we to think about the "someone" who assaulted Patsy? All we knew about him, apart from what could be inferred from his act, was that he was a man and that his skin was black.

NINE

USUALLY FULL of restless energy to get out into the day, Patsy did-
n't go outside for several days after the assault. The apartment came to
seem like a nest wrapped around her body: a nest constructed not of
twigs and string and scraps of paper but of artifacts and texts and
images. A nest lined with books and photographs.

Living among Patsy's images, I sometimes feel I inhabit her imagination. On the wall over the stove in the kitchen, among baskets and
wooden implements hanging in artful array, is a photo, taken before she
thought of herself as a photographer, of the rooftops of Kabul and
another of the terraced walls of the Chamba Valley in the Indian
Himalayas, the valley just north of the one where I had lived when I
first went to India. In the living room are several photos—documentary in character yet as mysterious as dream fragments—yielded by her
year in Paris. In one, a young Gypsy girl, smiling broadly, stands beside
a window that opens out on a ramshackle yard, while an older girl
looks back into the room from the outside. In another, a Gypsy woman
in a flowered dress, on a carpet with a flowery motif, extends her body,
smoke curling back from the cigarette in her mouth, and reaches out
to a small boy lying passively on his back. One must look closely to see
that she is pacifying the child by rubbing his penis.

Elsewhere in the living room: An army of litters, pushed by nuns, advances on the healing waters at Lourdes. A corner barbershop in Pilsen, a Latino neighborhood in Chicago, with a hat hanging from a hat rack and pictures of Pancho Villa in the window. A photo by a French photographer, Marc Riboud, of a camel bazaar in Rajasthan.

In the days after the assault, Patsy spent much of her time in bed, resting and reading. The children would often lie beside her; they would work on their projects and play their games on our bed. Her back supported by several pillows, a shawl across her shoulders, and the bedspread pulled up over her legs, she looked comfortable. Thinking of her body several days earlier lying, bloodied and alone, on the ground, I was flooded by a perception of the kindness residing in objects. The thought was new to me: physical comfort has moral claims. Not as self-indulgence or denial but as a humane and rational response to the pain and desolation that can be inflicted on a human body.

Our bedroom contains no photographs by Patsy, but there are, over the bed, two pictures that reflect her taste. One is a print of Manet's *Bar at the Folies-Bergère* which she had brought home from a French Impressionist exhibition at the Art Institute. The other is a poster for a centennial celebration of the work of Imogen Cunningham, a photographer we had known in San Francisco toward the end of her long life. The photo was taken in Yosemite Valley. Tiny and delightfully homely—an impish crone with a camera around her neck—Imogen peers around the trunk of a massive sequoia at her subject, a beautiful young woman, nude and vital, who meets the photographer's eyes with her own direct gaze. The image—old woman, young woman, ancient tree—is strangely consoling. Less evocative of erotic delights than of some larger history of desire.

PATSY REENTERED the world by degrees. Several days after the assault, she emerged from the apartment for the first time. Stepping outside, blinking in the light, she seemed, after a summer in the sun, pale and delicate. She was self-conscious about her bruised face. We walked around the block.

"I felt horribly exposed," she told me later. "I was terrified, even though you were with me, that someone might grab me."

What was so unnerving, she explained, was the knowledge of how *quickly* you can be ripped out of the world and isolated by violence.

The next day Deborah Epstein picked Patsy up and took her downtown. She insisted that Patsy, without regard to price, buy the sunglasses of her choice.

Two weeks after the assault, looking out at the world from behind her elegant new sunglasses, Patsy went out in public for the first time. The occasion was the rededication of Rockefeller Chapel at the University of Chicago. The chapel, which stands in imposing isolation at the center of campus, had been closed for a year for renovations necessitated by the discovery of a crack in the ceiling. At the request of Bernard Brown, the dean of the chapel and a friend, Patsy had made a photographic record of the restoration process.

This is the sort of work she loves. Some of her favorite assignments have involved documenting large building projects. Wearing a hard hat, she has explored various construction sites and once photographed from the ground up the construction of a large public sculpture by Joan Miró that stands opposite the Picasso sculpture in the Loop.

The word "chapel" is a misnomer applied to Rockefeller Chapel. (As someone once said upon seeing it for the first time, "Only a Rockefeller would call *that* a chapel.") Although built in 1928, it contains little structural steel. It was constructed in essentially the same manner as the great medieval cathedrals: stone upon stone. Hulking and austere, it doesn't possess the improbable lightness generally associated with the Gothic. (The Romanian historian of religions Mircea Eliade wrote in his journal, soon after his arrival at the University of Chicago, of "the mysterious Rockefeller Chapel, which resembles an Aztec imitation of a Gothic cathedral.") Yet within its thick walls, space soars. It's here that the community comes together to celebrate, to observe, to remember. Year after year, it's the setting for graduations and convocations, weddings and funerals, concerts and town meetings.

The strongest of my associations with the chapel is the memorial service for my father held there several months after his death. It was the moment I realized he was not coming back. I was brought to that recognition by a ritual called "the Tolling of the Bourdon." Slowly, the largest bell in the chapel belfry was struck, then struck again. It was a sound of piercing beauty. Each tolling of the bell marked a year of my father's life. Sixty years passed as if measured in heartbeats. Until that moment, I had adapted to his absence as to a long separation; it was as if he had gone on a journey and would someday come home. But the bells denied my accommodation. As they announced his passing, they seemed to bear him away. Finally, the last note was struck, drifted off over the South Side, and faded.

In order for workmen to reach the ceiling of the chapel, it was necessary to erect scaffolding to the height of eighty feet. A crew of eight worked for more than a month, building upward, section by section, level by level, occupying the space. In the process, they transformed the chapel into an immense tubular hive. Once the scaffolding was in place, craftsmen set to work. With rock and country music playing on transistor radios, they advanced on several fronts. Some cleaned the ceiling and rebonded loose tiles to the vault. Others applied coats of acoustical sealant to the porous limestone. Workers stripped and waxed the woodwork. Electricians cleaned and rewired the chandeliers. Painters brightened the plaster side walls. And Patsy happily clambered around on the scaffolding, talking with them and taking photographs.

As the work on the ceiling progressed, brightly colored mosaics— lost for decades beneath a layer of grime—emerged: bands of color running along the ribs that extend over the nave, medallions bearing more than a dozen different images which recur at intervals on the ribs and are concentrated over the chancel. Patsy spent many hours at the highest level of the scaffolding photographing these details. Another photographer, with whom she sometimes collaborates, was unwilling to go out on the more exposed parts of the scaffolding. So I occasionally helped carry her equipment and arrange the lighting. Working late at night, eighty feet up under the limestone vault, alone in the vast cathedral space, we reminisced about the rock climbing we had done earlier in our lives.

Before the scaffolding came down, Patsy took a series of photos that disclosed it to be a work of art. An intricate sculpture. As it was dismantled and the open space of the chapel was restored, we felt a touch of grief. Once gone, the scaffolding seemed like something we had dreamed.

The chapel was full on the day of the rededication. Again words were spoken and music sung in sacred space. Dean Brown expressed gratitude to those who had played roles in the restoration of the chapel—the Rockefeller family, the president of the university, the architects, the contractors, and so on. When he came to Patsy's name and spoke of her photos, his voice momentarily caught with emotion.

The time came to sing hymns. Patsy used to sing in choirs and in college was a member of a singing group. This is clearly something she misses in our nonchurchgoing life. When she opened the hymnal and read the words, she was overwhelmed by the power of the language. Here at last were words equal to her experience. Bread for the hungry. She was too moved to sing.

HAD I ever given thought to what the days following a sexual assault might be like, I doubt I would have imagined the quality of light that touched our lives during those first few weeks. The feelings that dominated were awe at the force that had struck Patsy down—such as one might feel toward a tornado or flood—and gratitude that she had survived. It was a time of thanksgiving.

At about this time, I read a newspaper account of a woman who had been kidnapped and, over a period of twelve hours, gang-raped. When the police had found her, naked and bleeding, on a West Side street, she was in a state of euphoria: she had *gotten away*, she had *survived*, she was *alive*. More vividly than the cruel details of the assault, her elation testified to what she had suffered. Patsy was clear about this: sexual violation, as she experienced it, had been an assault on her life. What had surrounded her, what she had struggled against, what she had escaped was annihilation.

During those first days, we didn't talk much about the sexual character of the assault. We didn't avoid the topic; it just wasn't at the center of our attention. We would, it appeared, pass through relief over what had not happened before engaging what had.

Patsy's physical wounds healed quickly. As the bruises faded, her face, looking out at the world, had a quality of unclouded clarity. She was radiant. She seemed to give off light. Others saw it too. "She's so beautiful," one friend remarked, "and I don't just mean in a physical sense."

Seventeen years after we met and more than a decade after we married, I felt, in my wife's presence, something akin to shyness. Like a soldier returning from combat, she had, in some mysterious way, been transfigured by what she had survived. Things had been disclosed about her that I might never have learned in the course of a long life together. Just what, I wasn't sure, but I sensed it was fundamental.

Patsy rejected any suggestion that her survival was her achievement. She insisted that it was "luck"—a fortuitous change in circumstances—and not her own actions that had enabled her to get away. Others countered that the changes in the circumstances might not have saved her were it not for her sustained resistance. She remained skeptical. She didn't think of herself as a helpless person; no need to dissuade her of that. In a way, that was the point: under assault, "inside that bubble," she had been completely overpowered and rendered helpless. She seemed determined not to lose sight of that.

Had the circumstances been different, her resistance might well have proved futile, but that didn't change its essential character. I recalled Dorothy's words: "God lays before us each a choice, life or death, and says to us—choose life. And you surely did." Barbara Engel had said that rape victims, at the moment of attack, are often disoriented and immobilized. Yet Patsy knew from the first instant what she was resisting; she had, in a sense, been resisting it most of her life. I almost laughed at my impulse to celebrate the habits of resistance to men which had so often confounded me. Was it possible that what, at the intimate center of our marriage, had seemed life-denying was really an expression of a fierce love of life?

Patsy was inside of something I was outside of. The assault had dislocated her from our shared life. At the same time, we were brought close by her willingness—her insistence—on trying to find words to share with me what she was experiencing. And by my hunger to know.

"There's knowing, and there's *knowing*." These words became a sort of shorthand between us for registering the perception that came at us, again and again, during those first weeks, that what had been inflicted on Patsy was *knowledge*.

"It's like childbirth," she said. "So common, but unknowable—until it happens to you."

In one sense, she was disabled, but in another sense she seemed to see more deeply into the marrow of things and to speak with new authority about what she saw. Two worlds had collided. The point of intersection had been her body. The perspective that had opened up was startling. It was as if certain connections had been made, as if she had been plugged into a huge network of kindred experiences. Again and again, she spoke of the vastness of what she had come in contact with.

"I feel in touch with something so large. I felt it from the first moments. I feel connected to cavewomen, to women who've been raped through history. It's like a weight bearing down on me. The knowledge that there are men so tormented and angry that they would do this to a woman."

TWO WEEKS after the attack, we resumed running. I had assumed we wouldn't run in the marathon, then less than a month away, but Patsy suggested we begin training again and see how we felt as the day approached. Training for the race became a central focus for her.

"It was a way of fighting back," she observed later. "At a time when I couldn't do anything else—couldn't work, couldn't even go shopping at the grocery store—it was something I could do."

She couldn't bear to run past the spot where she had been attacked. Nor could she run alone. So we ran elsewhere along the lakefront. And we ran together.

Those first runs were an immense effort of will for her. She was not *in* her body in the sense she had been before the attack. She had lost the capacity to yield to the experience. Her chest was constricted, her breathing shallow, her upper body tense. She was easily startled. The sound of footsteps behind her—another runner overtaking us—flooded her with fear. To run was to be brought back to the moment when cruel hands grabbed her from behind, not to all the happy moments before that. The lakefront had become a desolate and menacing place.

"It's like running in a tunnel," she said. "I can't *see* anything. I can no longer see the Lake."

One Sunday we went for an eighteen-mile run on the North Side of the city—from the downtown area north along the Gold Coast, then back downtown. Patsy was tense—her internal alarm system poised to go off—but eventually the distance wore her down and she began to relax. Running on the North Side, we felt rather like tourists. The sociological mix is very different. Downtown the lakefront population is homogeneous—white joggers in expensive sweat suits—but as one proceeds north one encounters a rich ethnic mix. There were pickup soccer games in which one could hear half a dozen different languages spoken. There were recent refugees from Southeast Asia who, I imagined, looked out at the Lake and recalled the South China Sea. When Patsy first returned from France, she discovered that Gypsies of the Kalderash tribe would congregate under a particular stand of trees on the lakefront, and she used to visit with them there.

As we headed back into the downtown area, with about a mile to go, Patsy suggested that I pick up the pace and run ahead, if I wanted to. I did so. It was the first time she had run alone since the attack. As soon as I passed out of hearing range, she panicked. Running between

Buckingham Fountain and Shedd Aquarium on a sidewalk full of tourists and parents pushing strollers, she was overcome by terror.

"It was as if I was moving through an alien world," she said later. "I felt like prey. Like a deer or a gazelle on the African plain. To have the herd all around me was no protection. It wouldn't make any difference if I was attacked."

For Patsy, brought down from behind on open ground, this was the ultimate reality. The prey move through the city. The predators stalk. If you are singled out for attack, the herd can't help you. It scatters and flees.

Some weeks later, I described this incident to our friend David Watts. A student of gorilla behavior, David had worked for a number of years with Dian Fossey and, after her murder, had replaced her as director of the Karisoke research facility in Rwanda. He was clearly affected by Patsy's image of the herd scattering at the moment of attack. That is, he said, a valid perception of certain species. In the case of such species, the only protection afforded by the herd is a matter of probabilities: the odds that another member will be attacked.

LIKE THE grinding gears of garbage trucks lumbering down the alley or drunken shouts from a fraternity party up the block, the 1988 presidential campaign—Bush vs. Dukakis—was unpleasant background music in our lives. I had the impulse to avert my eyes, as if from something embarrassing in which I was vaguely implicated. The spectacle of the Vice President, outlined against a blur of stars and stripes, expounding on the sanctity of the American flag was so remote from the conditions of life around me and so alien to First Amendment principles as I understood them that he might as well have been speaking in tongues.

The other symbol deployed by the Bush campaign, though, struck home with the force of a personal insult. During Dukakis's tenure as governor, Massachusetts, like most states, had a prison furlough program. A convicted murderer named Willie Horton, released for a weekend, fled and later terrorized a young couple, Clifford and Angela Barnes, beating him and raping her. The Bush campaign seized upon this episode and made frequent references to it. One television ad, prepared by an ostensibly independent group, used a picture of Horton's glowering face. The message: elect liberals, soft on crime, and a brutish black man will rape your wife.

I was confused by my reactions. I felt exposed, as if the violence that had struck Patsy had shifted the boundaries between private and public in our lives, leaving us in danger of being swept away by the swirling currents of racism and fear the Bush campaign was seeking to exploit. After all, my wife *had* been assaulted by a man about whom we knew only that, like Willie Horton, he was black and cruel. I felt an angry impulse to strike back. It was as if *our* household had been violated, as if our privacy had been invaded. The invasion took the form not of our private matters being forced into public but of the public realm intruding into our private space. And the intruder was not Willie Horton but the Vice President of the United States.

"DON'T USE your hand," Patsy whispered as we began to make love for the first time since the assault. Trying to be tender, I was aware of the weight and hardness of my body. I was grateful she didn't recoil from me. Afterward I realized I had somehow expected her insides to have the same spongy texture they had when we first made love after the children were born.

I WAS cleaning up in the kitchen after dinner when the second Bush-Dukakis debate aired. I stuck my head into the living room to hear the opening exchange. After introductory pleasantries, the moderator, Bernard Shaw, a television news correspondent, put the first question.

"Governor," he asked Michael Dukakis, "if Kitty Dukakis were raped and murdered, would you favor an irrevocable death penalty for the killer?"

"No, I don't, Bernard," Dukakis answered without apparent emotion. "And I think you know I've opposed the death penalty during all of my life. I don't see any evidence that it's a deterrent, and I think there are better and more effective ways to deal with violent crime."

He went on to talk about Massachusetts's success in controlling violent crime and about the need to address the drug problem in order to reduce crime.

A dreadful moment. Against the background of "Willie Horton," a journalist, who was confusingly a black man, asked the Democratic candidate for president how he would respond if his wife was raped and murdered. Dangerous ground. It opened up and swallowed Dukakis. His response confirmed impressions of him as a passionless social engineer. Together with a widely published photograph of him looking silly wearing a helmet in a tank, it contributed to the sense that he was unmanly.

I was unnerved by Dukakis's failure of response. Why didn't he challenge the question? Why didn't he attack the questioner? Yet I also identified with him. I was less appalled by the answer he gave than by the answer he was invited to give. Could there be any doubt he would have gained support had he cried out for blood and declared he would lead the lynch mob?

THE DAY Patsy was attacked, the clocks in our household stopped. Other clocks, however, kept running. I lived in a state of complete mobilization, concentrating on the demands of each day—attending to Patsy and the children, dealing with family and friends, trying somehow to discharge my professional responsibilities. About a week after the attack, deadlines for an article and a grant application bore down on me. The article was to be, in the words of the editor who commissioned it, "a celebratory essay on Chicago." Under the circumstances, a difficult dance to do. I allowed myself a private reference. "Nelson Algren put it best," I began. "'Loving Chicago,' he wrote, is 'like loving a woman with a broken nose.'"

During those first days, I was enveloped in the calm, at once detached and attentive, that comes over me in a crisis. A familiar clarity. Things slow down. Everything is focused on what to do next. Part of what attracted me to mountaineering was this disciplining of perception, this quality of attention. A matter of controlling your fear so that it sharpens rather than destroys your concentration. In this state of mind, I registered perceptions and said to myself, I'll have to think about that later.

Nothing is more important, my father used to say, than "staying in play." On our walks to the Lake, he would often talk with novelistic relish of other lives and the moral dramas they presented. Once, when we were talking about someone who was suffering a siege of depression, he spoke of the value he placed on "the dumb animal energy to keep going." To stay in play.

A man of great intellectual gaiety and charm, he was helplessly and contagiously interested in the world. (The greatest sin against life, he once remarked, is boredom—something he neither suffered nor inflicted.) Yet when I look at certain photographs of him now, what strikes me most is how sad he looks. The photos catch the moments-in-between—between witticisms, between kindnesses, between acts of engagement.

During the first weeks after the assault, I took refuge in action. Yet there were also the moments-in-between. Most often they came when I was alone in the car. As I drove from here to there, through the streets of my life, grief would balloon inside me, and I would sob. It felt good. It felt self-indulgent. It frightened me. A flood of sadness threatened to sweep away language and my capacity to act. To be without words. Not to be in play. Then all that would be left would be the pain. I hurried on to my next point of engagement.

TEN

On a clear, cold Sunday morning at the end of October, eight thousand runners gathered downtown in the plaza under the Picasso sculpture. We awaited the start of the marathon, in the chill air, under a great arch of red, white, and blue balloons. We stretched and hopped around to keep warm. As the moment approached, Patsy and I embraced. The balloons were released into the sky, a cheer went up from the massed bodies, and the race began.

In the days before the marathon, I had felt tired and overextended. The symptoms of a cold were closing in on me. I was so preoccupied I scarcely gave the race a thought. Without Patsy's clarity of purpose, I would never have made it to the starting line. But once in motion, I was delighted to be there. It seemed a respite, an unexpected vacation.

We had decided not to run together. Patsy was concerned that my pace would be too fast for her. The first ten miles seemed effortless. I felt as if I were being carried forward by the human current around me. The 26.2-mile course wound its way through the city. It went north from the Loop into the wealthy provinces of the Near North Side, turned south, and cut through Italian and Hispanic and Chinese neighborhoods to the South Side. Then, after a long haul back north, it went out to the lakefront and finally headed south to the finish line in Lincoln Park.

At about eighteen miles, I caved in. My body mutinied. I stopped counting miles and began counting steps. With two miles to go, my legs cramped up. With a mile to go, I stopped and, supporting myself on the guardrail, tried to work the cramps out of my legs. I felt a hand on my shoulder. It was Patsy. She looked at once spent and luminous. She urged me on and stayed with me as I hobbled the final mile. We finished together.

The park resembled a battlefield. There were bodies littered everywhere, in varying degrees of agony and exultation, attended by family and friends. It was hard to believe these were the same people who had assembled a few hours earlier under the Picasso. I imagined a film that would show only the moments before and after a marathon, but not the intervening event. Before: people awaiting the start, stretching, hopping around with nervous energy, stripping off their sweat clothes, tying and retying their shoes. After: the same people hobbled and ashen, straining to reach their feet with their hands in order to take off their shoes, helping one another put on their sweatpants, and so on. What, the viewer would be left to ask, had happened to this group of people?

I'm not sure how to answer that question. The idiom of athletics does not seem adequate to describe the phenomenon. For a handful of elite runners, the marathon is a competition; for the thousands of others who participate, while they may try to improve their times, it's something else. A ritual ordeal? A pilgrimage? A celebration of the city? I only know that for at least one runner that day, one who had known hellish isolation, it was deeply consoling to go out for a run with eight thousand others and, for several hours, to recover the city from the predators.

THE DAY after the marathon, our peculiar vacation continued as we boarded a plane for Los Angeles. The occasion for the trip was a ceremony at which I was to receive an award for my work on my father's book. This was the first time we had ever gone off together for more than an evening without the children. We had made arrangements for them to spend the week with our friends Deborah and David Epstein. It was Halloween, and their excitement about the holiday—Josh was to be an extraterrestrial, Betsy a rabbit—seemed to displace any anxieties about our leaving. As the plane took off, it almost seemed possible that we could simply be lifted out of the circumstances that had dominated our lives for the last six weeks. Our bodies spent from the marathon, it was a pleasure to sit quietly for the four-hour trip to L.A.

In the months before Patsy was assaulted, we had been savoring the reception of my father's book. Published earlier in the year under the title *A Worthy Tradition: Freedom of Speech in America*, the book had been widely reviewed. Feature articles had recounted the story of my effort—described, inevitably, as "a labor of love"—to complete my father's work.

That story eclipsed another, one only Patsy and I knew, about what the living out of my commitment to my father had meant in our marriage. She joked that she only really believed the book was finished when she read about it in the newspapers. The project had gone on for so long and demanded so much, she found it hard to imagine that things could be otherwise. Her life had been organized around mine; her work subordinated to mine. During the long intervals between the grants that came in to support the book, she was the principal wage earner, forced to take on assignments that held little interest for her. Plans for travel and other projects receded to the vanishing point.

Toward the end, her generosity and patience finally depleted, she became angry. She compared the manuscript to a severely handicapped child, beloved and all-consuming, sucking up all the human and material resources in the household. After Betsy was born, she became ever more insistent about asserting the claims of the present against the past. There were moments when she threatened to leave, taking the children with her, until I finished the book. I couldn't discount her words, for she spoke with care and measured force. In a sense, she did leave for a time, withdrawing emotionally and sexually into her anger.

I was confounded. The forms that gave shape to my life—the promise to my father embodied in the book, the promise to my wife embodied in our household—had come to seem at cross-purposes. I tried to find my way out of the manuscript. After a decade's labor, the revisions that remained were less in the manuscript than in the editor. At first, I had approached the project as a crisis, an emergency. Over time, my orientation had changed, as my understanding of tradition ripened. I had come to see the project as part of a larger, ongoing community of effort, extending into the future as well as emerging from the past. Now the time had come to act on that understanding: to bring to an end that which could never be finished.

One afternoon in the spring of 1987, we finally "got the book out of the house," as Patsy put it. I placed the manuscript in a large card-board box. No one besides Patsy knew what the contents of that box represented. Day to day, year to year, she had been the companion and the witness, never more so than during the final months of estrangement. Together we walked across campus and dispatched the box to the publisher. A moment of exquisite intimacy.

To a degree we hadn't expected, our private fate had public resonance. People were moved by the story of the book. My father's thinking and my efforts were generously acknowledged. In the months following publication, the book received an odd mix of awards. (I suppressed the thought that there must be something fishy about a work honored across such a spectrum.) Some were from predictable sources: the University of Chicago Law School, the American Bar Association. Some less so: I received a letter from Secretary of State George Shultz, informing me that he had presented a copy of the book to Soviet Foreign Minister Eduard Shevardnadze. ("Now that the Russians tell us they are for 'glasnost,'" he wrote, "I thought it might be salutary for them to see what openness and free speech really mean.") Honoring a son with his father's name, the Illinois chapter of the American Civil Liberties Union gave me an award it had established after my father's death, the Harry Kalven Freedom of Expression Award. The first recipients of the award had been close associates of my father's, legal scholars distinguished by their civic courage. More recently, reflecting something about the culture of the First Amendment as well as the role of such awards as draws to fund-raising dinners, the recipients had come from farther afield—for example, Phil Donahue, the television talk show host. The previous year the Kalven Award had been given to Christie Hefner, who had recently taken over from her father as CEO of Playboy Enterprises. This created a curious sort of kinship-by-award, for the award that awaited me in California was the Hugh M. Hefner First Amendment Award.

The award was to be given by the Playboy Foundation, the philanthropic arm of Playboy Enterprises. The foundation supports organizations and projects promoting freedom of expression, freedom of choice with respect to abortion, and so on. The First Amendment awards are the creation of Christie Hefner. Each year a panel of judges selects several individuals to be honored for their contributions to freedom of speech and given a check for $3,000. Among those to receive awards on this occasion were a scientist at Livermore Laboratory who risked his career by disclosing information that impeached claims made by Edward Teller about an aspect of Star Wars technology, and a librarian at the University of Maryland who had organized opposition to an FBI effort to get librarians to report to the agency on the reading habits of their patrons. The panel of judges had included Anthony Lewis and Tom Wicker of the *New York Times*, and Charlayne Hunter-Gault of the "MacNeil-Lehrer News Hour."

The participation of such individuals reflects Playboy Enterprises' success in advancing, by means of the foundation and awards, along the path toward respectability traveled in the past by other questionable enterprises associated with names like Rockefeller, Ford, and Guggenheim. This troubles many feminists. They argue that *Playboy* contributes to conditions that give rise to male violence against women. As they see it, to take *Playboy*'s money, even if it's put to the best of uses, lends legitimacy to a pernicious institution.

I could imagine how I must appear from such a perspective: the very model of the myopic civil libertarian, an unwitting apologist for pornographers, blind to his own corruption, unable to see that the institution whose largesse he accepts was implicated in the violence inflicted on his wife.

I didn't have settled views about the nature of *Playboy* as an institution. The question was open in my mind. Reading feminist arguments about the links between "objectification" and violence, I sometimes felt as if I were en route to perceptions I hadn't yet had. At the moment, though, such questions had an air of unreality for me. I was moved less by conviction than by curiosity. Given the opportunity, how could we not check it out? Besides, we needed the money.

I had grown up with *Playboy* in the family. In the early 1960s, my father's interest had been engaged by the constitutional issue of obscenity. The issue had only reached the Supreme Court in 1957; it was an uncharted and fast-developing area of the law. He wrote extensively about it. He participated in the defense of Lenny Bruce against charges of obscenity arising from a performance at a Chicago nightclub. And he occasionally advised *Playboy* on obscenity matters.

One by-product of this is that he was given a complimentary subscription to the magazine. So I grew up with the latest issue of *Playboy* on the coffee table, along with *The New Yorker*, *The New Republic*, and the *Bulletin of the Atomic Scientists*. Old issues ended up in the third-floor attic down the hall from my room—a private library I could explore at will. To this day, I associate the magazine with a certain musty attic odor. It has an almost Proustian quality for me—recalling the house I grew up in and the course of my unfolding adolescent sexuality. I recall the magazine, above all, as a safe place, a refuge. The many hours I spent thumbing through those back issues with one hand while touching myself with the other have in my memory an air of innocence. It seems to me now that I was engaged in a kind of reconnaissance. Shuffling through countless images of young women in various positions, I was discovering what moved me, what left me indifferent, and, in some instances, what repelled me. I was beginning to trace out the geography of my own sexuality, to learn the local dialect.

After I left home, I rarely saw the magazine. I couldn't bring myself to buy it. I'm not sure why. I was more put off by the commercialism than by the representation of women, sensing perhaps that there was something unhealthy about looking at advertisements while sexually aroused. Or perhaps it was the representation of women in the context of the commercialism: women presented as something to consume—along with all the other items advertised and promoted in the magazine. But it would be false to say that I came to experience the pictures in themselves as ugly or ceased to be aroused by them. My resistance to buying *Playboy* seems to have arisen less from a perception that the magazine exploits women than from the feeling that to buy it would be to collaborate in the commercial exploitation of *my own* sexuality.

Yet to this day, if I come upon a copy, I look through it hungrily. I have the impulse to go away alone with it—to try to relocate that refuge. It eludes me. What seemed to me as a boy such a wide world of human possibilities evoked and hinted at in the pages of the magazine now seems impossibly narrow. I am too aware of all that is left out: most of what I have known of delight and meaning as a sexual being lies outside its pages.

It's my impression that *Playboy* occupies a central place in feminist critiques of pornography not because its images are uniquely offensive but because it has come to be widely accepted as a part of mainstream culture. It's the magazine a woman's father, brother, husband, or boyfriend is most likely to have seen and, to some degree, been socialized by. Looking at *Playboy* from the perspective of violent pornography, feminists see a continuum. Violent porn, they argue, makes explicit that which is implicit elsewhere in the culture. *Playboy* doesn't depict explicitly violent acts, but it does present women as objects to be acted

7 3

upon by male power, to be used and abused; it presents them as rape-able. Viewed in this light, the adolescent boy leafing through back issues of the magazine in his parents' attic is being conditioned to associate sexual arousal with the subordination of women. This dynamic is particularly dangerous in the case of *Playboy*, feminists argue, because its objectification of women is legitimized by the context in which the images appear: legitimized, that is, by the prose of noted writers published alongside the images and by the use of money from the sale of those images to identify the magazine with the struggle for human rights—for example, by giving First Amendment awards.

UPON ARRIVING in Los Angeles, we went directly to our hotel: the Bel Age in West Hollywood. The suite Playboy had reserved for us was nearly as large as our apartment—and had more mirrors and telephones. Our weary bodies were at once grateful and disoriented. We went out for a walk, as we had in so many cities around the world in the years before we had children. On the plane, Patsy had read a *New Yorker* article about L.A. which described the phenomenon of people building houses on eroding hillsides and then having to reinforce them by various means. She was fascinated by the unstable world we were walking through and pointed out various precarious structures.

That night Christie Hefner hosted a dinner at a French restaurant on Sunset Boulevard. At our table: Christie, Tom Wicker, and several other award winners. The conversation over dinner, gracefully orchestrated by Christie, was genuinely interesting. I found her wide awake and intelligent—animated by a kind of feline alertness. A woman on a tightrope.

When someone at the table asked her what it was like for her as a woman to run Playboy Enterprises, her reply was practiced and deft. It was clearly a question she had fielded many times before. She made the case as well, I suspect, as it can be made that Playboy, far from being an exploiter of women, is an enlightened institution with respect to the rights and freedoms of women. She cited the high number of women in executive positions, the absence of sexism in the company, the support for feminist causes by the foundation, and so on. It angered her, she said, when feminist critics looked past all that and objected to the substance of the magazine. Listening to her, I was, for the moment, almost convinced that Playboy is a feminist institution. What made her stance finally unpersuasive was the fact that she acknowledged no doubt or ambivalence. Yet I was moved by her response, at the end of the evening, when she learned that Patsy had recently been assaulted. She simply embraced her.

By the time we got back to the hotel, the costs of running the marathon with a cold had come due for me. I had lost my voice. While Patsy fell into a deep, sedated sleep in my arms, I spent a restless night. Outside, a few blocks away, unbeknownst to us, a Halloween parade, some one hundred thousand strong, turned into a riot. It took police— some on horseback and in helicopters—several hours to restore order, as masked revelers smashed windows and looted shops on Hollywood Boulevard.

In the morning, I sat on the balcony and prepared my remarks for the award ceremony. I considered saying something about sexual violence—but what? I wasn't ready. I decided to stay on familiar ground and sketched out some thoughts about the First Amendment tradition. I wasn't sure I would be able to say anything at all: my voice had diminished to a whisper.

The award luncheon was to be held at the Playboy Mansion in Holmby Hills. We took a cab. When we reached the estate, we passed through a gate, attended by a guard, then up a winding road to a hilltop château: Hugh Hefner's castle.

Upon arrival, we were given a tour of the estate. There was a private zoo and aviary, which included a colony of squirrel monkeys, macaws, flamingos, peacocks, cranes, doves, pheasants, and, inevitably, assorted rabbits.

"I wish we'd brought the kids," Patsy joked.

We were also shown a game room, a gym, tennis courts. The grounds were heavily landscaped. There was a large free-form pool, crossed by an arched footbridge, with streams and smaller pools radiating out from it. And there was a rock "grotto" containing a Jacuzzi. The smaller pools contained varieties of fish, some quite large.

We saw nothing scandalous or titillating. The overall impression was of a kind of counterfeit gentility. An American male adolescent's vision of elegance—as if the governing taste were that of a sixteen-year-old boy with all the money in the world. It was, in ways altogether consistent with Hefner's success with the magazine, a monument to arrested development.

With drinks in hand, we wandered the grounds and chatted with other guests. A curious mix of people had assembled for the luncheon.

Civil libertarians and Playboy executives. The men around Hefner. The women around Christie, such as Cleo Wilson, the executive director of the foundation, a forceful and appealing black woman. Guests like Tom Hayden and Donald Woods, the South African newspaper editor. One minute I was talking with a smooth, vacant Playboy executive of Hefner's generation, and the next with Frank Wilkinson who had campaigned for decades against the House Un-American Activities Committee and had for a time been jailed for contempt of Congress in a particularly scandalous instance of the committee punishing one of its critics. I was keenly aware of Patsy beside me. Moving gingerly on marathon-blistered feet, she had a relaxed, dreamy air. I sensed that we were traversing complicated ground. The mix of principle and corruption was quite uncanny, and questions about the corruption of principle were obvious. But I decided to think about them later. For the moment, I was absorbed by the spectacle. As if the sight offered a clue to the phenomenon we were caught up in, we drifted back several times to look at the fish. Guests were encouraged to feed them. Beside the pond there were stands containing flakes of fish food. When one walked near the water, the fish surfaced en masse and avidly opened their mouths.

The luncheon was held outside beneath a canopy—with the cries of exotic birds in the background. We sat with Burton Joseph and his daughter. A Chicago lawyer and general counsel for Playboy Enterprises, Burt used to be director of the foundation. Fourteen years earlier, he had awarded me a grant for my work on my father's book at a time when the project was the most uncertain of undertakings.

As the award ceremony was about to begin, Hugh Hefner appeared. He was attended by two muscular young men. Various people got up to greet "Hef" as he made his way to a seat near us. The sight of him—a slight, pallid man in a silk sports coat and open collar—crystallized my impressions of the mansion: a perception of the layers and layers of insulation this man had wrapped around his body. He seemed less the satyr of legend than the Wizard of Oz stepping out from behind his curtain.

The ceremony began with opening remarks by Christie Hefner which included a gracious salute—heartfelt and unforced—to her father. Then Tom Wicker, acting as master of ceremonies, took over. In the case of each award, Wicker made a few remarks and introduced the presenter, who in turn made a presentation speech; then the recipient spoke about his work. (There were no women among the award recipients.)

I was the final recipient. Burt Joseph made a generous and emotional presentation. I apologized for my diminished voice, then spoke for several minutes. I began by observing that in accepting the award from Burt there was for me a sense of coming full circle.

"Yet there is another sense," I said, "in which I know that the circle doesn't close. It's the nature of a living tradition to be open-ended, ongoing, endlessly demanding. That's one of the things I learned in the course of working on my father's book.

"I took as an epigraph to the afterword of the book words from the Talmud: 'It is not upon you to finish the work, but neither are you free to desist from it.' I claimed those demanding, consoling words for myself, but as a reviewer later pointed out, they apply equally, and with special poignancy, to my father, who died at his desk working on the manuscript that would become *A Worthy Tradition*.

"It occurs to me that those words apply to all of us gathered here today. My deep hunch about this event is that we who are being so generously honored are really vehicles, occasions, for honoring and renewing that tradition—those great resources on which we draw and to which we seek, in our small ways, to contribute."

It was clear I had the audience's attention. I closed:

"I have had occasion over the years to reflect on Goethe's words: 'The sons must labor to possess what they have inherited from the fathers.' I have come to know something about what the word 'labor' means. My inheritance—a wealth of words—has at times been a burden, a riddle, a complex fate to be lived out. It has also been a gift. So I leave you with a mystery. At the end of this labor, I feel not depleted but enriched. In some mysterious way, I feel myself the beneficiary of a great gift."

As I finished, I sought out Patsy's eyes. Hefner was sitting nearby. To my amazement, I saw that he was in tears. Not wiping away a tear but weeping. Wicker made a few concluding remarks, and the ceremony was over.

Hefner came up to me, still teary, and warmly recalled my father. It was hard to know what to make of his emotion. Was he always like this? Was his emotional response a by-product of the small stroke he had suffered several years earlier? Did the theme of tradition perhaps have special meaning for him, having recently passed the leadership of Playboy Enterprises on to his daughter?

"Wow," he said. "The father, the son, and the First Amendment."

Good-natured and full of feeling, he spoke of the controversy over pledging allegiance to the flag that Vice President Bush had injected into the presidential campaign and of the Meese Commission on Pornography.

"I mean," he said, with a gesture that took in the gathering of civil libertarians on the lawn of the Playboy Mansion, "who could be against *this?*"

E L E V E N

————————

W<small>E TRAVELED</small> on to San Francisco, where we spent several days. Old friends we hadn't seen in a decade received us with great warmth. For us, time was organized around the assault; we measured out our lives in days and weeks since that September afternoon. Our friends, by contrast, saw us against a longer sweep of time. Again and again, they remarked on how beautiful and healthy Patsy looked—Patsy who six weeks earlier had been so badly beaten she was almost unrecognizable.

Wandering the streets of San Francisco was like visiting an archaeological site dating from the prehistory of our relationship. We stayed in the Castro neighborhood in the house, tiny and charming, of Florence Mischel, a dear friend who was out of town. In the mid-1970s, we had lived for some months in an apartment several blocks away from Florence's. The Castro had then been in the midst of its flowering as the capital of gay America. The tenor of life on its streets had been high-spirited—an ongoing celebration of the sexual feast. It was like living as a foreigner in a nation that had just declared independence. Now, more than a decade later, after years of the AIDS plague, the streets we walked were more subdued.

We regretted that Florence wasn't in town. She is an important person in our lives. Her biography is dense and full of incident. She had

grown up poor in a Russian Jewish family in Brooklyn. Intensely political, she had joined the Communist party in the 1930s. During the
McCarthy era, her husband, a Hollywood screenwriter, had been pil-
loried before congressional investigating committees and blacklisted by
the film industry. He had died young, leaving her with two small sons.
Our lives had intersected in the early 1960s, when my family spent a
summer in Santa Barbara, where my father participated in a series of
seminars at the Center for the Study of Democratic Institutions, the
enterprise Robert Maynard Hutchins had established some years after
he stepped down as president of the University of Chicago. Florence
worked at the center; her job was to tape the proceedings and edit the
tapes for radio broadcast. Inspired in part by a seminar on the First
Amendment my father conducted that summer, she entered law school
at the age of sixty and became a labor lawyer. Her life was full of ardent
friendships, occasional love affairs, many medical emergencies, world
travel underwritten by a wealthy friend who wanted the pleasure of
her company, and, always, passionate involvement in the lives of her
children and eventually grandchildren. When I phoned her after
months or years of not being in touch, she would say, her voice husky
with excitement, "How amazing! I was *just* thinking about you. I was
having a conversation with you in my head." And I, helplessly adoring,
didn't doubt it for a moment.

Through all her metamorphoses and reinventions of herself, she
was, simply, Florence. Absent, she remained a strong presence in her
house, reflected in her books and family photos, her furniture and art,
her kitchen and her plants. The matchbox house was as intimate as a
nest; it felt like an extension of her body.

The two days we spent there recalled our spell as house-sitting
nomads in the Bay Area. Living in someone else's domestic space in
their absence, you can look at their things with absolute frankness, as
you might stare at a blind person. So much is revealed by people's
bookshelves and medicine cabinets and kitchens. House-sitting, I recognize now, was an essential part of my apprenticeship as a writer.

Whatever the satisfactions of house-sitting, we were relieved, toward
the end of our years in San Francisco, when we found a place we could
afford to rent. It was an apartment, down by the water, across from
Ghirardelli Square. An old chocolate factory that had been converted
into a warren of shops and restaurants, Ghirardelli Square was a popu-
lar tourist spot. The main attraction was the Chocolate Factory, a soda

fountain and candy shop that sold chocolate of various kinds, much of it made on the premises. It amused us how *serious* tourists looked as they applied themselves to huge sundaes and banana splits. The smell of chocolate hung in the air like exhaust; it was the medium through which we moved.

We lived, among tourists, like hunter-gatherers. Patsy shopped for food with great care and ingenuity in the shops of North Beach and Chinatown. I gathered driftwood on the beach to feed the wood-burning stove in our kitchen. We prided ourselves on our resourcefulness. We even managed to eat out occasionally. The owner of an Indian restaurant at the edge of Chinatown befriended us and only rarely let us pay for our meals. We were also regulars at a decidedly nontrendy Italian restaurant named Original Joe's. We would get on the bus with a big bag of laundry, get off at Joe's, deposit our clothes in washing machines at the Laundromat across the street, then have a drink and share an entrée under the eyes of a tolerant waiter. (There is a dish we regularly have at home today—a spinach and ground beef concoction—that the children know as "Joe's Special.") In the middle of the meal, one of us would go across the street and transfer our clothes from washer to dryer.

I loved the sight of Patsy across a restaurant table. It was the setting in which I saw her most clearly. A mix of private and public space, at once intimate and out-in-the-world, where the light was just right. Sitting across from her, I would be stirred anew by her beauty and self-possession, by the candor and reserve that promised so much. When we got home and slipped into bed, she would often recede from me. We made love frequently. Her need for the physical connection was as strong as mine. Sometimes we delighted each other. Not predictably or reliably; it was more like an unexpected gift. Mostly, passion delivered us to loneliness.

One day I brought Patsy a gift. Returning from the library at the University of California in Berkeley, I came upon a cardboard box on Telegraph Avenue containing a squirming litter of puppies. I picked one out, put it in my shoulder bag, and brought it home. Patsy received the dog into her life with unrestrained joy. It was as if a channel of feeling opened up in her. We named the dog Farfelu after a term coined by André Malraux to describe a quixotic sort of adventurer.

Patsy was herself, I sometimes thought, like a wild animal living in captivity. She deeply inhabited her body, and through it the physical world. Yet she was precariously situated in the world of human relationships as if only half-domesticated. Freedom was not an abstraction for her but a deeply felt need. And men, especially in a sexual context, threatened that freedom. Mute and without language—when in distress, she would hold her hand over her mouth as if silencing herself—she resisted the loss of her animal freedom by withholding herself.

We saw Florence regularly during those years. Patsy confided to her of the inexplicable sadness that sometimes enveloped her. At Florence's urging, she went to her therapist several times. She found it helpful. The process was interrupted by my father's death and our move to Chicago. Years later, Patsy told me that when the therapist had asked her about sex, she had been unable to respond. She had no words.

AFTER FIVE days in California, we boarded a plane back to Chicago, bearing a check, a plaque that linked my name to Hugh Hefner's, and some questions. What did it mean to take Playboy's money? to stand before an audience at the Playboy Mansion and quote Goethe on what the sons have inherited from the fathers?

I knew there lay ahead of me renewed engagement with issues of freedom of speech I had thought behind me. Questions I had worked through and once thought settled now demanded to be engaged at a deeper level. Yet for the moment, those questions had an air of unreality for me. I tried to entertain the possibility that Playboy was moving its audience to violent acts, but I found it hard to get traction. The image that came to mind was millions of solitary men and boys masturbating over confected images of naked women. An institution afloat on a sea of spilt semen. A sad image, to be sure, but were these isolated consumers of pictures being incited to commit violent acts? I remained skeptical. Yet the image troubled me. Was it possible that the danger of pornography resided not in what it encouraged us to look at but what it discouraged us from looking at? Perhaps, as the old wives' tale warned, the real danger was that one would go blind—blind to the suffering and fear of the real women around one.

For all the generosity and personal warmth shown us, the dominant impression I took away from the Playboy Mansion was of an institution at war with the sorts of questions I was beginning to form, the thoughts I was trying to think. Hefner's tears, Christie's embrace of Patsy, Burt's friendship, Cleo's graciousness, acts of individual kindness multiplied many times could not obscure the basic fact that this was an institution mobilized against public acknowledgment of the knowledge inside the wounded woman sitting beside me.

IN THE emergency room on the day Patsy was assaulted, I caught a glimpse of a woman with whom I'd had an exchange in print some years earlier about pornography, sexual violence, and anger. Apparently, she worked in the hospital in some capacity.

The exchange was provoked by a review I had written for *The Reader*, a Chicago weekly, of a book titled *Take Back the Night*, a collection of essays by women on pornography. It was not a very good book, and I said so. A woman named Lynn Shepler wrote a letter to the editor:

> Mr. Kalven rather capriciously condemns the book while giving lip service to the basic issues presented. It is a position which allows him to escape feminist wrath through identifying with feminist concerns, yet which maintains and reinforces his superiority (as a male intellectual) in the condemnation of the book (written by females) on purely intellectual grounds. Mr. Kalven might have preferred a cool dissection of the issues, perhaps finding feminists' anger too alienating and blind in its ability to discriminate those sympathetic males from the rest, i.e., Mr. Kalven.

I had written that the design of the book "appears to have been dictated less by the possibilities of the subject than by the requirements of a united front." She disagreed: "For patently obvious reasons, the 'united front' to which Mr. Kalven refers reflects the universal outrage of women in response to misogynist ideologies and images." She went on to ask: "Would he have chosen to describe angry blacks or horrified and outraged Jews as 'foolish'?"

I had fun drafting my reply. Before submitting it, I read it over the phone to Alan Shapiro, a poet friend with whom I often exchanged manuscripts. As I read, I savored my rhetorical finesse:

> Note the operative words here: "*universal outrage* of women," "*angry blacks*," "*horrified and outraged* Jews." Ms. Shepler does not tell us what these hypothetical blacks and Jews are saying, only that they are angry, and then she challenges me to call them "foolish." What I object to here—and what bothered me about a number of the

pieces in *Take Back the Night*—is the notion that anger confers upon those enraged by injustice a kind of intellectual license which not only absolves them of deficiencies of analysis and argument but also converts such lapses into virtues. In this respect, Ms. Shepler is right: I do find the anger of certain feminists—their "wrath," as she puts it—"alienating and blind" in its inability "to discriminate." Anger is, of course, an appropriate response to various social evils, pornography among them. It can be an expression of conscience, a source of energy for meaningful action, and, at times, a condition of heightened lucidity. But, if indulged rather than disciplined, it can also be treacherous. A foolish statement is not alchemized into wisdom by the righteous anger of the speaker. And I think we owe it to those movements we care about to challenge such statements when we encounter them. There are other forms of solidarity besides the "united front."

Rereading these words now, I am prepared to stand by them. It's thus all the more unsettling to acknowledge that I wrote them without having *heard* the woman to whom they were addressed. I was too busy mobilizing my counterarguments to listen to Lynn Shepler or, earlier, to the voices assembled in the book I reviewed. I was deafened by the clamor of my own responses, stupefied by my insistence on winning the argument. What knowledge of the world, I wonder now, were they speaking out of? That question didn't occur to me then.

Over the years I had worked on *A Worthy Tradition*, I had become increasingly impatient with conventional defenses of freedom of speech, with the orthodoxy that had hardened around the First Amendment. From the perspective of liberal pieties about free speech, it's generally assumed that those who advocate censorship speak out of ignorance, that they are benighted, but in my experience they often seemed to speak out of knowledge—sometimes terrible knowledge—of the world. They might be wrong about censorship as a policy yet be profoundly right about something else. To my ear, the voices of those calling for censorship often had a resonance that made the voices of the civil libertarians who answered them sound thin by contrast.

The strongest example, in my experience, of this sort of asymmetrical public controversy in which some have terrible knowledge and others have opinions was the sequence of events that came to be known as the Skokie Case. The controversy was precipitated by the efforts of a small neo-Nazi group to hold a demonstration in a heavily Jewish suburb with a large number of concentration camp survivors. The neo-Nazi group was based in Marquette Park, a Southwest Side neighborhood that had resisted integration with great ferocity over the years. It was there in 1966 that Martin Luther King, Jr., leading an open housing march, had been struck in the head by a brick. (Fresh from Birmingham and Selma, he observed of the mob in Marquette Park, "I have never seen anything so hostile and so hate-filled.")

When the city of Chicago denied the Nazis a permit to hold a demonstration in their own neighborhood, they turned their attention to Skokie and then skillfully exploited the outrage this provoked, keeping the controversy alive for more than two years of demonstrations, counterdemonstrations, and sometimes hallucinatory public argument.

Immersed in legal abstractions by the work on my father's book, I felt driven to register this controversy on my nerve ends. Patsy and I followed it closely as journalists. We observed a number of violent clashes; in one instance we were the only witnesses to a bloody ambush of a group of Nazis by a far left group.

Over my desk are two photos. Patsy took both in the midst of angry mobs. One shows the heads of two youths, wearing Nazi insignias, shouting obscenities at counterdemonstrators. The other is of a survivor of Treblinka shrieking the word "Gestapo" over and over at Chicago policemen protecting a handful of Nazi demonstrators at a rally downtown.

These images retain their power to startle me. The animal vitality of the snarling youths. The agony of the elderly survivor whose expression—mouth open, nostrils wide, teeth bared—recalls the horse in Picasso's *Guernica*.

They also testify to Patsy's powers as a photographer. They are, in a sense, combat photos; and like the best of that genre, they leave one amazed that the photographer could remain so attentive and so in command of her craft in the midst of such frightening turbulence.

The woman who took those photographs was now—an hour away from Chicago, at an elevation of thirty thousand feet—overcome by panic. Sitting in the middle section of a 747, even more removed from the realities of flight than one usually is in a commercial airliner, she was seized by the perception that we were hurtling through space, at great speed, on an uncertain course. We were going to die. We would never see the children again. As the plane descended into O'Hare Airport, she gripped my arm with desperate force.

TWELVE

J osh and Betsy were waiting for us at the apartment, with Deborah and David, watching television. It was an emotionally confused moment—for them, for us. Within minutes of our return, Betsy fell and split her lip. Josh was at first remote, then burst out with great emotion, close to tears, "Dad, did you hear about what happened to Coach Ditka?" (Earlier in the week, the Chicago Bears coach had suffered a mild heart attack.)

We awoke the next day in our bed, in our apartment, on the South Side of Chicago, and resumed life as a family. We had arrived back on a Friday night. That Sunday morning we went out for brunch at Valois, a local diner, with Dave Light, a childhood friend of mine who was in town for the weekend. At about two in the afternoon, we left and began driving the several blocks home. Patsy sat in the back between the children, Dave beside me in the front. An orange station wagon lurched out of a shopping-center parking lot into the middle of the street. The driver was oblivious to traffic; he was looking the other way and didn't see us. I had to swerve to avoid hitting him. I stopped and glared back at him, expecting the sort of conciliatory gesture drivers customarily make to acknowledge a lapse of attention. Instead, he made an obscene gesture. I bristled and drove on.

Patsy was the first to realize he was coming after us. We turned south on Woodlawn Avenue. She looked back and saw him turn onto Woodlawn in the lane of oncoming traffic. She grabbed the children and began to scream. He came up on us fast. His face contorted with rage, he angled his car toward us. I swerved sharply. He came within inches of ramming into the side of the car where Josh was sitting.

He passed us and came to a stop, cutting us off. Patsy was hysterical—grabbing at me, screaming. I turned to try to calm her. When I turned back, he was out of his car and nearly upon us. He was a white man, wearing work clothes and a tool belt. He appeared drunk—in any case, unsteady—and he was waving a hammer.

"You gotta problem?" he shouted, and raised the hammer.

Dave got out on his side of the car, hoping, he said later, to create a diversion so I could get out. I tensed and prepared to hit the man with the hammer with the door.

Patsy screamed and screamed. A harrowing sound. It filled her. It filled the car. Beneath her screams, I heard Josh's voice.

"Dad, let's get out of here," he said in a choked whisper. "Let's get out of here, Dad."

It was a close thing. There was a moment when the man with the hammer appeared committed, when it seemed certain he would smash the windshield or my head. Then he backed off. I'm not sure why. Perhaps it was the realization that the car contained two men, both as big as he. Perhaps it was the sight of the children. Perhaps Patsy's screams penetrated his rage and forced a perception of the magnitude of what was about to happen.

He got back in his car, drove half a block, and parked, then disappeared into an alley. At that moment, a police car appeared, headed toward us. I waved it down and explained to the policeman what had happened: a man had tried to hit us with his car, had threatened us with a hammer, and was at that moment less than a block away. The policeman was unresponsive. He didn't get out of his squad car. He made no effort to take down a report.

"Okay," he said, "I'll check it out."

He drove at a slow, stately pace to the corner, waited out the red light, turned, and drove around the block. We remained at the scene of the incident, awaiting his return and watching to see that the man with the hammer didn't leave. Several minutes later, the police car approached at the same measured pace and drove past—past the assailant's car, past us. He didn't stop. He didn't make any effort to assess the situation. He drove on.

I was furious. The attack on Patsy hadn't been due to anyone's dereliction. Others may have witnessed a moment of the attack from passing cars and not stopped, but in the end a number of people did stop and help in various ways. And the police had done their job. Within several minutes of the attack, they came upon the scene—not by chance but because they were patrolling the lakefront. They couldn't be faulted for not being there at the moment the attack occurred. But in this instance a policeman *was* present at the scene of the crime in time to apprehend a violent man. And he did nothing.

When we got home, I called the police and the vice president of the university in charge of community affairs. The police came promptly and took a full report on the charge of aggravated assault and a complaint of professional misconduct against the police officer who had failed to investigate the incident. I was upset but also felt something akin to relief. It felt good to get angry. It felt good to have someone to blame, someone to hold accountable.

Dave, too, seemed more invigorated than unsettled by the incident. It was almost as if the encounter with the man with the hammer had provided a point of access to our situation—a chance to share with us, to act to protect us, to be of use.

Patsy didn't share in this peculiar mix of male emotions. She was horrified and exhausted. She looked spent; the rush of terror had left her drained.

Josh was the member of the family in the most obvious distress. He was pale and shivered with aftershocks of fear. He had seen everything: the car coming toward him, the depth of his mother's pain and fear, the hammer inches from his father's head. It was hard to know how to console him. In the weeks after Patsy was attacked, I had tried to reassure the children. I didn't deny that "crazy, angry" people like the man who hurt their mother are abroad in the world. The evidence was undeniable; they could see her wounds. But I told them, again and again, in a variety of ways, that if we behave sensibly, if we take care as individuals and as a community, if we look out for one another and help the police, such terrible incidents can be guarded against. They listened hard, hungry for reassurance. How confusing and undermining, then, to be set upon by "a crazy, angry man" with a hammer and have the police fail to respond.

Patsy and I were to attend a wedding reception that evening. We had arranged for a teenage baby-sitter to stay with the children. Dave, seeing Josh's distress, offered to stay with them instead. Later he told me that after we left, Josh had gone into his room and emerged wearing his baseball cap and carrying his bat, which he kept close at hand throughout the evening.

The three of them watched *South Pacific* on television. There was a scene in which a man and woman, silhouetted against the tropical sky and accompanied by swelling romantic music, kiss. As they embraced, Betsy asked Dave, "Is he going to hurt her now?"

Betsy had not been visibly upset by the hammer incident, but she was intensely curious about it. It wasn't clear how much she had seen from her four-year-old's perspective sunk down in the far corner of the backseat; nor was it clear how much of what she had seen she had understood. ("Why," she asked me, "was Mommy pulling on your jacket?") Several days later, she made a remarkable drawing: three figures (with heads, legs, feet, and belly buttons but no arms) and, beneath their feet, another, larger figure, horizontal, with teeth bared. Patsy asked her what the picture was about.

"It's a mommy and a daddy and a girl," she explained, "on a scary road."

MY MOTHER visited in November. She brought photos my aunt had taken on a visit a couple of weeks before the assault. Among them was a charming picture of Patsy and Betsy. They are in the garden. Green ivy embroiders the wall behind them. Patsy is wearing shorts and a T-shirt. Radiant in the golden autumn light, she holds barefoot Betsy on her hip in a secure and loving embrace. Their heads are close together. They are laughing.

When I came to bed the night after my mother's arrival, I found Patsy weeping. She had been looking at the photo.

"If I had been killed, this is what the children would have been left with—this photograph," she sobbed. "It's hard for me to believe there ever was a time when I didn't have this thing inside me."

I put my arms around her.

"I'm not the person in that picture anymore."

IN MID-NOVEMBER, Patsy entered Michael Reese Hospital, on an outpatient basis, to have a bunion on her right foot operated on. The operation had been scheduled long before the assault. She had expected to be released the same day. After the surgery, however, she was in acute discomfort. This surprised her. Apparently, she hadn't given a thought to the physical pain. Perhaps in the context of what she had been suffering it seemed trivial.

It was decided she should stay in the hospital overnight. I was to give a speech early the next morning and needed to go to my office to prepare my remarks. My mother, who was staying at a friend's, agreed to spend the night with the children and to see them off to school in the morning. I picked her up, then went to my office. I worked until about 6:00 A.M. As I approached the apartment, I saw that the lights were on and that a hole had been cut out of the back-door screen. My mother was awake.

She had been awakened, she reported, at about 3:00 A.M. by noises in the study. She got up and went to check, thinking it was probably the cat. The study window was wide open. The screen was lying across the desk with a hole cut in it. In the window she saw a face—a black man wearing a stocking cap. The man disappeared from view. For some reason she didn't articulate, she didn't call the police but went back to bed. An hour later, she heard sounds in the kitchen and went to investigate. It proved to be the same man trying to break in through the back door.

I checked for other signs of forced entry and found that he had also damaged the front door to the building in his attempts to get in. It was unnerving to think that the man had made a sustained effort to get into an apartment he knew contained people. What did he have in mind?

Patsy experienced the break-in attempt less intensely than she would have had she been home when it occurred. It disturbed her— "Is somebody after us?"—but it didn't seem to undermine her sense, so important in the months since the assault, of the apartment as a safe place in a perilous world. In any case, in the days that followed she stayed home, convalescing from surgery, wrapped in the cocoon of the apartment.

I was almost embarrassed to tell friends of our latest criminal encounter. When I mentioned it to Rebecca Janowitz, she offered a diagnosis. The sequence of misfortunes we had suffered, she said, clearly indicated that we were victims of "the evil eye." She suggested a remedy prescribed by Jewish tradition: we should change our names.

Betsy had another solution. About a week after the break-in attempt, she asked me to spell out a message—she was just learning to make letters—which she then wrote on sheets torn from a yellow Post-it pad. Her plan was to place the message on the front and back doors. Here is what she wrote before running out of space:

MY
DADD
Y C TA
KE BAD

What she intended: My Daddy is strong. He can take bad guys to jail.

A MAN forced a woman, a secretary heading home from work, from an El train and raped her in the stairwell of a downtown El station during rush hour. The attack was witnessed by commuters who said they were unable to intervene because they couldn't get past a turnstile exit.

A twenty-five-year-old man was indicted on charges of raping a woman in a gangway after he abducted her at gunpoint as she walked to a bus stop on her way to work.

A former janitor at a West Side convent was sentenced to twenty years for raping a nun at knifepoint. The nun was attacked as she was washing cups in the convent kitchen.

A thirty-three-year-old man was charged with raping a woman in a garage after abducting her as she walked home from work.

A grand jury indicted two men on charges that they abducted a woman as she walked her dog and raped her at knifepoint at a secluded railroad embankment.

A forty-five-year-old resident of a nursing home was charged with aggravated criminal sexual assault after an employee at the home allegedly caught him raping a senile resident.

An ex-convict pleaded guilty to raping a woman in the basement laundry room of her apartment building a month after he was paroled from prison for another rape conviction.

A twenty-six-year-old man accused of raping a woman at knifepoint in a vacant West Side apartment was ordered held without bail. The man allegedly abducted the woman as she sat in her car. He forced her to drive to his apartment building, where he took her to a vacant third-floor apartment and raped her. After the attack, the woman jumped out of the window to escape, suffering a fractured spine, pelvis, and shoulder. She was found naked on the ground by a nearby resident.

A thirty-year-old man was sentenced to life in prison for the rape and murder of a woman he and two other men abducted as she left her apartment to take her two-year-old son to a birthday party. The men took her and her son to a vacant apartment. She was tied to a radiator and raped. The boy was locked in a bathroom. She was then stabbed several times, including once in the heart, and shot in the forehead.

Almost every day, the *Tribune* contains stories reporting the violation—and sometimes the annihilation—of females. Reading such stories in the weeks after Patsy was assaulted, I was sickened. They corroborated her sense of the nature of the threat: any time, any place, any man. I felt close to the reality of what the words might mean. Yet I also felt something else that made me feel divided at my core. I was aware of a range of submerged responses I hadn't before, in a lifetime of reading such stories, allowed myself to acknowledge. The quickening of attention. The avidity with which I took in the words. The hyena grin shadowing my lips. These sensations were faint but distinct. I couldn't any longer disown them, but I didn't know what to do with them. Should I be ashamed? I felt implicated in the violence I read about—not through conscious hostility toward women but by way of the little jolt of energy the stories released in me.

During her moments filled with terror on the lakefront, Patsy had visualized a newspaper article. As she fought for her life, that was how she saw the fate she was struggling against: a newspaper story about a runner found raped and murdered beside the lakefront path. I imagined men throughout the city—men, like me, who were not rapists—reading that same story and silently purring.

WE NOTICED that the cat was behaving erratically. Among other things, she was urinating in the apartment, something she had never done before. Concerned that she might have a bladder infection, Patsy took her to the vet.

"Is there something going on in your household?" he asked. "Is she under stress?"

Of course, we realized, she hadn't been receiving the sort of affection she usually gets. Preoccupied and tense, we had tossed her aside when she sought our attention.

"Perhaps," the vet suggested, "she's urinating in the apartment as a way of redefining home."

I WAS downtown to run some errands. On Michigan Avenue, two young black men, precariously middle-class, walked by on the sidewalk engaged in cheerful conversation. I overheard the word "pussy." Before I could think, I growled—actually made a noise—and began to turn to follow them. I had to suppress the impulse to rush after them and berate them. The intensity of my reaction surprised me. What was I reacting to? The crudity of the language? the fact that the speaker was black? the cheerful tone?

DETECTIVE DOROCIAK called. The police had a suspect in custody and wanted to arrange a lineup. He called several more times before a date for the lineup was fixed. There was, he reported, a chance that the suspect would be released because of overcrowded conditions at Cook County Jail.

County officials were under a federal order to maintain the inmate population within the capacity of the jail, which had fifty-five hundred beds. The judicial intervention into the jail's day-to-day operations was the result of a lawsuit brought on behalf of inmates which argued that overcrowded conditions at the jail violated the constitutional guarantee against cruel and unusual punishment. Six months ago, in an effort to press county officials to relieve overcrowding, the judge had ordered the county to release defendants accused of nonviolent felony crimes on their own recognizance. His order had resulted in the release of thousands of suspects awaiting trial—including, by mistake, the man charged with raping a woman during rush hour at an El station.

The federal judge pressing for more humane jail conditions was Milton Shadur, a former student of my father's and a passionate civil libertarian, who before he had gone to the bench had been our family lawyer. His intervention in the jail case, in the service of constitutional values and in light of a history of default by other institutions of government, was precisely the sort of judicial activism I had been taught to applaud. But how would I feel if the man who had terrorized Patsy, released on his own recognizance, were to flee or to assault another woman?

It was a gray, wintry fall day when we climbed the steps of the courthouse adjacent to the jail. Patsy was bundled against the cold in a long coat and scarf. Leaning on crutches made necessary by her recent bunion surgery, she moved slowly and deliberately.

We met Dorociak in the "Homicide and Sex Crimes" section of the courthouse. He sat on a bench with us and chatted for a while. Then, with seeming casualness, he showed us the Polaroid photos the police photographer had taken of Patsy's face in the emergency room.

Patsy stared at the photos for a few moments, then passed them to me. I couldn't read her expression. I was shaken by the snapshots. They were images of such *hurt*.

Patsy later wondered if Dorociak had deliberately shown her the photos at that moment in order to sharpen her resolve to bring the man who had done this to her to justice.

She said she doubted whether she would be able to identify him. Dorociak replied that you can't really be sure what you saw or didn't see and assured her that no consequences would follow from naming the wrong man in the lineup. There was only one suspect. So she shouldn't hesitate to follow a hunch or intuition.

After a while, accompanied by Dorociak and another detective, we moved from the courthouse into the jail itself. A public defender appeared. A young woman with pinched features. She made an objection to the procedure. She was concerned that the composition of the lineup would somehow highlight her client. Dorociak became exasperated.

"When it happens to you," he said angrily, "don't expect us to come running."

Patsy hadn't taken off her coat and scarf. She remained bundled up. She seemed at once fragile and gallant.

Finally, after hours of waiting, we were taken deeper into the jail to a room with a thick door in which there was a small window. The room seemed crowded: the two detectives, another policeman, the public defender, Patsy and myself. Patsy stood at the window, the rest of us around her. She took my hand.

Through the window, in the background, were six young black men in white T-shirts. We could see them, but they couldn't see us. The scene was strangely lit. One by one, as instructed by the guard, they stepped forward. "Number One ... Number Two ..." Each stood inches away from Patsy on the other side of the thick door.

Except for the moment when he hit her in the face, blinding her, he had stayed behind her. She wasn't sure she had seen him, but she had heard his voice. There was thus a possibility she would recognize it if she heard it again. The police wanted each man in the lineup to say something. What should they say? Patsy said she couldn't bear to have six men step up to the window and say what the man who attacked her had said: "I'm going to kill you." She suggested instead that they say, "Take off the ring."

For the men on the other side of the heavy door, this was a kind of reverse audition: the goal was *not* to be selected. They said their line flatly, without emotion— except for one fellow with dreadlocks who gave the line a certain resonance, as if he actually wanted the part.

Pressed by the police to identify one of them and again assured that there would be no consequences if she identified anyone but the suspect, Patsy tentatively ventured that it might have been "Number One." He was ordered up to the window again. His face was impassive, opaque, unreadable. He had a thick neck, muscular arms.

The only thing Patsy was sure about was that it was not "Number Four"—the one with the dreadlocks. She was sure, she said, that the man who attacked her was clean-shaven, though his skin was rough, and that he had short hair. Throughout the attack, his head had been right beside hers. She would have been aware of it if he had had a beard or long hair.

The suspect, it turned out, was the youth with the long hair. He had been arrested in connection with an armed robbery of a woman on the lakefront.

Had Patsy chosen "Number One," I wondered, because of his evident strength? Because the man who had overpowered her and hurt her so must have been very strong?

"Imagine me fighting for my life with someone like Number One," Patsy said as we drove home. "Imagine him hitting me with all his force."

What would it have been like, what would it have meant, had her assailant been in the lineup? a particular human face? the hands that had violated her? As it was, our perceptions of the scale of the phenomenon were only deepened. Looking through a small window in a thick door, we had seen the generic urban criminal: young black men in a jail bursting with young black men.

Patsy again expressed doubts that she could ever identify the man who had attacked her. I suggested that perhaps the fact that she could confidently say it was *not* a particular individual—like the long-haired suspect or the boy the police had brought into the emergency room— meant that given the chance, she would be able to identify the man who had attacked her. She remained skeptical.

I recalled Barbara Engel's remark that the man who had assaulted Patsy probably wouldn't have recognized her had he seen her the next day. Was it possible that neither of the individuals involved in this cataclysmic event, this collision of worlds, would recognize the other if they passed on the street?

PART
II

1989–90

THIRTEEN

Betsy, for the first time in her life, is having trouble sleeping. Sometimes she gets up as many as eight or ten times in the night.

A few days before Christmas, she reported a "bad dream" to me.

"A big hairy monster got into the apartment. He grabbed me and threw me down. He grabbed Mommy and threw her down. I told the monster my daddy was going to get rid of him, but he grabbed you and threw you down. Then he ate our gingerbread house."

More often, she can't remember or find words for the images that fill her with fear. When she gets up in the night, her face is distorted; she speaks through clenched teeth. One night, at 3:00 A.M., I *saw* her pain. The sound of her feet as she ran from her bed to ours. The sight of her small form at the foot of the bed, waving her arms up and down—straight, unbent at the elbow, as if signaling from afar. A posture of the purest alarm.

By day, she is preoccupied with "bad guys." She has invested much intelligence in trying to figure out how they might break into the apartment—by shooting out the windows with bows and arrows, for example, or by getting copies of our keys. If Santa Claus can come down the chimney, she reasons, why can't bad guys?

One night when Patsy was out at a meeting, she asked me, "What if a bad guy kills Mommy and takes off her skin and puts it on and comes to the door and says, 'Hi, sweetie, I'm home'?"

Every day there are new questions.

"How do bad guys get made?"

"Are they rich or poor?"

"Do they know they're bad guys?"

And, en route to school, from the backseat, "Do bad guys wear seat belts?"

Betsy has great difficulty separating from Patsy. Twenty times a day she tells her how much she loves her. She demands many "hugs and kisses" from both of us as if only secure in the embrace of a strong, protective parent.

"I'll do everything you say," she told Patsy, "if you promise never to leave me."

PATSY, TOO, is having a hard time at night. For three months, since the day after the assault, she has slept with the aid of the sleeping pill Halcion. Now, concerned that she is becoming addicted, she is trying to reduce her dosage and by degrees to stop using the drug altogether. It's proving difficult.

"When I reduce the dosage even slightly," she reports, "my scalp seems to tighten and I can't get my eyes to close."

The day she was assaulted, she kept her eyes open all night in order "to make sure the world was still there." Since then Halcion has insulated her from nightmares. That's what the doctor said it would do: she would dream, but her awareness would be blunted enough that she would be able to sleep through the night.

As she has weaned herself from the drug, she has reverted to the stunned wakefulness of that first night. Sleep had been a sanctuary, but now to go to bed is to enter a universe of terrifying possibilities.

It's hard to know how much to attribute to withdrawal from the drug. Shock, too, seems to have provided a degree of insulation; now the veil is wearing thin. During the first few months, the assault had remained otherworldly—a dream in the waking world. She felt "dislocated" from her life, and once, in the course of describing the attack, had referred to "those first moments when I was still in my life." As time has passed, the incident has become more frightening rather than less so. The process has been like the opening, by degrees, of a lens.

"The further away the assault gets, the more frightening it

becomes," she said. "I used to think about how much worse it might have been. I don't anymore."

A few days before Christmas, she tried to characterize "the new phase" she felt she was entering.

"Having gone through the dream phase, the dislocated phase, I can imagine that if you lived alone or were a child, you might try to push what had happened from view and tell no one. The difference now is that it's coming to rest in my life. It feels more like depression now. It's becoming mixed in with everything else in my life."

She looks worn and is often tense and irritable. Preparing for Christmas, she was a storm of activity—shopping, shipping gifts off to far-flung relations in Canada and Vermont, making a gingerbread house for the children, and so on. Yet beneath all that purposeful movement, she seemed like a piece of machinery jarred out of alignment and in danger of shaking itself to pieces. Or perhaps it would be more accurate to say that she has been jarred *awake*. She can neither go back to sleep nor figure out, having awakened, how to function in the world.

"This describes exactly how I feel," she said. She showed me a page in a book by Susan Griffin titled *Rape: The Politics of Consciousness*.

It strikes me now that one of the untold burdens of the survivor of rape is what she has come to know. She has been left holding the truth. It is not only a threat of death she has encountered. That threat has carried with it a malevolence and an insanity with a long history. Before she is raped a woman may know statistics about the frequency of rape, and the atmosphere of violence cannot have escaped her. She, like other women, will have been careful at night. Perhaps she has even avoided going out alone after dark. But now, after being raped, the look of daily life is imbued with this event. Terror lies at the edge of the simplest habits. For her the world has changed. And in this understanding she is isolated, because for us who have not been raped the world remains the same. We keep the fact of rape at the periphery of consciousness and do not let it bear on our vision.

"There is knowing," Patsy has said repeatedly, "and there is *knowing*."

"I FEEL like I see something—a presence—that others don't. I'm healed in all the outside ways, but I'm left with these terrible feelings. Other people have gone on with their lives. They're supportive if I ask for it, but it's no longer immediate for them, and it's harder for me to ask. When I run into someone I haven't seen for a long time, someone who doesn't know what happened, I feel as though I'm talking across a great distance. A part of me wants to say, 'Don't you see, everything's changed. I'm a different person now.'"

WHEN PEOPLE called with photo assignments in the months following the assault, Patsy declined them. After a while, the phone stopped ringing. I have been encouraging her to think of the absence of assignments as an opportunity to focus on her own work. The problem is that she is a street photographer who is now afraid to be alone on the street.

She has one project that does not require her to work alone. Before the assault, our neighbor Rick Chrisman, the director of the ministry program at the University of Chicago Divinity School, had asked her to do a series of photographs of black storefront churches to complement an essay he is preparing. So, with Rick as her guide and companion, Patsy occasionally ventures out into the South Side, taking color slides of the exteriors of various churches.

We have also begun work on a project we have long talked about doing together: an article on a bookstore in our neighborhood. Under the circumstances, this seems an ideal project for Patsy: an engaging inquiry in a safe setting. Located two blocks from our apartment, the Seminary Co-op Bookstore ranges through the basement of the Chicago Theological Seminary. It is often said to be one of the best bookstores in North America—a subterranean labyrinth of books, as intellectually spacious as it is physically dense. It offers a huge range of titles in the humanities and social sciences, yet its role in the community is larger, and more mysterious, than simply a place to get books. That is what we want to explore and evoke. In a sense, our aim is to do a portrait of the community by way of the bookstore: a portrait of a village of readers.

The bookstore may be a secure environment for Patsy to work in, but her darkroom no longer feels safe to her. Photography, as she practices it, has two distinct phases. She goes out into the world and exposes herself—her sensibilities, her nerve ends—as well as her film. Then she returns to the darkroom, where, alone and in the dark, she works with the images she has retrieved. Her medium is as much the darkness in which she prints as the light in which she shoots.

Her darkroom is located in the home of friends, Kate and Bill

Morrison. It is a beautiful house—a large wood frame structure in a neighborhood where brick predominates. At once elegant and comfortable, it calls to mind the word "household": all a house holds—the life it embraces. Bill is a lawyer, Kate a teacher. They have raised four children: a doctor, a poet, a painter, a classicist. All four have left home, yet their presences remain. It is the house of passionate readers: there are books everywhere and many inviting places to read. The large sun-lit living room contains both a piano and a harpsichord.

Patsy's darkroom is in the basement. Like a carpenter's workshop, a cook's kitchen, or a potter's studio, it is an environment shaped by the demands of craft and the idiosyncracies of the craftsman. Over the twelve years she has worked there, Patsy has minutely organized the space around her patterns and rhythms. The design of the space establishes an intricate system of pathways through which, when the work goes well, her concentration flows. Sealed off from the world, insulated against light and distractions, the darkroom is almost a physical expression of concentration: an environment in which everything works together to focus her attention on the task at hand.

Before the attack, Patsy spent long hours in the darkroom. It was her space, private and autonomous. The darkness was consoling, the solitude centering.

"It was secure. It was quiet. It was a place completely my own. It felt very safe. Psychologically safe. I never thought of physical harm."

Now this sanctuary has become a frightening place. "It's a big problem. It's like working in a broken eggshell. I have to force myself to go." The solitude she used to savor is now unnerving—"an aloneness within a larger aloneness." The darkness in which she looks deeply into her images now seems a condition of blindness: she can't see *out*, can't see threats approaching. The quiet that used to console her is now edged with tension: she listens for the ominous sound that will break the silence.

She will only go to the darkroom if someone is home at the Morrisons' or if I accompany her. When she has an assignment and must go to the darkroom, I bring my papers and work at the Morrisons' dining room table while she works downstairs developing images in the uneasy dark.

ON A Monday evening in late January, as we were preparing dinner, Detective Dorociak called. He told Patsy that a woman had been raped that afternoon at the same spot where she was attacked. A young woman out taking a walk. The rapist attacked her from behind, hit her in the face, tied her up, put some sort of cloth over her head, dragged her past the basketball courts to the rocks, and raped her. Dorociak had little doubt it was the same man.

"He's improved his technique," he said.

Patsy was sickened by the news. She told Dorociak to give the woman her name, in case she wants to talk at some point.

"If he'd put something over my head," she said, "I wouldn't have been able to talk with him."

Two weeks later, Dorociak called again. There had been another attack on the lakefront: a woman, walking on the bike path, had been grabbed near Forty-ninth Street. She struggled to get away and was stabbed in the back. Her assailant fled when a motorist, who witnessed the assault as he passed, drove off the highway to help the woman.

I experienced a strange mix of emotions. I was excited by the possibility that evil might now assume a particular human form. This prospect released hope as well as anger. The news of the other attacks sharpened my awareness of *him* as an individual abroad in the world. Perhaps he would now be caught. For the first time, I had fantasies of catching him myself. I imagined that on one of my runs I would see him and somehow *know* or that I would come upon an attack in progress.

One afternoon, running on the lakefront, I slipped into imagining what it would be like to be grabbed from behind as I ran. What made the thought so unsettling was less the location or the time of day than the activity I was engaged in. For me, as for Patsy, running is a private time, when I am deep in my body and at home in the world. We run as pilgrims: this is our path, by way of the body, into the world. We immerse ourselves in the world, breathe it in, take it in through the senses. To be attacked at such a moment, to have the world go dark, to have your body taken from you and turned against you . . .

As I approached the place where Patsy had been attacked, I registered the features that made it such a good spot for an ambush. The overpass across Lake Shore Drive: a point of access, an escape route. The building, containing rest rooms, behind which he could hide. The hill, beyond the building, beside the basketball courts—a slight rise just high enough to provide cover. Behind that hill one is not visible from Lake Shore Drive or the running path. Presumably, that is where he was trying to drag Patsy and where he succeeded in taking the woman he raped several weeks ago.

Did he set out that day with the intention of raping a woman? Was he strategic or swept by sudden impulse? Did he lie in wait, looking out at the world with a hunter's heightened attention? Or was he stupefied, oblivious to his surroundings, blindly lunging at a passing form?

What did he see as Patsy ran toward him? I imagine he looked out at this woman, this universe, and saw something akin to a pornographic image: a woman as meat, faceless, rapeable.

She ran past. Then he launched his attack and ran her down. I recall the sensations I used to feel in races when I overtook and passed another runner. Although you don't touch, the excitement of that moment is carnal. It strikes something deep in the psyche. The animal impulse to bring down from behind. The predator's exuberance. The moment you know you have broken the other is like biting through a bone with your teeth.

Can I more easily imagine being the rapist than his victim? To be rendered powerless, to be in the absolute control of someone who wants only to destroy me—my every cell resists the thought. I also resist imagining the rapist's experience beyond a certain point, but do I back off because it's too alien or because it's too familiar?

JANUARY WAS unusually mild; at one point the temperature reached sixty degrees. In February winter reasserted itself. The temperature dropped to zero, and nearly a foot of snow accumulated. For Patsy, the snow was a reprieve, freshening the world, muffling threatening urban noises, and engendering a consoling sense of "inside the house" as something other than a bunker.

One evening I came home from my office to find that Patsy had let the cat out and had forgotten about her. It was below zero, windy, with nine inches of snow on the ground. Casey had disappeared. Although she soon returned, I remained upset.

This is not a new issue for us: Patsy's insistence that the cat have a life out in the natural world vs. my concerns about her safety and about the complaints of neighbors who object to pets in our common yard. What is new is that my concern over the cat surfaced feelings about the attack I hadn't acknowledged before. I bit back words I could taste on my tongue: What good will it do for her to be free if it gets her killed?

BETSY'S SLEEPING problems continue. She gets up again and again in the night. Her feet pad rapidly across the living room floor, our bedroom door opens, and a voice urgently whispers, "I can't sleep. I'm scared. Come tuck me in." One of us gets up, walks her back to her room, tucks her in, and, having extracted a promise that she will stay in bed until morning, kisses her yet again. Within a few minutes, she is back. "This is the last time, I promise."

At first we are calm and reassuring, but as the sequence is repeated again and again, frustration builds, and we respond erratically. Each of us has had moments when we have lost control and approached the point, beyond spanking, where one strikes a child. When one of us becomes harsh with her, the other takes over.

Late one night, I became angry, swatted her on the behind, and roughly marched her back to her bedroom. Biting my lower lip to contain my anger, I tasted the violence I might do. When I returned to bed, Patsy was upset.

"You're taking out on Betsy what you feel toward me," she said sharply. "It's not fair."

I was surprised. I didn't contest the point, but I wasn't sure whether it was true.

It's hard to know to what extent Betsy's sleeping problems are due to the attack on Patsy and to what extent they arise from developmental factors. For several weeks in the spring of his sixth year—two years before his mother was assaulted—Josh suffered a similar siege of night fears. It was as if he had, all at once, awakened to the fact that the world doesn't cease while he sleeps, that only the fragile shell of our household stands between us and the world's power and violence and chance. As he took this truth in, his eyes widened, then stayed open.

The smallness of a child's body makes certain things easier to see. When the children as infants got sick, I was struck by how disease invaded and occupied their little bodies: So *that's* what it means to be sick. As Josh struggled with night terrors, I had a kindred perception of what it means to be afraid. Holding him in my arms in the night, I could feel his heart beating fast and hard inside the delicate latticework of his rib cage.

The gray of fatigue settled over the family. I became increasingly exasperated and volatile. Soon I had exhausted my strategies for reassuring him and began to threaten him—"This is a terrible thing to do to Mommy and me . . ." "If you get up one more time . . ."

One day, over breakfast cereal, he told me, "Last night, when you came in my room, you looked like a bad guy."

Early one morning he came into our bedroom, panicked by a noise in the street. "It's only the damned milkman!" I growled at him. Then, seeing his alarmed expression, I laughed, realizing that the word "milk-man" meant nothing to him. It's been years since there were early-morning milk deliveries in our neighborhood. I might as well have said, "It's only the bogeyman!"

Finally, late one night, I hit upon a new strategy. I turned on the lights in the kitchen, sat him in a chair, and told him he could remain there until he was ready to go to bed and stay in bed. It was up to him. He could stay there all night as far as I was concerned. I lay down on the sofa in the living room and slept intermittently. Each time I woke, I craned my neck to peek at the dignified little figure in pajamas sitting under the kitchen light, resisting me, standing guard over the household, remaining true to his perceptions of the world.

Several times I asked softly, "Ready for bed yet?" No, he said, not yet.

Finally, as the day began to dawn, he woke me.

"Daddy, I'm ready now."

Our test of wills ended with an embrace. At the end of that long night, it was as if we had accomplished something together. Thereafter his sleeping patterns returned to normal.

I tried the same strategy with Betsy. I placed her in a chair in the kitchen with the lights on and told her to stay there until she was ready to go to bed. It didn't work. She promised too readily, then within a few minutes leapt out of bed again as if her pillow were on fire.

We consulted a book recommended by a friend, *Solve Your Child's Sleep Problems* by Richard Ferber. He writes:

> Your child may also have trouble sleeping from time to time because of anxieties that do not seem realistic to you. She may think that there is a monster in the closet, a goblin under the bed, or a robber outside the window. Although she will be genuinely frightened by these times, she will not usually show overwhelming panic. Simply reassure her firmly and matter-of-factly that she is safe and that you will take care of her; then put her to bed with her usual story or quiet talk. Your child will be more reassured in the long run if you show her that you can take care of her than if you give in to these "fears."

Elsewhere he observes: "She can be most reassured if she knows that you are in complete control of yourself and of her and that you can and will protect her and keep her safe. If you can convince her that you will do this, then she will be able to relax."

I liked the tone of this. It made good sense. Yet what was one to do when the child does at times show "overwhelming panic," when her fears are grounded in reality, and when the central issue in your mind, as well as hers, is whether you can in fact protect her?

Beyond my fatigue and impatience, at a deeper stratum, this is perhaps the source of the emotional turbulence I feel when awakened in the night by a frightened child. I'm oppressed by the hard knowledge that there are things I can't protect my children from, that there are assurances I can't give them. I can show Betsy that our doors are locked and double-locked. I can remind her that she is not alone, that we are close at hand. But I can't, in light of what she already knows about the world, tell her that there are not bad guys who would hurt her if they had the chance. Nor can I tell her we can always protect her.

I don't try to talk her out of her fears. Instead, we have developed a ritual to help her sleep. Think about a happy time and place, I say. Most often, she chooses the pond on her grandparents' land in Vermont. She closes her eyes as I describe the pond and the things we do there.

"It's a beautiful warm day. We're down at the pond. You're swimming like a fish—strong and fast and graceful. We play the game you like. I throw you up in the air and catch you. 'Too high,' you say. Then the next time, 'Too low.' We laugh and do it again and again. Then it's dinnertime. We dry off and run up the path to the house. When we come into the kitchen, Mommy is just putting fresh corn from the garden into the water boiling in the big pot. . . ."

Unable to tell her that her fears are groundless, I try to tell a story that evokes the beauty and goodness that is also part of the world—a narrative that will wrap its wings around her in the night.

"Daddy," she asks me now, "what should I dream about?"

FOURTEEN

P ATSY RETURNED from lunch with our friend Mary Hynes-Berry intrigued by an image out of Greek mythology: a woman, threatened by a man, turns into a tree. A writer and school reform activist, Mary is also a storyteller. In classrooms and via cable television, she gathers children around her and tells them stories. Over lunch she reported to Patsy that she had recently told the story of Daphne and Apollo to a group of children. In the midst of recounting the myth, she heard it anew, in light of Patsy's experience, and realized that it's a story of rape.

Ovid tells the story. Daphne, the daughter of the river god Peneus, "took her delight in woodland haunts and in the spoils of captured beasts, emulating Diana, the maiden goddess, with her hair carelessly caught back by a single ribbon." Daphne is intensely physical but not sexually in play. Her happiness lies deep in the forest, beyond the world of men. Much to her father's frustration, she turns away from the young men who woo her, preferring to roam the woods.

When Apollo sees her, he wants her. A strong runner, Daphne flees his attentions. He runs after her.

"Though I pursue you, I am no enemy. Stay, sweet nymph!" he implores her. "You flee as the lamb flees the wolf, or the deer the lion, as doves on fluttering wings fly from an eagle, as all creatures flee their natural foes!"

He urges her to stop: "Alas, how I fear lest you trip and fall, lest briars scratch your innocent legs, and I be the cause of your hurting yourself. There are rough places through which you are running—go less swiftly, I beg of you, slow your flight, and I in turn shall pursue less swiftly!"

Then he tries another tack. "I am not a peasant living in a mountain hut, nor am I a shepherd or boorish herdsman who tends his flocks and cattle in this region," he declares. "Silly girl, you do not know from whom you are fleeing: indeed, you do not, or else you would not flee. I am lord of Delphi, Claros, and Tenedos, and of the realms of Patara too. I am the son of Jupiter."

Daphne, in terror, runs on. Silent now, Apollo closes in on her. Ovid likens the scene to a hound running down a hare in an open meadow: "The dog, seeming just about to fasten on his quarry, hopes at every moment that he has her, and grazes her hind quarters with outstretched muzzle, but the hare, uncertain whether she has not already been caught, snatches herself out of his very jaws, and escapes the teeth which almost touch her."

Apollo is upon her, about to seize her, when she sees the waters of her father's river.

"O Father," she cries, "help me!" She appeals to him to transform her and free her from the beauty that has inflamed the god.

As she speaks, her limbs become heavy, her flesh is enclosed in bark, her hair turns into leaves and her arms into branches. Her feet become roots, and her face becomes the treetop. All that remains is her loveliness.

So it is, concludes Ovid, that Apollo thereafter regarded the laurel as his tree. Sprigs of laurel adorned his hair, lyre, and quiver; and the victors in athletic contests and war were crowned in wreaths of laurel.

This story held great resonance for Patsy. What struck her most was not the obvious parallel: a woman running, in flight from a predatory male. It was, as she put it, "the option of becoming a tree."

"I mean," she explained, "both the alternative of giving up sex, of withdrawing from men, and the alternative of moving to the woods. Back to nature."

In the geography of our lives, the latter alternative is represented by the area in Vermont where Patsy grew up. Her parents live on the western flank of Mount Mansfield. Among the highest privately owned property on the mountain, their land borders on state forest. The woods are dense with birch and ash, maple and beech. On a clear day, one looks up at the mountain and down the valley to Lake Champlain shimmering in the distance and, beyond, to the Adirondacks.

When we visit during the summer, we stay in a cottage Patsy's parents had built several years ago near their house on Mount Mansfield. For nine months of the year they rent it; and in the summers it's available to us. There is a small room I use as an office, and we built a darkroom in the basement for Patsy. By degrees, the cottage has become a second home for us and the children.

Known to their grandchildren as "Grammy Dot" and "Wis," Dot and Lew Evans are effortlessly hospitable. Yet their house is full of restlessness. It's easy to see Patsy as their daughter. They move through the world with the same lean vitality and hunger for physical activity. This is a family in which everyone seeks refuge in physical activity—gardening, hiking, skiing, tinkering—outside the house.

In March, during spring vacation, Patsy and the children went to Vermont for ten days. It was the first time we had been apart since the assault. When she called the day after they arrived, she sounded good.

"For the first time since the attack, I've noticed physical beauty. There was a spring snow the day we arrived. I went cross-country skiing. It's as if it had snowed just for me."

Several days later, her tone began to change.

"There's no outlet for my feelings here," she complained. "I don't get what I need. But I can get out into the world. I've been skiing every day. As the weather has gotten nice in Chicago, I've felt cut off from the world. *Caged.*"

I had been uneasy about the prospect of being separated. Then, the night before she and the children left for Vermont, we had made love. Patsy's recoil from me had been immediate; she could scarcely stand being touched or kissed. It was as if she wanted me to make love without touching her.

I can't bear this much longer, I thought. An uncharacteristic thought—allowed, I suspect, by the knowledge that she was about to leave.

Alone in the apartment, I worked long hours and slept deeply. I became aware of how hollowed out by fatigue and stress I was. As the days passed, I resumed friendly relations with my body.

IN THE absence of the family, the cat became a larger presence in my life and I in hers. Small, bright-eyed, and deaf, Casey is the source of much delight for the children. At night she often sleeps with her head nestled under Josh's chin. Her primary bond is with Patsy; this has been especially true in recent months, when Patsy has been home more than usual. The sight of Casey, curled up on the sofa, deeply asleep, is consoling for Patsy. "It's an image of peace," she once remarked, "of the world as it should be."

Now, with the family gone, Casey gently but insistently demands attention from me. Sometimes she just wants to be touched, to be petted, to make contact, but mostly she wants me to open the back door for her. She hungers to be out in the world, and Patsy, despite the obvious dangers and the irritation of certain neighbors, has insisted that she have this freedom. Casey's comings and goings create in our lives a rhythm of anxiety followed by relief when we hear the ringing of her bell—a sound she herself can't hear as she trots across the yard toward our back door with her head cocked to one side.

We put the bell on her collar after she brought home several birds and presented them to us. It's amusing now to watch her hunt in the backyard. She stalks a bird, then pounces, setting the bell to ringing and alerting her intended prey. As the bird flies away, she looks confused, as if trying to figure out what she did wrong.

One afternoon, as I left the apartment to do some errands, I released Casey into the yard. It was a beautiful early spring day, and she was keen to be out. When I came back an hour later, she wasn't around. I went for a run and came back. Still no Casey. I checked the basement and the Spooky House. I became more and more anxious. I stayed in the kitchen, near the back door. At seven-thirty, she had still not returned. I checked the basement again. Alone in the apartment, six months after the attack on Patsy, I realized that if Casey didn't come back, I would weep and weep. I went to check the Spooky House again. As I approached, I heard her mewing; she must have been asleep when I checked earlier. I was overjoyed.

THE CHILDREN returned from Vermont in high spirits. Josh was excited about the approaching start of the Pee Wee League baseball season. And Betsy no longer seemed oppressed by fears and questions. Occupied by the project of learning how to whistle, she was imperturbably cheerful. Soon after their return, she sat on my lap with a book. I told her how pleased I was to see her happy after the period during which she had been so distressed. She had no idea what I meant.

Patsy, by contrast, was rigid with tension. The day after her return, we argued.

"Don't you understand?" she wept. "I have a great hole in me."

That evening Patsy lay beside Betsy in her bed, among stuffed animals, reading her a bedtime story. She began, silently, to cry. Betsy wiped away the tears. No words were exchanged.

FIFTEEN

AFTER SIX months, Patsy is suffering more rather than less. Barbara Engel told us to expect this. Still, it's a surprise. One expects recovery, no matter how protracted, to be a matter of feeling progressively better. But this process clearly has its own shape and logic. We are coming to recognize that things will almost certainly get worse before they get better.

Patsy now uses words she didn't use at first. She sometimes talks as if her suffering were her fault.

"I'm starting to feel ashamed and embarrassed," she said one night, in tears, in bed. "In some strange way, I'm beginning to feel humiliated."

Six months after the attack, she says, "the fog is lifting." A harsh new world is being revealed.

"It's as if the world is an alien sea, and the apartment, the children, and you are a boat."

It has taken time for certain questions to form, for vague dread to crystallize into specific perceptions of risk. She speaks, with amazement, of things she used to do in the months following the assault which she would never do now, like drive downtown alone at night, park in a parking lot, go up alone in an elevator.

"I'm so afraid. Every time I have to go from the car to the front door, all I can think about are all the possibilities, all the things that could happen. I wish I thought there was another world out there beyond this one."

She is taking the measure of the loss. "He really took something away from me. He wouldn't be a person who could actually know what it would be like to go through what a woman has to go through after this. Yet I feel that in some way it must have been intended."

She speaks often of the loss of her freedom. "I never was a fearful person. And I'm someone who really values my freedom. So I have to find some way to feel that again. I don't feel free anymore."

She used to be free by "defying" her fears, but that won't work any-more. She cannot *not* acknowledge her fears, cannot push past them by acts of raw will.

"I've got to change the way I live."

Since the first shaky days after returning from Vermont in March, she has moved decisively on several fronts. She has begun to see a ther-apist recommended by Barbara Engel named Barbara Brodley. She has purchased a bicycle—a sturdy red mountain bike—so that she can ride on the lakefront with me when I run. (Her foot is still healing from bunion surgery.) And she has enrolled in a self-defense course.

I encourage her to see such countermeasures not as evidence of oppression but as exercises of freedom. She listens closely, but is not persuaded.

"It doesn't feel like my life. It's like having someone else living inside me. What if I had behaved like this before the attack? What if I had been afraid to walk from the car to the door? What if I had asked you to come and sit outside the darkroom while I worked? What would you have thought? What would *I* have thought? That I was a timid, paranoid person?"

She has no doubt that her fears have a basis and that her precautions are warranted, but that only sharpens the question. "What if I had behaved like this before the attack? What sort of person would I have been?"

THE DARKROOM remains a frightening place. She feels exposed there. As a result, she goes there as little as possible, and her work suffers.

"Before there was no separation between shooting and printing. It was one process. Now it's completely different. Printing means going to the darkroom. It means feeling afraid."

The transformation of the darkroom into a place where she feels caged and imperiled was "a completely unexpected development." At first, she thought it was a displaced phobic reaction that would eventually go away. She was mystified. "The rape didn't happen there, so why am I afraid to enter the Morrisons' basement?" The fears haven't passed with time, however, and she no longer expects that they will.

"I don't now think it's as crazy as it seemed in the beginning. I don't think it's going to change."

As she has remapped her world in light of the assault, the possibility of being attacked in the Morrisons' basement has become real and immediate. She worries that someone might break into the house to rob it and, finding her there alone, assault her; she worries that an intruder may already be in the house when she enters it. There is a basis for such fears. The house has been broken into several times—once when the family was at home, asleep. She knew this before, but the knowledge has a different weight now that she knows in her marrow what it means to be assaulted. "There is knowing, and there is *knowing.*"

For some months after the attack, she could only use the darkroom if someone was home—a family member or the housekeeper—or if I accompanied her. Then, for a time, she was able to go there alone. She would coax Hector, the Morrisons' arthritic, twelve-year-old Labrador retriever, down the basement stairs and get him to lie down outside the darkroom door. But Hector died, and the problem again became acute. She began to research alternative possibilities—other sites for the darkroom, the possibility of putting bars on the windows or installing a panic button. Finally, she arranged to have the Morrisons' alarm system extended to the basement and installed in her darkroom.

The workplace of an artist is, in a sense, a state of mind; it's a quality of attention. As I walk to my office, I try to enter into the day's work, to begin to write in my head. I cultivate a dreamy, brooding state of mind. Patsy, by contrast, approaches her darkroom in a state of vigilance, making constant strategic calculations and moment-to-moment assessments of risk. If the security system is on, she enters the house, turns the system off, and opens the basement door. She then gets an eight-inch knife from the kitchen and goes downstairs. Once in the basement, she turns the system back on and places the knife on a table near the darkroom door. Before she leaves, she returns the knife to the kitchen.

Sometimes the Morrisons forget to turn the system on. At first, when this happened, she would turn around and go home or would ask a neighbor (and her dog) to escort her into the house and down to the basement. Now, when she finds no one home and the system off, she walks around the house checking windows and doors for signs of forced entry. She then enters the house, gets the knife from the kitchen, and goes downstairs. She always latches the darkroom door when she leaves; that way, she knows that if the latch is on, there is no one inside. Once down in the basement, she turns on the system, puts the knife in its place by the door, and goes to work.

She finds it hard to stay in the darkroom for long periods. She frequently goes upstairs. (Every time she does so, she must turn the system off; then turn it back on again when she returns.) If she hears a noise, she checks it out. She frequently checks the security-system light in the darkroom—shielded by black plastic—to see that the system is on.

"When I come down the stairs from the kitchen with a cup of tea, I never fail to think that I have a weapon in my hand—a cup of hot tea I could throw in a guy's face."

When she looks at large houses like the Morrisons', she sees not security but vulnerability. She thinks not of thick walls that enclose and protect but of how isolating those walls would be if she were attacked within them; no one could hear her scream.

She is aware that others experience the world differently. While she works in the Morrisons' basement with a knife close at hand, people in houses around her, many without alarm systems, go about their lives feeling secure. When Kate Morrison is home alone, she doesn't see any need to turn the security system on.

"I feel so safe in this house," she once told Patsy. "It makes me sad to think you feel the way you do."

Risk assessment remains a great puzzle for Patsy. Attacked in midafternoon, in full view, beside a busy highway, she knows how isolated you can be in the midst of life, knows how little time it takes for the world to shatter. She extrapolates from that situation to others and lives with a moment-to-moment awareness of the cracks in the world through which violence can come rushing at you.

"The fact is that I could have been attacked not on the lakefront but at the bottom of those basement stairs."

She has no doubt about the reality of the threat. She knows what she knows. Yet she keeps coming back to "that unsettling question:

what if I behaved this way before it happened? Imagine if I had gone down the stairs with a kitchen knife. Would I have been crazy?"

The security measures serve to get her into the darkroom, but they don't help her to work once she is there. They don't provide the sort of security that creative work requires. How can you make art if you are afraid?

Two blocks away, an artist friend works in a studio behind her house. Ringed with windows, sunlit and open to the world, it is, in a way, the opposite of a darkroom, but her dilemma is the same. She has a panic button but still feels exposed and vulnerable. A friend of hers offered to assemble a device for her: a very loud buzzer she could wear around her neck and trigger if she felt at risk.

"Can you imagine," she said, "what wearing such a thing around my neck would do to my creative process?"

Patsy feels the same way.

"I could wrap the darkroom in barbed wire, but it wouldn't help. Every time I looked at it, I would be reminded of what I fear."

SIXTEEN

O NE EVENING, after the children were in bed, Dorociak, accompanied by two other detectives, came by with some photos of suspects he wanted Patsy to look at. He also gave her the Polaroid photos of her battered face which she had requested.

There is something oddly comforting about these large, beefy cops. They seemed very big in our small apartment.

They described the pattern that has emerged: three white women, out jogging or walking, have been attacked from behind by a black man who says, "Be quiet or I'll kill you." Patsy was the first. The second was a student at Loyola University. The attacker pulled her clothes up over her head—she never saw him—dragged her off, and raped her. The third woman, a doctor, managed to get away, but not before she was stabbed. All three attacks occurred during breaks in the weather when the temperature went up into the fifties and sixties.

The pictures they showed Patsy: tough-looking young black men. The face of urban crime.

"After looking at those faces and my own battered face," Patsy reported the next morning, "I woke up in the night and could remember exactly what it felt like."

THIS SPRING a New York rape case captured the nation's attention: a woman, out for a run in Central Park, was attacked by a group of young men. She was beaten, raped, and left for dead. When she was discovered, she was in a coma and had lost two thirds of the blood in her body. The victim—universally referred to as "the Central Park jogger"—is a twenty-eight-year-old white, educated at an elite university and employed as an investment banker. The accused are black and Hispanic teenagers. Much of the public discussion of the crime has been cast along racial lines.

A horrible crime, but does that explain why it has commanded people's interest to the degree it has? During the same week that the jogger was brutalized in Central Park, a woman was gang-raped and thrown from a Harlem rooftop. The incident received virtually no press coverage; it didn't occasion editorials and op-ed pieces; it was not *a story*.

Beyond the mystery of why some occurrences capture our imaginations and others don't, the tidal wave of public discussion prompted by "the jogger case" has been disorienting for Patsy and me. It's impossible not to hear much of what is said about the Central Park case as a comment on what happened to Patsy. There are obvious differences between the two incidents—the group attack, the disfiguring severity of the physical injuries suffered by the jogger—but there are also strong parallels: a privileged white woman attacked while running on common ground. The public clamor about the New York case has thus far been more confusing than clarifying for us. It is noise that drowns out the story Patsy is trying to voice and I am trying to hear.

The attention of others creates the space in which one's story emerges; the telling requires the hearing. It would be terrible to have no one attend to one's story, but it would also be terrible to have *too much* attention brought to bear—to have the world seize on one's emerging story and appropriate it for purposes not one's own.

"THERE IS anger now, but I don't know where to put it. It's so unfocused. Where should it be directed? At one faceless man?   at all black men? at all men? It's very confusing. I wish I had some strong focus for it. Even if I felt really racist, that would be something. I can't find a way to be angry at a person I never saw, a person I'll never see again. He's not the person who's going to hurt me next time. It's going to be someone just like him. I know there are hundreds more out there who would do the same thing. I'm angry at all the things that cause people to do this, but it's hard for me to focus my anger on one man. I don't want to let anybody off the hook. I just don't feel it.

"It's like a weight I can't shed. The burden is that there is this problem in the world that I feel like I have to solve—the causes and the conditions that make them strike out in this way at women. It's too big for me to deal with. I can't take that on. Yet I have felt from the beginning as though that's what I was facing—the question of how to deal with this enormous problem."

SEVERAL FEMALE medical students share an apartment in our building. Each regularly runs alone on the lakefront. The sight of one of them heading out or returning through the backyard confuses and upsets Patsy. She feels she should warn them but worries about what they would think. Would they see her as timid and paranoid? At the same time, their exercise of freedom, however misguided she may think it, underscores her lack of freedom.

These feelings extend to me. One day when I came back from a run, I found Patsy in the kitchen. She was agitated.

"It makes me furious that you can go out for a run without fearing for your life. I feel like my territory is the backyard. *Casey's* got a larger range than I do."

"I HAVE an image in my mind of myself running along that day with all of my ties to my life—the kids, you, my schedule, how I was feeling, what the day was like—then all of a sudden they were cut. And I was left there, totally alone, to be killed."

In the first days after the attack, Patsy directed my attention not to her wounds or to the element of sexual violation but to something that lay beyond them. She spoke of the horror of being so hellishly alone: the loneliness beyond loneliness of being in the complete control of someone who wants only to hurt you. Lying in bed the first night, she had been afraid to close her eyes for fear she would be sucked back into the black hole she had looked into. Now, months later, she can close her eyes, she can sleep without sedation, but she still feels dislocated from her life.

"It's as if the moment I was hit I was cut off from myself. It's as if all my connections to the world were slashed. All my pleasures are gone. All those little pleasures that make you peaceful, all the ways you have in your day to relax, the things you notice as you're driving or cooking or whatever. All those little things are gone. Nothing tastes good. Nothing looks good."

She has always attended closely to nature—no less in the city than in the country. She loves to garden. She needs to be out in the world. One of the reasons she is so attached to running is that it gets her out into all sorts of weather.

"But now I can't even *notice* what it's like outside. I mean, I notice but it doesn't *fill* me with anything. The world looks different. It seems shrouded. It's as if everything has this gray cloud on it. The world looks like it's covered with ashes.

"There is a hole in the place where I used to be able to rest and be secure. Every day I consciously try to find one thing that makes me feel peaceful. I struggle to find this little connection here and that little connection there that might make me feel everything is going to be okay."

A meal enjoyed. A stretch of concentrated work. Absorption in a book. Shared laughter. Every small act of attention, every *noticing* of the world, every unshadowed moment is a small step in her effort to recover the fullness of her life from fear.

"I feel like this floating ship that's come unmoored. Even though I look the same, and I'm in exactly the same life, I'm really not. I'm floating. It's terrifying to feel that way, to realize that I haven't been able to get those ties back. I don't know how long it will take. I would have thought six months was lots of time."

I AM reading the report of the Argentine National Commission on the Disappeared. One of the first acts of the democratically elected government of Raúl Alfonsín, when it assumed power in 1983, was to appoint an independent commission, chaired by the novelist Ernesto Sabato, to investigate the fate of *los desaparecidos*—the thousands of Argentines who disappeared under the military regime that had ruled the country since 1976. Titled *Nunca Mas* (Never Again), the commission's report is an extraordinary document. A painstaking description of the machinery of repression based largely on the testimony of those who survived abduction and torture, it evokes a world of utter cruelty.

After seizing power in 1976 in the chaos following the second coming of Juan Perón, the military junta responded to left-wing terrorist activity by waging what it called a "dirty war" against "subversion," which it defined to include any form of dissent whatsoever. Thousands of people disappeared. They were "sucked" off the streets or taken from their homes in the middle of the night by heavily armed men in plain clothes who drove Ford Falcons without license plates. Most of those abducted were never seen again. Few had any connection to left-wing terrorist groups. They were, in Sabato's words, "trade union leaders fighting for better wages; youngsters in student unions; journalists who did not support the regime; psychologists and sociologists simply for belonging to suspicious professions; young pacifists, nuns and priests who had taken the teachings of Christ to shanty areas; the friends of these people, too, and the friends of friends, plus others whose names were given out of motives of personal vengeance, or by the kidnapped under torture."

In the accounts of the victims who survived, the same pattern is repeated again and again. The individual is seized on the street or at home by men driving an unmarked car, blindfolded or hooded, taken to an unknown place, tied to a table or bed, and tortured. The torture techniques almost invariably include electric shocks and savage beatings. Many other techniques are described as well. Much perverse ingenuity was invested in finding new ways of inflicting the most extreme and humiliating pain. Often there was not even the pretext of seeking information. The objective was to crush the spirit by way of the body. Most of those who were disappeared and tortured were ultimately killed.

"The original point of the 'dirty war'—to create a climate of fear in which subversion would be impossible—was superseded, for the officers who actually carried it out, by an even more repellent purpose: the perverse exhilaration of absolute, uncontrolled dominion over others, which became an end in itself, a way of life," writes the legal philosopher Ronald Dworkin in the introduction to the English edition of *Nunca Mas*. "Nothing can seem out of bounds in a room where people are deliberately made to suffer excruciating pain. Every instinct of dignity was violated there: nuns and pregnant women were tortured with special glee, husbands and wives and children tortured in each other's presence, and babies taken from their mothers for military families who wanted children."

Forcing myself to read on, I was drawn into a nightmare. I could readily identify with victims of such state terror. My point of access, my way in, was my role as a writer. I imagined living in a society where, because of things I had written, I might be sucked up and swallowed by the violence of the state. It was, for me, a vision of personal and political hell.

I imagined being disappeared: I am at home, sitting at my desk writing, or out on the street, taking a walk. Several men jump out of a Ford Falcon and seize me. They immediately overpower me—they have superior numbers, they are stronger, they have weapons, they are prepared to apply violence without restraint. They put a hood over my head. They take me away to a room somewhere. They beat me and taunt me. They tell me they are going to kill me. They hold me down and abuse my genitals. They treat me like garbage.

Now, months after Patsy's ordeal on the lakefront, I am startled by the realization that my personal vision of hell is a common rape scenario. The abduction ... the blinding ... the malign human presence that wants only to terrify and humiliate you ... the harrowing isolation ... the immediacy of death ... the assault on one's world by way of one's body. How extraordinary that rape should be seen as "a woman's issue" and not as a fundamental human rights violation.

Sexual violence, *Nunca Mas* makes clear, was central to the world the torturers created. Female victims were routinely raped. Males, too, were often raped, castrated, tortured in ways that exploited the vulnerability of the soul by way of the genitals. But the perception that struck me with such trembling force was not that rapes are often committed in torture cells but that rape, wherever it occurs, is a form of torture.

ALMOST DAILY Patsy has occasion to drive past the spot where she was assaulted. To go downtown on Lake Shore Drive, one must pass it. What can it be like for her? When I am in the car, we exchange glances or I squeeze her hand.

Since purchasing her red mountain bike, she has often gone out on the lakefront with me when I run. She pedals hard in one direction until she is about to lose sight of me, then circles back.

At first, she couldn't bear to go past the place where she was attacked. As we approached it, we would stop, reverse direction, and retrace our course. Then, one day, after a couple of weeks of doing this, Patsy and Josh on bikes joined me on a long run. They were ahead of me. When the time came to turn around, they kept going.

"I was filled with grief and fear as we passed the spot," Patsy told me later. "It seemed like the most desolate place on earth."

After that we routinely passed the spot. One day, in mid-May, when we reached the basketball courts, Patsy stopped and looked around.

"It was here," she said. "I recognize that tree."

A WATERCOLOR hangs in our kitchen. It was painted by Josh at the age of six. It's a picture of the table that stands at the center of our apartment. On the table there is a vase filled with flowers. The shape of the vase is full and generous; the flowers are deep red. Beside the flowers, Casey, seen from behind, gazes out at the world beyond the window. And in the window there is the head, in silhouette, of someone passing by our first-floor apartment.

That someone, Josh explained when he first showed us the picture, is our neighbor Ben Brown, the retired auto worker who lives with his wife Abby in an apartment above ours. No less than the table at which we take our meals, no less than his cat and his mother's flowers, Ben was an essential part of Josh's vision of home. The same was true for the rest of us. It was even true for Casey. Although she is deaf, Ben was convinced he could communicate with her by whistling in a high register. Perhaps he could. In any case, he looked out for her, as he did for all of us.

Vigorous and purposeful, Ben was always heading off somewhere— to one of several libraries, to the Lake for a swim, to a lecture or a political meeting, to a farmers' market from which he would return with crates of fruits and vegetables to share with his neighbors. Then, this spring, he began to lose his bearings. He suffered memory lapses. He would become lost a block away from the building—or in the middle of a sentence. Lost at home. Within weeks he was dead, struck down by a brain tumor at the age of sixty-six.

Death came so swiftly that we responded much as the children did. With pure wonder. Where did he go? Ben's comings and goings— walking past our window, stopping at our door to exchange a few words—had been so much a part of the rhythm of our lives that when he died, it seemed as if the clocks had again stopped.

In the days that followed, we felt bound to Abby in the kinship of grief. It seemed for a time as if all the sorrows in the world were part of one big sorrow, as if the subterranean current of grief flowing through our household joined other griefs, past and present, in other lives and households to form a broad river.

At the same time, Ben's death made us aware that Patsy's grieving was somehow different from that demanded by the death of a loved one from natural causes. Ben's death was so unfair, so wasteful, so unacceptable. Yet, ultimately, to be accepted. However unimaginably painful and protracted it might be, Abby's process of grieving, if it ran true, would eventually bring her to a measure of acceptance of his death. Could that possibly be the outcome of Patsy's process? Acceptance of cruelty and violence as part of life? Acceptance of the circumstance that, in a world already full of unavoidable suffering, some people claim the power of death, become death's agents, and inflict unnecessary suffering on others? Or was it possible that the outcome of the process Patsy was suffering through, if it ran true, would be not acceptance but an absolute refusal to accept violence as part of life?

ONE MORNING we discovered when we went out into the garden that burglars had broken into the Spooky House during the night—they had ripped the locks completely out of the door—and had stolen several bicycles, including Patsy's new red mountain bike. She was outraged. The bike had been a vehicle for recovering her freedom. *This* was something she could get angry about.

THE DAY before we left for Vermont, Patsy and I drove out to the lakefront and walked from the highway to the spot where she was assaulted. She wanted to take some photographs. She continues to think about doing a photo-montage that would somehow render the experience. I stood by while she set up her tripod, checked her light meter, and shot from various perspectives. Birds sang in the knot of trees that stand at the spot. There was a steady hum of automobile traffic and, intermittently, the click-clickety-click of bicycle wheels.

The geography of our world comes to a point here. It is a spot from which, in a sense, the whole city is visible. The downtown skyline across the water. The public housing high-rises and tenements on the other side of the Drive. The industrial wasteland of South Chicago and Gary to the south. It feels like the center of our world. Standing on this sliver of green between Lake and highway, I have a sense, as on a battlefield, of the immensity of what happened here. This is hallowed ground.

SEVENTEEN

THE DAYS begin early in Vermont. There is no need to set an alarm clock. We awake to birdsong and light radiating through the green trees outside our bedroom windows. While I brew coffee, Patsy, wrapped in a towel, barefoot in the dew-wet grass, walks down the path, past her father's vegetable garden, to the pond. She hangs her towel on the branch of a tree. Then, naked in the morning air, she dives into the water. After swimming for a few minutes, she dries herself and walks back to the cottage—for coffee and an hour of reading on the porch before the children get up. On the rare occasions she misses her morning swim—because of illness, perhaps, or a storm—she seems disoriented, as if she can't find the entrance to the day. Even at the end of our stay in September, when the grass underfoot is brittle with chill, she continues her dawn ritual. Most mornings she is not the first woman to dive, naked, into the pond. Her seventy-five-year-old mother has been there before her.

We spend the mornings working. Patsy dives into the darkness of her darkroom as if into the pond. Working without fear, she is recovering her pleasure in printing.

My relationship to my work, too, undergoes a change. A different quality of light falls across the page. The window in my office looks out on a meadow and a stand of woods. One day I looked up from my papers and saw a moose and its calf emerge from the woods, explore for a while, then fade back into the green, leaving the woods transformed. For the rest of the summer, whenever I looked at that wall of green, I smiled.

We devote the afternoons to physical activity—to running and cycling and playing in the pond with the children. Running has added drama because of the hills. Every run ends with a half-mile climb up the mountain to the house. And cycling is thrilling. Thigh-bursting climbs are rewarded by swift descents.

Mount Mansfield is the highest mountain in Vermont. Once a peak of Himalayan stature, its elevation today is a mere 4,393 feet. It's an old mountain, worn down to a comfortable human scale. Its lines are said to resemble the profile of a man's face turned toward the sky; different points on the summit ridge are known as the Chin, the Nose, the Forehead. But for me, the qualities of the mountain are feminine. Turning up the road that leads to the house, I am drawn into the familiar folds and openings of the terrain. The welcoming embrace of the land.

We are in constant relationship to the mountain—ranging around it, traversing it, climbing it again and again by different routes, looking back at it from afar. (It reveals a different aspect from the north—more rugged, more dignified.) Running and cycling during the summer, we follow some of the same lines on the mountain which we ski in the winter. We also enjoy less strenuous perspectives: looking up at it while floating in the pond, or sitting with a drink in the evening. Even when swallowed by darkness or obscured by clouds, the mountain remains a strong presence. Lying in bed on stormy nights, we listen as water rushes down its flanks.

For the children, the pond—"Grammy Dot's pond"—is the center of the world. When they can persuade an adult to accompany them, they swim, play with rubber rafts and inner tubes, hunt for frogs and salamanders. Sometimes they skinny-dip, and we joke about "butt fish." After returning from a run or bike trip, Patsy and I dive in. Betsy is exuberant in the water. Nothing delights her more than frolicking in the pond. I swing her around. I throw her up in the air and catch her. Her appetite for such play is unlimited. Her lips blue with cold, she pleads, "Throw me up one more time."

Perhaps because the setting is so unthreatening, Patsy's sexual anguish seems more acute here, her fear more pointed. When physically engaged—running or climbing or cycling—she is strong and graceful, poised and alert. She fully inhabits her body. I love the sight of her—her open face, her appetite for life, her generous stance in the world. But on intimate ground her body becomes awkward in its nakedness, disabled by tension, stricken by fear. Like a porcupine curling into a bristling ball, she stubbornly withholds herself.

Watching Betsy at play in Vermont, I imagine Patsy as a child. A young Diana, Betsy lives intensely in the physical world. She is without fear. I am so moved by her strong, exuberant body, by her unshadowed sexuality. It infuriates me to think that her sense of herself-in-the-world might be diminished by male stupidity and cruelty.

I am equally moved by Josh's body—his delicacy and grace, his gentleness and high spirits. He seems every bit as vulnerable to the injuries blind power inflicts. While pregnant with Josh, Patsy, one of three daughters, was amazed that a male body could come out of her body. When he was six months old, she took a picture of me, bare-chested, holding him naked on my hip. We called it "Beefcake and Cupcake." I am relaxed and spent, in the afterglow of a hard workout. Plump Josh is full of intensity: it's time to nurse. The photographer is reflected in the ardor in two sets of eyes. Looking at the photo now, in light of how he has grown, Josh's round little form seems like a tightly coiled spring. The unfolding of his male body has been astonishing. Each successive stage has swallowed the last, yielding an elegant, long-limbed creature who can't pass through a doorway without leaping to touch the top of the frame. The trajectory of his explosive growth is clear. Yet how inconceivable it seems that this body might someday be threatening in its maleness, that it might inspire fear in another.

One day in Burlington, I drove past a man sitting on a bench. Thirtyish, overweight, kind of a slob. His black T-shirt and posture declared a certain sense of himself as a male. That passing glance delivered a jolt. I had a perception I had never had before: a visceral sense of how a woman might simply dislike men—as a category, as a form of life.

I look at myself in the mirror. How many hours—days? weeks?—of my life have I spent studying my reflection? In the weight room, I am embarrassed for the men standing in front of the mirrors—ostensibly perfecting their technique—who stare so frankly, so hungrily at their bodies. (A macho form of anorexia: as their bodies become increasingly deformed by bulk, they become ever more convinced they are approaching perfection.) Yet alone in our bathroom, as the shower mist clears from the glass, I, too, look, with unrestrained intensity, at my body. I consider the definition of my muscles and fret over the flesh I want to shed from my middle. I check out my penis with the usual ambivalence—at once pleased to find it still there and disappointed it hasn't grown. I wonder about my face. How do the features I see clearly enough in isolation come together to form the face I have never quite been able to bring into focus?

At times when Patsy's sexual grief has left me feeling invisible at the center of my life, I have stared in the mirror and consoled myself with the thought that there are other women who are moved by this body. I have tried to see myself through their eyes. But now it is through Patsy's eyes that I try to see. What is it like for her? I am all too aware (or think I am) of what she doesn't see, but what *does* she see? I consider the question with curiosity edged by vertigo.

I imagine my body is, for her, at once familiar and alien. It can, I know, at times (when sexually spent) be a comforting presence. Most of the time, though, it's too threatening to be comforting or interesting. Nor is it, in any sense, *home* for her—as her body is for me (albeit a home from which I often feel exiled). It's deeply other. I try to imagine what it's like to be frightened by the body of one's beloved. Is it like sleeping with another species? with an animal, stronger and unpredictable, exciting perhaps but also frightening, like a gorilla or a bear?

How ambivalent women must be about male strength—attracted to it and fearing it, seeking its protection and fleeing its violence. Strength is something Patsy requires in a man—it's difficult to imagine her with someone soft and unathletic—and it's something she fears in a man. She lives with the awareness that I am stronger. The knowledge that I could force her is more immediate than the knowledge that I never have. While I long for a loving touch upon my skin, she is aware of the capacity for violence that resides beneath that skin. Reflected back at me by her pain and fear, the way male sexuality comes to a point—this thrusting hardness—seems wounding. Sometimes I wish I could assume another form. Be present but not controlling, enveloping but not oppressive. A source of renewal and delight. I wish I were the pond.

BEFORE RETURNING to Chicago, Patsy and I made a trip to western Massachusetts to visit her sister Betsy and to investigate a possible journalistic project. Randy Kehler, a nonviolent activist whom I had interviewed several years earlier when he was one of the leaders of the nuclear freeze campaign, is at the center of an intriguing controversy. For some twelve years, Kehler and his wife Betsy Corner have refused to pay federal income taxes in protest against U.S. nuclear weapons policy and wars of foreign intervention. In recent years, they have informed the IRS of the exact amount of their tax liability, then have contributed that amount to nonprofit organizations. They have given half to local groups (a homeless shelter, a veterans' center, a peace group) and half to a group that provides artificial limbs to victims of the "contra" war in Nicaragua. Earlier this summer, the IRS responded by taking possession of their house in order to sell it and recover some of what they owe in taxes. Kehler, Corner, and their nine-year-old daughter Lillian continue to live in the house but may at any moment be evicted.

This is the sort of story I love. What interests me is the fateful unfolding of lives lived in fidelity to passionately held values. I know from my prior contact with Kehler that he is a lucid witness to his own experience, full of narrative energy, for whom activism is a form of inquiry. I am drawn to such individuals out of admiration but also because for me as a journalist their lives provide vehicles for exploring the world.

We drove south to Massachusetts through the great, consoling forests of New England. Land that a century ago had been cleared for farming is today heavily forested. And it is inhabited by returning wildlife: deer and bears, coyotes and bobcats; there have even been sightings of mountain lions. It was a joy to set out with Patsy to work on a story together—to be released from our preoccupations into the spacious world.

Born to privilege—he was raised in Westchester County and educated at Exeter and Harvard—Randy Kehler has devoted his life to working for democratic renewal at the grassroots level. After graduating from college in the late 1960s, he organized resistance to the Vietnam War. During 1970–71 he served twenty-two months in federal prison as a draft resister. While in prison, he continued to organize— moving widely through the prison population, initiating various efforts to reform prison practices. Upon his release, he was offered the position of secretary-general of the War Resisters International, an organization with chapters throughout the world. He declined. He wanted, he told me in our earlier interview, to work locally before he worked globally—"to practice a politics that had to do with neighbors."

He ended up settling, more by chance than design, in Franklin County in western Massachusetts. A constellation of small towns, Franklin County is rural hill country. The political culture of the area arises out of a distinctive mix of conservative Yankees, whose families have lived there for generations, and progressive "back-to-the-landers," who settled there in the early 1970s. During the sixteen years he has lived in the area, Kehler has been a moving force behind a variety of community projects and initiatives. Working with all segments of the community, he has sought to develop those themes—self-sufficiency, local autonomy, stewardship—on which the conservative politics of the Yankees and the progressive politics of the "newcomers" coincide. While challenging U.S. defense policy, he has also participated in the life of his community in more conventional ways: for example, by serving on the local school board.

This is the setting out of which the nuclear freeze movement emerged. Kehler and his associates fashioned the strategy of using the institutions of local democracy—town meetings, local referenda, and so on—to build support for the freeze proposal. When this approach succeeded in western Massachusetts, it was pursued across the country, and Kehler became the national coordinator of the Nuclear Weapons Freeze Campaign.

It's against this background that Kehler's confrontation with the IRS is unfolding: a man who has lived in a particular place for close to two decades, practicing "a politics of neighbors" and crafting strategies to engage global issues at the local level, is now threatened with the loss of his home because of his stand on issues of state violence. Many tax resisters are marginal figures in their communities who can be dismissed as cranks and eccentrics, or at best as quixotic figures to be admired perhaps but not emulated. Kehler, by contrast, has been deeply involved in the life of the community on a variety of fronts for many years. It's as if Thoreau had served on the PTA.

Kehler and Corner's house is nestled among trees, bushes, and flowers. It appears to grow out of the earth. There is a flower garden in front which in late summer included phlox, bee balm, gladioli, asters, black-eyed Susans, and hydrangeas. A crab apple tree and ferns stand beside the front door. Much of their property is devoted to a large vegetable garden.

When we arrived, Randy gave us a tour of the house. The small, simple kitchen was full of baskets of various sizes containing vegetables harvested from the garden. There was a woodcut beside the sink: a picture of two peasants, a man and a woman, picking apples from a tree, under the words "Rejoice in the Fruits of the Earth."

Although the house has often been shown on television, it doesn't contain a television set. There is a small piano in the dining room. Over the piano a Matisse poster of a vase of flowers mirrors the flowers on the dining room table and the flowers outside the windows. A small greenhouse cobbled onto the side of the house gives the impression of a home that opens out on the world.

Betsy Corner was working in the garden. We joined her, and she gave us a tour. There were tomatoes, corn, peppers, eggplant, zucchini, squash, potatoes, cucumber, Savoy cabbage, purple beans and green, carrots, onions, broccoli, Swiss chard, leeks, celery, and basil plants. Bean plants spiraled up fence posts which earlier in the summer had supported peas. Grapevines grew along a fence built for the purpose. Under shrouds to protect them from birds and insects, blueberries were ripening. We removed some of the shrouds and picked berries for dessert.

As we were about to sit down to dinner, Randy took the phone off the hook. It remained disengaged for the rest of the night. After dinner, we stayed at the table and talked for several hours while shelling peas and snapping beans.

Randy has fine features, bright eyes, and a quick smile. His erect carriage and deliberate way of moving testify to a bad back. He suffers from an advancing arthritic condition that may eventually cripple him. Throughout the evening, he sat straight in a chair with a cushion behind his back. An animated, articulate talker, he is a curious combination of rigid control and generous emotion. He is easily moved. Several times in the course of the evening, he was swept by emotion and came close to tears. His anger is equally fluent; controlled but powerfully present, it sharpens his words.

Betsy is more reserved than Randy. A careful and somewhat hesitant speaker, she gives each word its proper weight. She immediately reminded me of Patsy in her vitality, her reticence, and her forthrightness.

We talked about how their willingness to risk their home for their beliefs has affected those around them. Their stand has provoked a wide range of responses.

"One of the ways this whole experience has deepened my awareness is the meaning of *home* for most people," said Randy. "Some people look at me with terror in their eyes. They want to reach out and take my hand as if the guillotine is about three millimeters from my neck. I look in their eyes and wonder, What are you seeing?"

Randy was eloquent on the subject of resistance as a form of awareness—a way of gaining access to perception. One must listen deeply to the voices of the outcast, the marginalized, the oppressed, he said, for they see and hear things to which the privileged are blind and deaf.

As he spoke, an image came to my mind of their imperiled home as a vessel carrying them deeper into the world.

Patsy was deeply engaged by the conversation, as if she had come upon people speaking a dialect she understood. We talked about the parallels and differences between the lucidity she has been burdened with since the assault—the things she cannot *not* see—and the current of perception flowing through Randy and Betsy's lives.

"Suddenly you're in touch with a whole range of things," Patsy said. "You don't know what to do with the knowledge."

"It's almost a division in time," observed Randy.

"Yes," said Patsy, "a before and an after."

As our conversation moved deeper into the night, Randy spoke with great intensity of a fundamental tension in his life.

"Within me I feel these two impulses that are often in conflict. One is to reach out to people, to make and strengthen connections, which you can only do out of some kind of humility. That is to say: listening, accepting people for where they are, being part of what's already there before you got there, as you do in a community. It's also the impulse in me that wants to be loved and accepted. I don't want to cause waves. I don't want to insult, injure, disrupt. I want to strengthen my connections. At the same time, I have values, beliefs, principles that are very important to me, and I feel the need to stand firm with them. It's in standing firm that I shake the connections and sometimes sever them. I risk losing people's affection, respect, love. That's very upsetting to me. Yet the impulse to stand firm is equally strong. I try to hold these two impulses in creative tension with one another. It's been a constant theme. I have all sorts of images of it in my head. I mean, standing firm, holding your ground, and yet reaching out."

He gestured, evoking the twin principles that govern his life. Elbows tight against his sides, hands to his chest, fists clenched, he assumed an

erect posture of concentrated power—"standing firm"—as if to withstand blows, to be immovable, to *resist*. This stubborn verticality then
yielded to an open, embracing posture as he extended his arms to the
left and the right—"reaching out"—with fists open and palms up. The
gestures, one after the other, sketched a cross in the air. When he
repeated the sequence, the tension and strain imposed by fidelity to
these competing principles were for a moment visible. As he went from
"reach out" to "stand firm," there was an instant—before he resumed
his upright posture of resistance—when his hands, withheld from others, seemed grief-stricken and his stance seemed anything but immovable.

"No wonder my back hurts," he joked.

A FEW days after our return from Franklin County, we set out on the
drive back to Chicago from Vermont. With the children nesting in the
backseat amid books, games, and tapes, we talked en route about the
possibility of doing a long article or even a book about the Kehler-
Corner controversy. Although Patsy had not taken any photographs,
she had been working as a photographer during our visit. Now she
talked about the images and angles of inquiry she had noted, about
ways in which it might be possible to evoke the sense in which Kehler
and Corner had exposed their deeply inhabited home—both symbol-
ically and in fact—to violence. Seen in light of the confrontation with
the IRS, she observed, simple household objects—a bowl of fruit, a
child's drawing, a gardening implement—took on an almost radiant
poignancy.

I was delighted to see Patsy so engaged. It's been a long time since
we collaborated on a substantial project. Working together has always
been central to our understanding of our relationship, but my years of
immersion in my father's book had denied us much opportunity to do
so.

I was stirred by Kehler and Corner's principled stand. Perhaps
because of the temperamental affinities between Patsy and Betsy
Corner, it occurred to me that there was a kinship between Patsy's
resistance to male coercion and the sort of steadfast political resistance
I so admire in people like Kehler and Corner. There are, I suspect,
forms of resistance woven into everyday life which are not recognized
as such or which are dismissed as neurotic when in fact they are vital

responses to injustice. Patsy's sense of her freedom is not abstract; it's something *felt* in the body. She responds to what she perceives as threats to that freedom by withholding herself. It's my fate to love her for qualities that sometimes cause me pain. And it's her fate to be called upon again and again by me to join in a dance which requires that she summon the balance and grace to reach out while standing firm.

EIGHTEEN

THE TRANSITION back to Chicago was difficult for Patsy. After the pleasures of being abroad in the world, the horizon seemed to collapse in on her. She carried herself like someone returning to jail. The moment she reached our door after three days on the road, she began frantically cleaning the apartment. There was nothing consoling or centering for her in the rhythms of housework. She was agitated and volatile—a storm of anxieties. It was as if she were making a desperate bid to control the one domain she could hope to control in a dangerous world she can't control. I was reminded of Casey urinating around the apartment in an effort to restore *home*.

Within a few days of our return, Patsy was openly distraught. It took me a while to realize that she was upset not only by the transition back to Chicago from Vermont but by the prospect of the one-year anniversary of the assault. As the day approached, we learned from a newspaper article that movements of sun and earth are implicated in this grim occasion: the assault occurred at the time of the autumnal equinox when the sun crosses the plane of the equator, making day and night of equal length all over the world.

"I'm troubled coming back," she said, "by some sense of the light."

"HAVE YOU considered moving?" We have heard this question many times. We *could* move. Our work allows us to live almost anywhere, and we have the immediate alternative of Vermont. My answer to this question may differ from Patsy's.

For me, this place is home. To leave under these circumstances wouldn't simply be a matter of relocating. It would be a surrender. It would be a matter of being driven from my home by violence. The thought fills me with grief. I *belong* to this place. To move would be a banishment.

I don't know how Patsy regards this question these days. I'm afraid to ask. She is less deeply rooted here than I am. Although she has lived here longer than anywhere else, she never refers to Chicago as *home*. It's my unspoken prayer that she won't ask me to move.

EACH TIME Patsy tells the story of the assault, I hear things I didn't hear before.

"He dragged me out of sight," she recounted to a friend, "where no one could see."

HARDLY A day passes when we don't hear from Hans Zeisel, the Viennese statistician, now in his eighties, who collaborated with my father on a massive study of the American jury system and in the process became part of our extended family. Hans phones daily and visits frequently. He rarely mentions the assault on Patsy; and when he does, he reassures himself by talking of it in the past tense. Yet in his way—by turns courtly and imperious—he is deeply solicitous of Patsy and the most steadfast of friends.

When I returned to Chicago after my father's death in the mid-1970s, Hans extended to me the good opinion, affection, and loyalty he felt toward my father. Despite the forty-odd-year difference in our ages, we became close friends. Youth is said to look to age for wisdom, but what makes Hans such a heartening presence in my life is his turbulent energy and appetite for the world. He continues to work with undiminished intensity and ambition on a wide range of projects—defending the jury system against attack, challenging the death penalty, writing articles, hatching various schemes.

Hans always has a certain *edge*. I have never known anyone whose relationship to the world is more direct and unmediated. He is never less than fully present. He always seeks to go to the heart of the matter. In every situation, from the most personal to the global, he looks for ways to intervene. This can yield splendid results; it can also be meddlesome and intrusive. I have slammed the phone down in the middle of a conversation perhaps half a dozen times in my life. Every time the person on the other end of the line was Hans.

Born in Czechoslovakia and raised in Austria, he was active in the Austrian Socialist party during the years between the world wars. When the Nazis occupied Austria in 1938, he fled to the United States. He was accompanied by Eva Polanyi Stricker, whom he had just married in England. A celebrated ceramic designer, Eva had gone to the Soviet Union in 1932 and had worked as a designer in the Russian china and glass industry. In 1936 she had been arrested and charged with conspiring to assassinate Stalin; Trotsky was alleged to be among those with whom she conspired. She was held in prison for more than a year, then mysteriously released in the fall of 1937. (She was one of the sources for her friend Arthur Koestler's novel *Darkness at Noon*.) Hans and Eva settled in New York. Then, in 1952, he joined the faculty of the University of Chicago. Eva, after a brief try at life in Chicago, decided to return to New York. Hans took up residence at the faculty club and was a frequent visitor at my parents' house.

My earliest memories include Hans. He is there from the beginning—talking, arguing, cajoling, telling stories, eating overripe fruit, standing on his head, shedding tears, laughing, always in motion, never in repose. There was often a place for him at my parents' table—set with china designed by Eva. We had a complete set of Zeisel china which we ate off almost every night. It was white with blue decorative patterns. The shapes were gentle and often witty; there were frequent bird motifs. My single favorite piece was a bowl in the form of a bird looking back across its body—its neck and head formed the handle of the top—which my mother kept walnuts in. Those lovely shapes—especially the kindly birds—are deeply imprinted on my memory. A few surviving pieces—cracked, glued, treasured—today grace the table where Hans frequently joins Patsy, Josh, Betsy, and me for dinner.

At first, Patsy didn't know what to make of such a mercurial personality, so ardent and quarrelsome, so sweet and irascible. (He could always get a rise out of her with his statistician's argument that if you took *enough* photographs, some of them would be of the highest quality.) But over time she got the hang of being Hans's friend. And they became close.

Hans is a delightful storyteller. (In a tribute written on the occasion of his retirement from the University of Chicago Law School, my father disclosed the punch lines to several classic Zeisel stories and encouraged readers to ask Hans to tell the full stories.) His singular gift, however, is not narrative but his ability, as he put it in the title to one of his books, to "say it with figures." The power and eloquence of statistical analysis in his hands is due to the fact that he never loses sight of the human realities to which his figures refer. He is a storyteller with numbers.

In this respect, as in others, he is helplessly of a piece. A story illustrates this. As a longtime resident of Hyde Park, he had often heard the conventional wisdom about street crime and had rehearsed in his mind what he would do if accosted. Don't resist. Be sure to have some cash on you, so you have something to give. And so on. For many years, as he thought about crime and wrote about crime, he remained personally untouched by crime. Then one day, crossing the Midway after lunch at the faculty club, he was approached by two youths. They asked him how to get to Sixty-third and Cottage Grove. He gave them directions.

"That's too far to walk," they said.

He suggested they take a bus.

"But we don't have any money for a bus," they said.

Hans reached in his pocket, pulled out a money clip thick with bills, and peeled off a couple of dollars. The boys lunged forward.

"This is a stickup," one of them said.

The moment for prudence and restraint was at hand. Hans responded characteristically.

"You *idiots*," he exploded, "do you want to go to jail for 2.3 years for a lousy fifty dollars?"

Utterly baffled, the boys fled.

In my conversations with Hans, I probe what he has learned about rape from his inquiries into the workings of the legal system. He directed me to a striking finding in the study he and my father did of the jury system. Drawing on massive empirical data, they demonstrate that in a wide variety of cases the decisions of the citizen nonlawyers who make up juries are consistent with how the presiding judge would have decided the particular case. One area where there is a sharp divergence, however, is rape. They found that juries "closely, and often harshly, scrutinize the female defendant whenever there are suggestions of contributory behavior on her part." In other words, if the victim knew her assailant, had been drinking with him, had a "promiscuous" sexual history, etc., the jury, departing from the law, was disposed to acquit. They characterized the degree of divergence between jury and judge in rape cases as "startling" and observed, "This rewriting of the law to accommodate the defendant when the female victim has taken a risk is on occasion carried to a cruel extreme."

"Rape is a peculiarly elusive crime," Hans remarked one day as we sat in the garden. It goes to the core of the victim's physical being, yet it is also, in a sense, invisible. The *deniability* of rape—by the defendant, by the community—rests on this circumstance.

"Unlike homicide," he said, "you don't have a dead body."

PATSY AND I have decided to do a book together, but it will not be the book about Randy Kehler and Betsy Corner which we contemplated over the summer. It will be about the aftermath of the assault. The idea was first proposed to us months ago by a friend in publishing who had herself been raped some years ago. We lived with it for a while and gradually made it our own. Now we have decided to go forward.

Since the day Patsy was attacked, I have been writing about it. With no sense of form or occasion, I have been scribbling barely legible notes—a fragment of conversation, an image, a child's question—on odd scraps of paper and in the margins of other manuscripts, never looking back or rereading, not even establishing a folder to hold the notes, as if hiding from myself what I was doing. I couldn't *not* record what was happening, couldn't *not* respond as a writer. It was as if, at some level, I knew what to do, or perhaps, to be more exact, didn't know what else to do.

The book, as we conceive it, is a journalistic inquiry—an effort to explore the world by way of our own experience. I have no impulse to write in a confessional mode, to tell a story of personal woe as an end in itself. Nor do we see ourselves as offering a recipe for recovery. I know from talking with Barbara Engel that individuals respond to rape in a variety of ways; they possess different strengths and draw on different constellations of resources. The point is not that Patsy's story offers *the* model for how to respond to rape. It's rather that her distinctive strengths—among them, her fierce insistence on keeping certain questions open—coupled with her relationship to me as a writer create a space in which some illumination might be possible.

The impetus for this project has arisen as much from her need to tell and be heard as from my need to listen and record. It's as if she knew from the start that her psychic survival depended on this. The book is thus a form wrapped around a process already unfolding; it's a vehicle for energies already in play.

For me as a writer, there are so many questions. I know how to approach writing about Randy Kehler and Betsy Corner, but where am I to stand in relation to Patsy, the children, myself? Can I report as a journalist from the innermost circle of my life? Is it possible to tell *this* story from *this* perspective?

From the first moments after the assault, we have been swamped on all sides by contending narratives of what happened. Narratives shaped to serve different purposes. Narratives urged on us from different perspectives. Narratives advancing different agendas. I have tried to hold these narratives at bay, to clear a space in which to pay attention to the unfolding of *Patsy's* story. Now I must confront the fact that I don't know what happened.

LUNCH AT a local restaurant with Barbara Engel. We talked for a couple of hours—somewhat tentatively at first, then with growing momentum.

Like many anti-rape activists, Barbara was herself a victim of rape. It happened on a February night in 1972. She was twenty years old, a student at the University of Chicago, returning home from the library. She lived in an apartment over a storefront on Fifty-fifth Street. She pulled her car into a vacant lot across the street from her apartment. As she opened the car door, a hooded man put a knife to her throat and forced her back into the car. She struggled, but he quickly subdued her.

"During the rape, a phrase went over and over in my head: 'This has happened so many times before. This has happened so many times before.' At that moment, I felt connected to this river of women from the past and into the future who were assaulted and who would be assaulted. I'd tapped into this horrible underground truth—this deep river of pain."

A person of embracing warmth and good humor, Barbara becomes sharply focused and her presence takes on a quality of gravity when she talks about violence against women.

After the rapist left, she went upstairs to the apartment she shared with several roommates and did something that years later still seemed to surprise her. She took plates made by one of her roommates, a potter, and threw them to the floor, smashing them to pieces. At first, she spoke as if this were an expression of rage. Then she interrupted herself.

"I've always interpreted this as anger, but I know it wasn't anger. This is the first time I've really been honest about it. I think I was trying to find a way of *showing* others what had happened to me."

Within a few months of the rape, Barbara left Chicago and went to Boston, where she helped set up one of the first rape crisis hot lines in the country. When the hot line went into operation, the first call she received was from an eighty-seven-year-old woman.

"It sounded like it had just happened. She was so relieved to have someone to tell and someplace she could say the words out loud."

The woman, it turned out, had been raped when she was seventeen years old and had never spoken with anyone about it.

"I was completely undone. I had felt that I was recovering from the effects of the rape, that I was functioning well." She had been educating herself about rape, preparing to work in the area. But the elderly woman's phone call derailed her. "It threw me back into my own pain. I realized I was nowhere near ready."

She retreated from anti-rape work. It would be several years before she could even bring herself to read about rape. She circled back by way of travel in Europe, academic study, and a job working with abused children. Then, in 1978, she became director of Women's Services at the YWCA in downtown Chicago.

Over the next decade, under her direction, Women's Services grew from two staff members to fourteen and took on a range of functions, but the heart of the operation was always the counseling sessions with individual women who had suffered violence at the hands of men. The effort was to create "a safe place" where victims could tell their stories and struggle to make sense of what had happened.

I asked Barbara what she tells rape victims when she first meets with them.

"I usually say very little. I try to follow the victim's lead—to provide a generosity of listening, without being prescriptive or directive. You must recognize that you can't make it better for the victim—you can't fix it. What you can do is listen deeply and well and thereby contribute to the conditions for her to heal herself."

She tries to discern what the issues are for the individual. If the victim expresses concern about the intense and turbulent emotions she is feeling, Barbara reassures her that what she is feeling has been felt by many other women.

"And I always tell her," Barbara said, her eyes flooding with tears, "how sorry I am that this terrible thing happened to her."

We ordered coffee. When we resumed, the conversation moved in another direction.

"I've been working full-time on this issue since 1971. Hundreds of other women like me around the country have been doing the same. So why has there been so little progress?"

Positive changes have occurred over the years, she observed. There are more services for victims. There is greater openness. The front-line institutions—the police, the criminal justice system—have, to some degree, been sensitized.

"Yet despite all these changes, it almost seems that denial has grown stronger. There remain not just pockets of denial in the society but solid strata of denial. I find it hard not to agree with those feminists who argue that rape is an exercise of male power, a means of maintaining the prerogatives of patriarchy."

Barbara said this with force and conviction. Yet she did not seem fully satisfied with it as an explanation. She continued.

"The truth is that even those who've been victims of sexual assault engage in denial. For example, we know of rape trials in which jurors who had themselves been raped were strongly inclined to blame the victim."

I had been struck, I said, by how some people have reacted to the assault on Patsy—seizing on the particular circumstances of the attack as if they provide a rational explanation of why it occurred. This seems not so much a matter of "blaming the victim" (though at times it felt that way) as of reassuring themselves that the world is manageable by distinguishing themselves from the victim: Patsy was assaulted *because* she was running north of Forty-seventh Street, *because* she was running alone, *because* she was running. I don't do these things, so I'm safe.

Patsy's sense of the world is very different. In the course of her daily routine, she was struck down by a random act of terror. It happened in the middle of the day, next to a busy highway, in full view of those driving by. If it could happen there, it could happen anywhere—when she took the garbage out to the alley, when she walked from the car to the front door, when she descended the stairs to her darkroom. As she sees it, she was assaulted not because she was in a particular place at a particular time but because she is a woman. This way of looking at things makes it very hard to move through the world.

"You can't live with moment-to-moment awareness that you might be assaulted anywhere at any time," Barbara said. "If you're going to function in the world, a certain degree of denial is necessary. I know better, but I deny what I know in order to function."

There is something else as well, she said, that facilitates denial and contributes to the invisibility of the phenomenon: the sheer difficulty of communicating the nature of the injury.

"In all the years I've been speaking about this, I've never been able to find words to describe the *loss of control* rape victims experience."

She recalled that a year before she was raped a close friend of hers had been raped. She had tried to support her friend, to share what she was going through. When she herself was raped, this friend was the first person she called. In the emergency room, Barbara told her, "I didn't understand until now."

She went on to talk about the aftermath. "The violence doesn't end when the guy zips up his pants and leaves. The sense of loss of control—of powerlessness and vulnerability—deepen and pervade your life long after the assault. They enter into your sense of the world."

We got up from the table and put on our coats.

"A lot of people," said Barbara, "never heal."

NINETEEN

As WINTER yields to spring, Patsy is in renewed distress. Irritable, anxious, full of foreboding. Overwhelmed by the day-to-day demands of the household, she flails around. She has little patience with the children. When they are around, she is almost continuously in low-level conflict with one or the other.

One night, at her request, we sat at the table, after putting the children to bed, and talked.

"I'm in terrible shape," she said. "I feel like there are a thousand broken pieces inside me. I feel so isolated. I can't talk to others. I don't *want* to talk to others. It's gone on for too long. I hate myself for feeling this way. So weak. During the first year, I had a strong sense of being swept forward by a process. I felt I was doing fine. But I don't feel in touch with that process anymore. It's so hard to figure out whether what I'm feeling is part of the process or just me screwing up. If I'd never been depressed before, or if I'd never had problems with sex before, maybe I would know, but I don't. What I *do* know, what *is* different, is the loss of pleasure—never being able to experience anything with genuine relaxation or pleasure. I can't even imagine what used to give me pleasure. In the last few weeks, I haven't even taken pleasure in reading. There's not much left."

She seems defeated by time. "It's humiliating to be in this condition after so long. I feel ashamed. I feel like I'm a terrible person. Sometimes I can't even remember what happened to me."

She spoke, once again, of feeling "disconnected"—from the world, from the things that used to give her pleasure and a sense of security. "I feel so cut off. Like I'm from another planet. Free-floating. Unable to connect."

Every day she wakes up feeling frightened and tired. "I'm so worn out from living with fear all the time. The constant vigilance is exhausting. What if this? What if that? Will I ever be able to look forward with anticipation? I keep waiting for the next terrible thing to happen—to the children or to you."

"Fear is the enemy," I said. "It displaces everything else."

"Yes," she said. "Fear and the sense of being disconnected. It's as though you escaped death, which would have been absolute, but suffered another kind of death. The death of your sense of the world."

We stood up from the table. I put my arms around her.

"It's amazing to think what happened to my soul during those minutes of struggling with him." She began to cry. "I never imagined it would be like this."

WE WATCHED a television documentary on rape. It was built around interviews with victims—mostly women, a couple of men. It was most effective when it simply attended to their words. When it moved to commentary and analysis, the intensity eased; it was possible to relax, to become distracted. Generalizations about "rape trauma syndrome" seemed hollow by contrast with the direct testimony of the victims.

The faces of some of those interviewed were electronically blocked out. This was done to protect their privacy, but it had a strange effect. It was as if an aspect of the injury inflicted on them was the erasure of their features, the obliteration of their particularity. Others agreed to have their faces shown. I saw something in those faces I had often seen in Patsy's: the upsurge of unmastered emotion flooding eyes and voice as they spoke, in some instances years later, about being raped. If only, I thought, I could listen to one woman after another speaking this way—words arising out of experience with such authority—I might eventually come to understand things I don't now understand.

Each had a different story. One woman had been jumped on a Chicago street by a stranger who dragged her to a nearby vacant lot, threw her down on the grass, and, with a knife at her throat, raped her.

A woman from Los Angeles in town on business was waiting to use a public phone in a bar when a man approached her and said she could use the phone in his office around the corner. Once in his office, he raped her. A young woman recalled being sexually assaulted by three men when she was eleven years old. She was returning from a roller-skating rink a couple of blocks from her home when they grabbed her. A middle-aged woman was working late at the office when a man posing as a job applicant attacked, tortured, and raped her.

One of the central voices was that of a young woman who had been raped by an acquaintance. She had given a party on Christmas Eve for a group of close friends. There had been much drinking and dancing. When the time came for people to leave, her best friend's brother appeared to have passed out on the sofa. She covered him with a blanket and went to bed. Waking from a deep sleep and an alcohol fog, she found he was in bed with her and had penetrated her. Afterward she curled up in a ball, in fetal position. When she awoke the next morning, he was still in her bed. He got up, used the toilet, and brushed his teeth with her toothbrush. Then he wished her "Merry Christmas" and left.

Patsy responded intensely to this woman. "Most people wouldn't regard what happened to her as rape. They would see it as her fault. That's why it was important the filmmakers included her on an equal footing with the other women who had been assaulted by strangers."

Several of those interviewed spoke of how difficult it was to get what they needed from those around them.

"I felt as if I'd survived an airline crash," said one woman. "I felt as if I should be in head-to-toe traction. My boyfriend at the time got impatient with me three weeks afterward."

The woman who had been raped by her friend's brother received little support from her family and friends. They said things like "You weren't raped. You knew him." And: "That's what you get for letting him stay in your home. What did you think he would think?" She went back to work immediately following the rape. Several months later, her employer found her under a desk curled up in fetal position. Thereafter she couldn't work for more than a year. She never reported the assault to the police. "I would be laughed at," she said. "Who would believe me?"

Patsy said she found the documentary "confirming." She was struck by the fact that the women interviewed were all still suffering years after being assaulted. "All of them spoke with such incredible intensity," she said, "even years later." In view of what she had recently been feeling, this was reassuring. Perhaps her process had not derailed after all.

She noted that the women spoke in similar terms about the impact of being assaulted on their lives:

"The most significant thing that ever happened to me."

"The most devastating thing I will ever endure in my whole life."

"Nothing can compare with it."

Several said the experience had fundamentally changed them. "I'm not that happy-go-lucky girl anymore who always had a smile," said the woman raped by her friend's brother. "She's gone."

These comments resonated for Patsy. "It's a profound change in your life," she said. "It isn't a matter of 'getting over' something. It's a break. From then on, everything's different. You have to find ways to make that change. For a long time, you wait to feel better, to have it heal and go away, as though you were wounded. But the reality is that it's changed your way of looking at the world, and it's changed you as a person."

Watching the documentary seemed to ease her sense of isolation. It occurred to me that her recent tendency to blame herself for how she feels, for the slowness of the process, may be due in part to the absence of the sort of perspective afforded by regular contact with others who are going through similar processes. Presumably that is what support groups are intended to provide. As one of the women in the documentary put it, recognizing that the others are "innocent," you realize that you are too.

Several days after we saw the documentary, Patsy, over a late dinner, said that the story of the woman assaulted by her best friend's brother had prompted her to remember something. A few years after college, she had driven across the country with the husband of a college friend. En route, they stayed at the home of people he knew. They slept in the attic, on the floor.

"I woke up in the night and found him on top of me. I had to push him off and talk him out of it. He was angry with me. I felt terrible. It sickened me. I was so angry with him. But I never thought of it as rape. There was a sense that I was being a prude: Oh, come on, what's the matter with you?"

She felt that something *was* wrong with her, that it was somehow her fault.

"It never occurred to me that it would have been rape," she said, "but that's what it was. The amazing thing is that I never thought of it again. I buried it. I forgot about it. I never let it come back into my mind until two days ago, when we saw the documentary."

If she could take an episode like that and "put it away someplace," she speculated, then surely it was possible that something had happened much earlier that she had pushed from view.

"Maybe I pushed this episode out of sight *because* there's something earlier. An alarm went off and said, Oh, no, you can't deal with this. Just bury it. Put it somewhere."

She went on to talk about high school and college, about the constant pressure to have sex and about her resistance. "High school wasn't so bad—there was a sweetness about some of those relationships—but college was horrible." In high school she'd had ongoing, day-to-day relationships with those she dated, but not in college. She had attended Skidmore, a women's college in upstate New York, during the early 1960s. The established pattern—the way to meet men—was weekends away at various Ivy League colleges ("Dartmouth, Williams, Amherst, all those places"). Parties at fraternities. Drunken men trying to force her to have sex—cornering her, practicing various deceptions like not arranging for a room for her, coercing her.

"You'd find yourself stuck in some room with a guy who was trying to push you down on a bed. I think it was just assumed you would sleep with somebody, even if you didn't know them. And I wouldn't do it. But I never thought of it as rape. I never even thought of my friend's husband on top of me as attempted rape."

Often she would dump her date, she said, and make her way back to Skidmore. "You would be hundreds of miles away. Without a ride. Everyone was drunk. It was really awful. When I think about it now, it's sickening. But it was accepted behavior. I'm sure many, many girls got raped and never said anything. I don't think the men thought of it as rape. Get a girl drunk and you could do anything you wanted— including gang rape. That happened. Not in my view, but I heard about it. And it was always put on the girl. 'She was drunk and she let all these guys do it.' But of course that's not what happened. She was drunk, and they all raped her."

Her memories of weekends at Ivy League colleges illuminated by what she now knows about sexual violence, Patsy was not describing deviant behavior. Rape was not a breakdown of the system, it was one of its predictable outcomes. *She* was the one who felt deviant. While she knew that the men who tried to force her to have sex were boors, she also felt bad about herself.

"It didn't seem like fun to me. It seemed extremely serious. There was a quality of violence to it in those social situations that I couldn't bear. There was no way—I could've been passed out—that I would have gone through with it under those circumstances. But still I kept wondering what was wrong with me. Why couldn't I just let them?"

EARLY IN our relationship, Patsy's anger was submerged. By contrast, I indulged my temper. Most of the time I am patient and forbearing to a fault—so I am told—but I can also flash with sudden anger, can slam my fist on the table in frustration, can cut those close to me with a sharp remark before it can be intercepted by a second thought. I grew up in a household in which anger was expressed fluently, sometimes operatically. I didn't fear my own anger; I was familiar with its trajectory and knew it didn't lead to violence. But Patsy's distress in reaction to my occasional outbursts reflected back an image of myself I came to hate. Around her I felt something I had never felt before: I felt I was a bully.

Over time, the dynamic between us became more balanced. Patsy learned to express her anger; I learned to contain mine. But there were moments, frequent enough to constitute a pattern, when we would ambush ourselves. I would blow up over something—slam my fist against a table, door, or wall—and Patsy would become hysterical. My anger would trigger something deep in her, and she would strike out at me. When this happened, the delicate structure of accommodations, understandings, and reticences supporting the union of two difficult lives would collapse. "Go ahead, hit me!" she would cry as she flailed at me. "Kill me!"

After such fights, Patsy would for a time seem relieved, as if some tension within her had been released, while I would feel burdened and filled with self-reproach. I was so hurt and confused that it took me a long time to realize that the ultimate target of her violence was herself.

My most violent act toward Patsy occurred during a particularly stressful period in our lives. It was early in the day. I had just put down the phone after a frustrating conversation with Hans. Emerging from the kitchen with a cup of coffee, I encountered sharp words from Patsy.

I can't now remember those words nor what the issue was, but I vividly remember the sensation of yielding to helplessness. Standing in the middle of the living room, I dropped my cup and saucer—our wedding china—to the floor. They shattered and broadcast hot coffee across the room. I didn't hurl the cup and saucer in a gesture of muscular rage. I just released my grip, and they fell from my open hand.

Patsy was appalled. It was as if I had struck her.

WE WERE about to make love. I sensed Patsy's distress and stopped.

"I don't think we should do this now," I said. "We're both too fragile."

We lay beside one another and talked. Patsy had seen Barbara Brodley, her therapist, that afternoon and was full of perception.

"When we start to make love, I feel as if everything has been taken from me—my body, my freedom, any possibility of pleasure. I feel I've been robbed. I realize now I've always felt this.

"When it comes to sex," she said, "it's as if the wires inside me are crossed." Her hunch why this might be so: Sex brings on feelings of being violated, imposed upon, of having her freedom taken from her, but she can't release the anger this makes her feel because she doesn't want to hurt me.

"I know it's not you," she reassures me. "I've always known that."

So she is left paralyzed and in agony. Lately she has had fluent access to anger in other contexts. In recent weeks, she has been able to say with great force: I don't like so-and-so. This is a new development. Barbara Brodley is encouraging her to let her anger out, to let herself feel the full force of it.

Once again, Patsy seems to have a sense of process, of movement. Her hope is that releasing her anger will be "a cleansing process," that it will help restore her sense of herself. She is convinced that something is happening, that things can't go on as they are.

"It's just too painful."

PART

III

1990–91

TWENTY

Mʏ ᴅᴀʏ begins early. I wake to birdsong and garbage trucks. Concentric circles of sound radiate out and penetrate in: my heartbeat, Patsy breathing beside me, the garden and street beyond the bedroom wall. I get up, make coffee, and set to work. I enter the day with a sense of possibility. That which resists me at night sometimes yields to language in early-morning light. When the weather permits, I take my coffee and papers out to the glass table. Set in the deepest corner of the garden, among waist-high ferns, marsh marigolds, daylilies, and hosta, the table is shaded by an ornamental cherry tree. Embedded in green, I inhabit a privacy so deep I disappear into it. If Casey isn't around, birds and squirrels go about their business as if I weren't there. Often people walk past without seeing me.

A few know to look for me there. The first person I see is usually John Feil, the janitor of the building. A Romanian, John has worked for the co-op for close to forty years; he is the memory of the building. Although past retirement age and well-to-do (he owns a couple of buildings in the neighborhood), he has retained his appetite for physical work. He lives the life of a peasant, moving vigorously and purposefully, at a measured pace, through his daily round, stopping to talk with friends and neighbors he encounters on the way. We salute each other from afar. Later in the day, we will talk, but he knows I'm not available for conversation now.

Sitting at the glass table, I'm a few feet from the tall wooden fence that marks the boundary of our yard. On the other side is the alley. I have come to think of the alley as a river. I sit on the bank as its varied life flows by. The laboring engines of garbage trucks. Urban hunter-gatherers pushing shopping carts and winnowing through other people's garbage. The clang of Dumpster covers. The rhythmic beat of a scavenger flattening cans.

One of the pleasures of waking early is the relative quiet. At this point in the day, sounds remain distinct. When I first go outside, I'm aware of strata of sound—the rush of water in the sewers, the hum of transformers—that will be submerged in larger sounds as the day progresses. As the morning advances, the sounds of households entering the day issue from the building. Alarm clocks. Showers. Coffee grinders. Domestic turbulence. Laughter. Voices raised against children. The intelligent drone of National Public Radio.

I watch Patsy move through the garden.

"One of the most distressing things," she recently observed of the spring following the assault, "was my lack of interest in the garden. I had no appetite for it."

This spring she has spent every free moment in the garden. Her appetite is returning.

Over the last few weeks, she has prepared the garden by weeding and enriching the soil with compost. She has returned from nurseries and garden fairs with flats full of annuals—petunias, impatiens, marigolds, zinnias, alyssum, etc. Now, at dawn, while the building sleeps, she works in the garden, attended by Casey, observed by me.

The cat darts off to chase a squirrel up a tree, or checks in with me, brushing the length of her body against my ankles and addressing me with a soft, inquiring meow, but mostly she stays in Patsy's orbit, luxuriating and stretching, looking for action. At large in the garden, Casey conveys a sense of the sufficiency of the world—it's enough, it's good, it's her domain. It's been a long time since she brought us a bird. What she stalks these days is human affection. When we go inside, she will leave the garden and address herself to the ankles of people passing on the sidewalk.

This spring Robert Pohill, a hostage held for more than three years by an Islamic fundamentalist group, was released in Beirut. Patsy was taken with an observation he made to reporters.

"A man regains his freedom," he said, "in the small details of life, in the ability to walk about or to choose when and what to eat."

Watching her now in the garden as she moves purposefully from one small act of attention and care to the next, I am aware of her fragility and her concentration. The techniques of gardening are lifelines. Working this patch of land, she ministers to herself by way of the world.

PATSY'S WORK as a photographer these days has something of the same quality. It's as if she is recovering the world image by image. The project that most engages her now, that has taken on the force of necessity, is the photo essay on storefront churches. Conceived initially as a study of the exteriors of the churches to complement an essay by Rick Chrisman on their names, her inquiry has broadened and deepened. Invited inside, she is now documenting the life of the churches—photographing the interiors, doing portraits, and taking photographs during the services. When she showed some of her work to the photo curator at a major Chicago gallery, he expressed interest in the possibility of an exhibition. This has had a galvanizing effect on her. The project is now her central focus. On Sundays she gets dressed up and, together with Rick, goes to various South Side churches. So her impulse after the assault to go to church has now been satisfied.

WHAT CAN it be like for Patsy to have Betsy's vivid sexuality at the center of her life? She says that when Betsy kisses her—hungrily, licking—she can feel the transition from nipple to lips. Betsy is asserting herself; she is rehearsing independence. "I am the boss of my own body," she declares—most often when contending with Patsy over clothes. Yet her need for connection to her mother's body remains strong.

"When I think of Josh as a baby," Patsy remarked one day, "I think of a sweet round little koala bear. When I think of Bets, I think of a little kangaroo clinging to me."

Betsy burns brightly. She is almost explosively full of energy and high spirits. Yet she still has immediate access to her mode of complete rest—fingers in mouth, pillow to cheek, eyes extinguished. She has taken to putting her pillow on the radiator to warm it up in preparation for these moments when she steps out of the dance. Pillow and fingers function as a portable mom—a consoling connection.

Her teacher Peggy Malone told us this story: One day this spring Patsy had come to her school in the morning to take photos. She had told Betsy that she would come to her room and say good-bye before she left. As it got to be later in the morning, Betsy became anxious. She told Peggy she was worried her mother would not come back.

"Let's wait half an hour. If she still hasn't come, then we'll start to worry about it. Why don't you go draw something?" Peggy suggested. "I'll tell you when it's ten o'clock."

Betsy went off and occupied herself with a piece of paper. At ten o'clock Peggy went over to her. She found that Betsy had covered the paper with the word "MOM."

Although she no longer seems as obsessed by it, Betsy has not abandoned her inquiry into what happened to her mother and what it means about the world. Out of the blue, with no context of conversation, she will ask questions like "When are there not going to be bad guys anymore?"

One day Patsy took Betsy grocery shopping with her. In the supermarket parking lot she saw a woman from whom she had taken several self-defense courses. They hugged and talked for a few minutes. Betsy looked on.

"Who was that woman?" she asked.

"Her name is G. C. Guard."

"Is she a good friend of yours?"

"Yeah. She taught me self-defense."

"When am I going to learn that?" Betsy asked.

Patsy explained that maybe when she is a little older she can take a course, perhaps even with G. C. as the instructor.

"What do they teach you? Do they teach you about guns?" Betsy asked.

Patsy explained that they teach you how to use your strength to defend yourself if someone tries to grab you.

"You mean like when someone puts their hands around your neck?"

"Yes," Patsy replied, "things like that."

"But I need that *now*," insisted Betsy.

PATSY CAME into the study with a strange look on her face. She began to cry. While making Josh's bed—he sleeps in the top bunk bed—she had straightened up suddenly, forgetting where she was, and struck her head on a ceiling beam. She had blacked out for an instant, then, as she came to, had been brought back to the assault, to what it was like to be smashed in the face. It was almost as if she was reliving the attack, was in touch with the *force* of it. I wrapped my arms around her.

"I remember saying, 'What are you doing? Why are you doing this?'" she sobbed. "Why? Why?"

Betsy came upon us embracing and intervened. She herself delights in kissing, but says of grown-ups (especially her mother and father) kissing, "That's gross."

"No kissing, no kissing," she said as she tried to force her body between ours. I told her that Mommy had hurt her head. She disappeared. A few moments later, she returned and joined the embrace, hugging Patsy from behind.

In bed that night, Patsy was deeply shaken.

"I went right back to the moment," she said. "I feel like something was ripped open inside of me, like a scab was torn off. My dreams often explore the moment of the attack. It's as if they keep testing the spot. But hitting my head made me realize that there's something I haven't been able to take in yet—the *hate*."

She became more and more upset.

"I can't find any peace," she sobbed. "There is no peace in sex, no peace in work, no peace in sleep. I'm so tired."

That night, eighteen months after the assault, exhausted, her head throbbing, Patsy couldn't close her eyes. She took a sleeping pill.

TWENTY-ONE

A Sunday afternoon in June. I was reading at the glass table in the garden. Betsy came running out. She was excited, her face wide open. Patsy followed, looking stricken. Jennifer, a neighbor's child, had just come to the door. There was a dead cat in the street, hit by a car. She thought it might be Casey.

I went out to the street. Jennifer was standing by the front door.

"I'm not *sure* it's her," she said.

It was. Casey lay by the curb outside our bedroom window. Her body was rigid. Even her fur seemed stiff. There was a small pool of dried blood on the pavement beside her head. It appeared to have flowed from her ears. Flies and ants were crawling on the body.

I returned to Patsy and the children.

"It's her."

Patsy wept. Horror passed across Josh's face; then he composed himself.

"I want to see her," said Betsy. She was insistent. "I want to see her."

Patsy took the children inside. I went back out to the street, wrapped the body in a towel, and carried it into the backyard. In life, Casey had always seemed so light—as if grace exempted her from gravity—but the stiff bundle in my hands was heavy. I placed it on a table in the Spooky House among objects waiting to be discarded.

The rest of the evening it was as if the household had come unstuck and swung out of its orbit. Each of us drifted around the apartment and the garden, intersecting with one another, exchanging a hug or consoling word, then ricocheting off in some new direction.

I approached Josh to comfort him. He was in the backyard, standing alone beside the building, under our living room window.

"I want to be alone, Dad," he said softly.

I wanted to wrap him in my arms, but he wasn't open to that. Later I suggested we play ball. We went to a nearby field, and I hit him some flies.

When we returned to the apartment, I found Betsy sitting on the floor in her room, looking at a photograph on the wall of Josh holding Casey.

"I don't want Casey to be dead," she said.

Her tears seemed willed, as if she was confused about what to feel. We sat together for a while. I told her that all living things die. Casey died today, I explained, and in the days to come we'll find out what that means for us—all the little ways we'll miss her, all the little holes her death will leave in our lives.

She brightened.

"We don't have to be sad, because we'll see Casey in heaven," she said. "Do you think Casey is in heaven now with Ben? Maybe Ben is whistling to her."

She crouched down and imitated the way Ben—convinced Casey could hear his high-pitched whistle—used to address the cat.

That night she chose a bedtime story about cats. When I came in to kiss her good night, Patsy, reading the story, was in tears.

"You'd better kiss her too," said Betsy.

Once the children were in bed, Patsy released the full force of her grief.

"When I think of Casey out there so alone, lying cold and rigid in the Spooky House, it's the black hole I looked into. The reason I felt so euphoric after being attacked is that somehow the natural order of things got reversed. I saw where things were heading. I knew I was going to die. Then somehow it got reversed. That's what I want for her—for the natural order of things to be reversed."

She woke me in the night.

"Are you sure," she asked, "that it's her?"

The next day, at dawn, I dug a hole in the garden and placed the towel-shrouded form in it. Then Patsy and the children came out. Patsy and I each said a few words. She spoke of how much she loved Casey and of how much she would miss her. I spoke of how Casey made the world—the garden, the children—more beautiful. Josh said nothing. Betsy was eager to put flowers and dirt in the grave. I filled the hole with earth, and Patsy transplanted some hosta to the spot. Casey became part of the garden she used to animate.

"It doesn't feel like a cat out there in the ground," Patsy said later that day. "It feels like somebody I was taking care of. It's as if there's a baby buried out there in the garden."

That night she dreamt that the doorbell woke her in the night. It was a student bringing Casey home. "Here's your cat," he said. "She was in the street."

In the days that followed, Patsy's grief seemed to grow in intensity and emotional clarity. She withheld nothing.

"I want to feel it all," she said. "I don't want to let go of her. I know I'll just forget. It doesn't seem right."

Night after night, before coming to bed, she would stand in the darkened living room, look out at the garden, and weep. Sometimes I would go to her and try to comfort her.

"Something's not right," she said one night, looking out at the garden. "You can't see it or touch it, but something is terribly wrong. It's so ominous. It's as if my worst fears about the world have been confirmed."

"CASEY WAS so centering for me. So reassuring. So deeply in the world. Since she died, I just haven't been able to *rest*. I realize now that she was an important part of my healing. It's taken so long to recover pleasure in life, in the little things that make up the fabric of my life. And Casey was part of that fabric. She was one of life's pleasures, and they aren't enough.

"I hate to come back to the apartment now. It seems so empty without her sweet little spirit. The garden is not the same. I can't believe I'll never see her come walking across the yard again, with her head cocked to one side. It's so sad for me here. I feel caught between the darkroom and the house."

Patsy was oppressed by the knowledge that Casey had suffered a violent death outside our bedroom window—by the thought that while we slept, the cat lay a few feet away, suffering and alone.

"It could have been me," she said one night. "That could have been my body lying by the curb. Without even a tag to identify it. Just a body."

The image pierced me: Patsy's body, like Casey's, a lifeless thing on the side of the road. Dead weight in my arms.

"What would the kids have done then? The death of a cat leaves so many holes in their lives. Imagine what it would have been like for them if I had been killed. What would you have done? It would have been just like this, wouldn't it?" she said. "Suddenly I would have been gone. Disappeared."

She studied the children's responses to the cat's death as if looking for clues of how they would have responded had she been killed.

As always, Betsy was alert to her mother's pain. One morning, preparing breakfast, Patsy came upon a jar of cat treats in the bread box. She threw it away with a sigh. Betsy, in the living room, heard her and asked, "Mom, Casey?"

"Are you still sad about Casey?" she asked Patsy one day. "Don't worry. We'll see her again in heaven." Then, after a pause, "I know you don't believe that stuff."

As time passed, Betsy talked more and more about Casey. Her vision of heaven didn't keep her from simply missing the cat.

"I liked to scratch her between the ears and under the chin," she recalled one night at bedtime. "She had such a pretty little face."

One night, lying in bed at story-time, she said, "I wish we were all dead, and Grammy Dot and Wis were dead, so that we could be together with Casey." Heaven for Betsy, it seems, is a place much like Vermont.

Josh disclosed little of what he was feeling. "I'm trying not to think about it," he told Patsy the next day. And several days later: "I don't think about her at all."

We were concerned about him. I wanted him to open up, to cry, to grieve openly for the cat he was so loving toward when she was alive. I had to contain my impatience with him. I wanted to embrace him, and I wanted to shake him.

Three weeks after Casey's death, he was exhausted, tense, hollow-eyed. He hadn't written anything or drawn anything or read anything since Casey's death. He hadn't let himself be alone; he had maintained a frenzied level of activity with his friends. He had been irritable and harsh with Betsy. And he had been remote and volatile in his dealings with Patsy and me.

We speculated about what he might be feeling. He has such a powerful sense of responsibility, such a demanding conscience. Did he feel, at some level, that it was his fault? Might he be feeling guilty that he didn't feel more, that he didn't feel sadder, especially in view of Patsy's fierce grief? Did his handling of the loss reflect in some way his understanding of what it means to be male?

We were perplexed. Patsy sought the advice of our friend Bill Pinsof, a family therapist. Bill pointed out that Josh may be dealing not only with feelings about Casey but also with feelings of loss and grief and anger over what happened to her. He suggested that we press the matter with Josh, that we help him make the connection, help him see that he is angry about what happened to Casey, that his sadness is issuing in that form. The point, Bill cautioned, was not to present Josh with an analysis of his condition but to help him experience the connection between his anger and Casey's death.

Patsy followed Bill's advice. Josh had just blown up at Betsy. Tense and agitated, he was in the kitchen pouring a glass of juice. She stood behind him and put her hands on his shoulders.

"It's okay to feel sad about Casey," she began.

He said nothing, but stood absolutely still. As she talked, she could feel his body relax. Her words, and his silent acknowledgment, seemed to release a tension in him. That night, lying on the living room sofa, he began to read again: Dr. Dolittle, the friend and protector of animals.

Betsy continued her metaphysical speculations.

"What if," she asked one day, "we're in heaven now?"

A SATURDAY night in July. 1:00 A.M. Sounds of violence outside our bedroom window. Angry male voices. A woman screaming. A gang rape? I told Patsy to call the police, pulled on my pants, and went outside.

It was a strange scene—not at all what I expected. About a dozen well-dressed Hispanic youths in their twenties. Two of the men were fighting. The others were simultaneously separating them and egging them on. The women were screaming. One of them shrieked again and again, "You motherfucker. Motherfucker."

I walked out into the middle of the street, into the middle of the rumble. I looked for a point at which to intervene but saw none. They were not threatening toward me; it was almost as if I were invisible to them. The action swirling around me seemed choreographed. It was like standing among a herd of wild animals as they played out highly patterned conflict behavior. Eventually, the police came, and they dispersed.

Patsy, who observed the episode from our shuttered bedroom window, was undone by the woman's screaming, by the force and immediacy of the violence.

"Our beautiful children are going to go out on those streets," she said.

The next day her body ached. Her shoulders and rib cage were sore. Bruised by tension.

THE PHOTO-MONTAGE continues to evolve in Patsy's mind. She now envisions a set of images that would take in the setting—the building with rest rooms, the playground, the highway, the overpass, the public housing high-rises, the trees, the basketball courts, the skyline across the water.

As we did last year, we visited the attack site, on the eve of our departure for Vermont, so she could take some more pictures. We drive or run past the spot daily. I never fail to register it and often notice new things. Yet these occasions have a different quality, as Patsy explores the place with her camera—searching for clues, for meanings.

Lake Shore Drive seemed a long way away from the bicycle path. The point on the path where he grabbed Patsy is completely exposed and visible from the highway, but when I crouched down in the area where he pulled her to the ground, the cars on the highway largely disappeared from my view.

Patsy wanted to take some photos from the overpass that connects the lakefront to the vacant, boarded-up public housing high-rises on the other side of the Drive. This was his escape route. She recalls that he walked across it at a leisurely pace—daring others to come after him? demonstrating his lack of contact with reality?—and disappeared into one of the most desolate, impoverished areas of the city.

From the overpass, we had a commanding view of the lakefront. Did he look back at the scene his actions had caused: the sobbing, blood-drenched woman on the shoulder of the busy highway being attended by two cyclists, a doctor, and a nurse?

We stood for a while at midpoint on the overpass, between the lakefront park and the public housing buildings, between worlds.

"It's a long way," Patsy observed, "from here to there."

TWENTY-TWO

THE DARKNESS in Vermont is deep and rich. On clear nights, the sky
is dense with stars. When the moon is full, one can see the outline
of the mountain in the moonlight. But the fact that Patsy lies down
to sleep in a safe place, wrapped in consoling quiet and darkness,
doesn't alter her dream life. For many months, she has regularly had
nightmares in which she is assaulted. The scenarios are endlessly varied, but they always deliver her to a moment of terror as a man seizes
control of her body and her life. This probing of experience by imagination does not relent in Vermont; if anything, it intensifies. The day
after we arrived in Vermont, she described a dream she had had the
night before.

"I was in this large house with a group of young girls. There was a
group of boys outside, armed with knives, trying to get in. I ran
through the house calling for my father to come and save us. I finally
found him off in his room and realized that he was a little old man
who couldn't protect us."

She dreamt the children drowned, and we couldn't save them. . . .
She dreamt she was attacked and managed to get away by biting her
attacker's hand. With the taste of blood in her mouth, she woke up
worrying about AIDS. . . . She dreamt she was playing a board game
on the floor with Josh and a friend. One of them asked, as Betsy asks

about Casey, "Are you still sad about Betsy?" And she became hysterical.

One night we made love. I was full of ardor and affection. Patsy, it soon became clear, was tense and unhappy.

"Are you almost done?" she whispered. "I've got a great knot of tension inside."

This is such a confusing moment. Should I continue? Should I stop? Desire ebbs. Patsy insists on going forward, on getting it over with. It feels violent to me; it feels like I'm hurting her.

We went to sleep. In the morning, she reported a dream:

"We were living in a new apartment, one I didn't like. It was night. Thinking I was stepping out onto the deck for fresh air, I went out into the street, wearing only my nightgown. When I realized what I'd done, I turned to come back. A black face appeared in front of me. At that moment, from behind, a black hand closed over my mouth. I knew you were inside the apartment. So close, yet too far."

Fighting feelings of suffocation, she had struggled to wake up.

"This is the first time in all my dreams that the attackers have been black."

IN VERMONT, unlike in Chicago, Patsy sometimes goes out for runs alone if I am unavailable. She does so uneasily. Sometimes when she is on a remote stretch of road and hears a vehicle approaching, she hides in the woods until it passes.

"Am I crazy to think every car or pickup truck that passes might contain a rapist?" she asked one day after returning from a solitary run. "Any one of them could carry something bigger and stronger. Something hungry."

It's hard to know how to think about safety and risk here, about violence in general and sexual violence in particular. Seen from the perspective of Vermont, the conditions of our life in Chicago are extraordinary. It is incomprehensible to our family and friends in Vermont why anyone would be willing to live under such conditions. Have you ever, they ask, considered moving? They put the question gently but persistently, with the air of someone pointing out the obvious. It's as if we lived at the site of a recurring natural disaster—tidal wave, earthquake, mud slide—and inexplicably refused to relocate.

Why *don't* we move? The question has such a different feel when it comes up in Vermont. How to explain the ways one's life comes to be implicated in the fate of a place? How to explain that what one most values and what one most deplores—the most humane and civilized, the most savage and cruel—can inhabit the same place? How to explain such feelings of connectedness and membership to those who don't share them? We don't try.

There is no question that we feel much safer in Vermont than we do in Chicago. Crime statistics support these feelings. In 1989 only North Dakota and Montana had lower rates of violent crime than Vermont. When the figures are broken down into specific crime categories, there can be no doubt that one is vastly safer in Vermont than in, say, New York. In 1989 the rate of murder was almost fourteen times higher in New York than in Vermont, the rate of robbery seventy times higher, and aggravated assault almost eleven times higher. The one exception is rape. The rate in New York is slightly less than twice as high.

It's hard to know what to make of such figures in light of the under-reporting of rape. Conceivably, a high rate of reported rapes in a particular area could mean not that one is more likely to be raped there but that the quality of law enforcement and community support is such that victims are more likely to report.

There is, however, one thing that can be said with some confidence on the basis of these figures. If the statistics are corrected for underreporting—survey data suggest that only one in ten rape victims report—a woman in Vermont is far more likely to be raped than to suffer any other sort of violence.

The geography of sexual violence is thus not so simple. The crucial division is not between haves and have-nots nor between blacks and whites but between men and women. It's not so easy to remove one-self from the threat.

It requires little imagination to be frightened in a city like Chicago. The city *feels* dangerous. The veil has worn thin. But what cruelties lie behind the opaque normalcy of the Vermont countryside? Running past picture-postcard farmhouses, I wonder about sexual abuse.

The newsstand in Essex Junction where I sometimes buy *The New York Times* has an extensive magazine rack. Much of it is devoted to skin magazines. Is there, I wonder, among men in this diverse and divided country a common culture of pornography: alien to one another, yet brothers in their attitudes toward women?

There are, I notice, regional differences. The magazines may be the same, but in Vermont they tend to be presented side by side with gun and hunting magazines. At the newsstand in Essex Junction, *Hunting, Bowhunter,* and *Guns & Ammo* repose on the rack beside *Boobs & Butts, Thigh High,* and *Rear Action.* Surveying the covers in juxtaposition—*Knives Illustrated* and *Tail Ends*—I'm swept for a moment by an impression of vast waste and carnage, as if women were a species threatened with extinction, like buffalo slaughtered for their tongues.

When I pointed out the interplay of skin and gun magazines to Patsy, she recalled a scene she had witnessed years earlier in Colorado. Walking in the woods after hunting season, she had come upon a campsite recently vacated by hunters. Amid garbage and beer cans, there was a bloody pile of deer legs. And ringing the camp, there were photos of naked women torn out of magazines. They were nailed to trees.

TOWARD THE end of August, we know without consulting the calendar that it will soon be time to leave. Autumn colors—red, gold—begin, almost surreptitiously, to appear amid the green. Winter notes softly enter the melody; they will grow steadily stronger but for the moment remain subtle and elusive—something in the quality of the light and, even if the temperature remains unchanged, in the feel of the air upon one's skin.

The emotional tone of the household changes too. There is a heightened sense of focus. An awareness that this bike ride, this hike, this swim is among the last. Anticipation yields to regret. Over dinners designed around late-summer vegetables—sweet corn, tomatoes, squash—Lew speaks wistfully of the things we didn't do, the trips to the Adirondacks we didn't make. With glistening eyes, Dot looks hard at the children as if memorizing them.

I am aware of how intensely Patsy now concentrates on her pleasures; she seems to be storing them up for the winter. Concentration is required, too, to hold at bay her anxieties about returning to the city.

A series of ritual occasions fall at the end of the summer—Josh's birthday, followed by Patsy's, then our anniversary. As his tenth birthday approached, some two months after Casey's death, Josh expressed a desire for a stuffed animal—"something soft and furry." Among his various other gift desires (for a fishing rod and rap tapes, the latest Roald Dahl book and computer software), this one had the force of need. We gave him a teddy bear. He immediately took it to his heart.

He named it Mitch and adopted an unselfconsciously affectionate tone with it. At night he sleeps with it in his arms or nestled under his chin.

We celebrated our anniversary by going out to dinner. Lying in bed together that night, Patsy said, "I can't imagine what it would be like for me to go through this by myself. I think I would have gone crazy. I would have become completely depressed."

In the final week, we helped Lew move the split wood that had been drying in the meadow to the wood shed. Throughout New England, as cold weather approaches, houses seem to turn inward. The emblem of security is a pile of firewood, split and tightly stacked, beside the house. Some mornings I built a fire in the stove to warm Patsy when she returned, shivering, from the pond.

As our departure approached, tension built in Patsy. Betsy picked up these adult themes. She'd had a wonderful summer but was now looking forward to going home—to her room and her friends. I was to return to Chicago several days earlier than the rest of the family. Before leaving for the train station, I kissed Betsy good-bye.

"The next time you see me," she said cheerfully, "I'll be heartbroken."

TWENTY-THREE

I ENJOYED the train trip home. Solitude was restful and movement consoling. I read and dozed and looked out the window. Moving through other people's places en route to my own, I recalled a time in my life when the only place I felt at home was on the road.

The train approached Chicago through Gary and South Chicago. Entering the city from the south, I saw what Southern migrants to Chicago, drawn by the promise of jobs and the air of freedom saw: the astonishing industrial landscape of Gary and South Chicago. With the decline of the steel industry, much of this area has reverted to industrial wasteland. Hulking structures stand derelict—mysterious and sad, like landlocked ships. It's hard to imagine an environment more remote from the Vermont mountainside where I had awakened the day before. Yet here, too, amid the ruins, it's possible to look past abandoned structures to the underlying vitality of the wild. There are marshes and small bodies of water. Hardy weeds grow everywhere. Nature, having bided its time, is reclaiming ground.

The train entered Chicago by way of impoverished South Side neighborhoods. At one point, it passed within blocks of the University of Chicago campus. For a moment, the thick spire of Rockefeller Chapel was visible through the dirty train windows. It seemed worlds away. The area through which the train passed was like a Third World shantytown. In the distance I could see the public-housing developments—the Robert Taylor Homes and Stateway Gardens—that line South State Street for several miles, a city within the city, ringed by an expressway moat. Looking at those monolithic blocks, it's hard not to see the populations within them as an undifferentiated mass. Here, by contrast, I was struck by the fragility and particularity of the dwellings. A house must withstand more than the elements in this setting. Seen from the window of the train lumbering by, small amenities (a chair on the porch), evidence of repairs (a fresh paint job amid the mud and debris), and security measures (grates over windows, fences) seemed poignant emblems of households straining to hold on.

I took a cab home from Union Station. Before I had a chance to prepare myself, we passed the spot where Patsy was assaulted. The sight triggered a clamor of alarm, surprise, anger. The spot seemed so *public*. It was as if the city radiated out from this place. Although still in motion, I was no longer detached. The path to our door went past the place where my wife was tormented. I was home.

"ABOUT AN hour away from the city, I was overcome by grief," Patsy said the day after her return. "This is home for you and the kids, but not for me. I feel homeless. Yesterday I didn't think I could bear it. I felt as if I'd been put back in a cage."

Several days later, I was awakened in the night by the sound of her whimpering. She was deep in a nightmare. It wasn't easy to wake her. The dream was long and complicated. She was alone in a room with a strange woman. The windows were of frosted glass. The woman attacked her and pulled her down to the floor. She had coarse, dry hands. As the attack progressed, the woman turned into a man.

"Am I dead?" Patsy asked. "Will I ever see my family again?"

"You're in prison," said the person with rough hands. "This is prison."

We lay in the dark and talked. As she had in the first hours after the attack, Patsy tried to find words to describe the experience of pure terror. She spoke of the terrible aloneness at the core of the experience, of being alone before death—death forced on one by cruel human hands. "I'll never be able to describe how the woman cyclist looked to me. To see another face. She was so beautiful."

We lay in silence for a while. I rubbed her back and stroked her hair.

"I feel like I've been to hell," she said, "like I know where hell is."

In the weeks following our return to Chicago, Patsy's dream life became almost unbearably intense.

"When I go to sleep," she said, "it's as if I enter a vast world. Every night I go to great depths and have to fight my way back to the surface. I'm afraid that if I don't break out of the dream, it will turn out to be happening in reality."

This was, I suppose, a measure of progress. During the first weeks and months after the attack, she had awakened from dreamless, drug-induced sleep to the realization that the nightmare had really happened.

As the two-year anniversary of the assault approached, Patsy, tense and agitated since our return from Vermont, grew quiet, as if paying close attention to something invisible to me. She later told me that for several days prior to the anniversary the ominous sense of the world she had experienced in the aftermath of the attack had returned.

We spent the day together: lunch at a favorite restaurant, some errands downtown, a run on the lakefront. Over lunch, driving around the city, running, we talked, trying to take the measure of things.

"Can it really have been two years?" said Patsy.

It occurred to me that we operate with two different time scales. On one hand, we never quite shed the child's sense of time—the year as the measure of all things, the year as almost-infinity. On the other, grief teaches a very different sense of time—teaches how much of life is consumed by the suffering through of our losses.

Looking at Patsy throughout the day—across a restaurant table, driving through the city, running side by side—I thought: How beautiful she is, how precious to me.

That night she cried out in her sleep. I woke her. She held me tight, as if I were an anchor, for she was not yet free of the nightmare and feared she might be swept back into it.

"I was out in the city doing errands. I got in the car and reached back for something in the backseat. Someone grabbed my hand and starting biting it. It was a white man. He jumped into the front seat—snarling and biting me on the neck and face. I somehow got away from him and climbed out of the car. He chased me into a flower shop. There were other people there, but they didn't do anything. They ran away. In this little shop full of flowers, he grabbed me and tore at me with his teeth. I can still feel where he bit me on the neck."

She was having trouble getting back from the depths to which the dream had taken her. I held her and rubbed her back. She clung to me and took comfort from my touch. As in the first days after the attack, it was clear to us both that my body, though male, is no threat to her, that I am not a man with rough hands. How I have longed, over our years together, for this moment: when she would draw close to me, when she would no longer resist, no longer withhold herself. I have dreamt of it, waited for it, sought to prepare a place for it. Never did I imagine we would be brought to it not by passion but by terror.

A NEW presence has entered our lives. A. K. Ramanujan—known to his friends and colleagues as Raman—moved into our building this fall. A man of about sixty, he is one of the most honored members of the University of Chicago faculty. A poet, translator, and scholar, he has moved back and forth throughout his career between languages, genres, and disciplines. He is presently working on a collection of Indian folktales.

Several years ago Raman and his wife Molly divorced. They have two children, both of whom are in their twenties—a son, Krishna, and a daughter, Krittika. The divorce left Raman in a state of depression, uncertainty, and homelessness. He spent the better part of two years away from Chicago—as a visiting professor at the University of Michigan in Ann Arbor and at the Hebrew University in Jerusalem. He considered offers from other universities.

It was during this period of rootlessness that he contacted me. We had known each other for several years, and he had a good impression of the building. He could see himself living there. Were any apartments available? As it happened, one was.

Slight and graceful, Raman is an engaging presence in my life. I love talking with him. He is at once cosmopolitan and unworldly as only a Brahman intellectual can be. I orchestrate his dealings with Croatian painters, Scottish plumbers, and so on. And he tells me tales.

The first time he walked into our apartment, he stood before one of the photographs on the wall—a Marc Riboud photo of a camel bazaar in Rajasthan.

"I once had a dream about this picture," he said. "I was in such a place, and a beggar approached me with his hand out. I didn't know what to do. I was paralyzed. As I equivocated, the man began to vibrate and disintegrated in front of me."

When we talk, Raman always asks me about my work on sexual

violence and listens intensely to my responses. One day, standing in the garden, he told me a story that may explain his interest. When he first came to this country, close to thirty years ago, he lived in the apartment building across the street from our co-op. One day, soon after his arrival, he entered the building and found a black man and a white woman on the stairs ahead of him; he assumed they were a couple. The man turned on him, threw him to the ground, and demanded his money. Raman was baffled. He didn't understand what was happening. The man, unable to understand Raman's accent, left in disgust. It turned out that he had grabbed the woman as she entered the vestibule of the building and was taking her up to her apartment to rob and rape her when Raman, an inadvertent hero, arrived on the scene.

Some weeks later, Raman was taken by the police to a lineup in the basement of the police station. He found himself the only man in a large group of rape victims. A man in a room full of violated women.

"After that," he said, "I saw it everywhere."

EARLY OCTOBER. We had been out to dinner. I took the baby-sitter home at about eleven-thirty. After dropping him off, I came on a disturbing scene at Fifty-fourth and Harper. In the middle of the poorly lit street there was a large dark form. Standing over it, waving cars away, was a man I recognized—a computer specialist who plays the harmonica in local blues bands. I pulled over and got out. The form on the ground proved to be a large black man dressed in layers of ragged clothes. He was lying facedown. We spoke to him, asked what was the matter, asked if we could help. He moaned and grunted. We each grabbed an arm and struggled to bring him to his feet. It wasn't easy. He seemed impossibly heavy.

A tall, knife-thin black man appeared.

"I should kick your ass, Juke, you stupid asshole. What do you think you're doing?"

Juke grunted. He seemed beyond language; I never heard him speak a word. Now that he was up off the street, we could see his face: swollen and bruised, a face stupefied by abuse.

Juke's harsh companion directed us to "Juke's bench" in the park on Blackstone behind Giordano's Pizzeria. The bench proved to be far from the street in the darkest corner of the park. As we walked, the man continued to verbally abuse Juke. He seemed barely able to restrain his impulse to strike him. When we reached the bench, we sat

Juke on it. He immediately lay down, his head coming to rest a few inches from a pile of turds. (Dog or human? I wasn't sure. Would a dog shit on a bench?) We stood there for a moment, as if we should somehow tuck him in, then walked away.

When I got home, I looked in on my sleeping children—Josh on his stomach, clutching his pillow like a life preserver; Betsy on her back, mouth open, arms flung out. I checked that the doors were double-locked, turned out the lights, and slipped into our bed—warm and fragrant from Patsy's sleeping presence.

MID-OCTOBER. As the weekend approached, I felt free, for the first time since our return from Vermont, to relax. I had had a speaking engagement on Thursday night on the topic of freedom of speech during wartime occasioned by the growing threat of war in the Persian Gulf. On Friday I felt spent and restless. I attended to odds and ends. In late afternoon, drawn outside by the unusually warm weather, I worked in the yard and in the Spooky House, removing debris left by recent roof repairs. It was so mild I was able to work in cutoff jeans and without a shirt.

My friend Len Ackland dropped by after work. A journalist who reported from Vietnam early in his career and today specializes in arms control issues, Len is a kindred spirit. We sat at the picnic table, downed a couple of beers, and talked about the prospect of war. I walked him to his car. He asked me what our plans were for the weekend. We had no plans, I said, and that was fine with me. It promised to be the sort of weekend I have come most to enjoy—time with Patsy, physical work around the building, a long run or bike ride. Domestic pleasures.

Suzan Pinsof was to come to dinner. Her mother, terminally ill with cancer, was in swift decline. We had invited Suzan for dinner in the hope of giving her a few hours' respite. She was delayed en route, so I resumed working outside.

Eventually, Suzan arrived. She and Patsy talked in the kitchen as Patsy prepared the meal. Bare-chested and sweaty, my tool belt slung over my shoulder, I came in and joined them. I poured a Scotch and joined their conversation about doctors, chemotherapy, and a dying woman.

It was not a relaxing evening. Patsy and I were tired; and Suzan was, understandably, preoccupied. We sat over dinner, drinking wine and talking. I was only half in the conversation. While Suzan talked, I snuck affectionate looks at Patsy.

The evening wound down. Suzan left. I set to work on the dirty dishes, while Patsy put the children to bed. When the dish rack was full, I began to put clean dishes on the counter. A plastic glass fell to the floor. The sound brought Patsy into the room.

"I think we should get the dishwasher fixed," she said. "Every night I feel guilty while you do the dishes."

She spoke sharply. I responded badly. We began to argue.

"I don't want to have this conversation," I said. "Listen to yourself. Can you hear the crazy intensity in your voice?"

We couldn't disengage. Feeling trapped, I slammed my fist down. It struck the edge of the kitchen counter, opening a cut on the heel of my hand. Blood dripped on the floor.

We were launched on a familiar pattern—one we both had hoped was in the past. It was clear to her at such moments that divorce was the solution: "Go! Leave! I can't bear another minute." Most devastating was her absolute certainty that I was the source of her suffering. At other times, when she was deep in depression or in the grips of sexual agony, one of her kindnesses to me—an act of love—was to say, "It's not you." But at these moments she confirms what I fear is true. "It's you," her every angry word declares. "It's you."

It had been some four years since we had last had such an episode. Now, as we lashed out at each other, unable to walk away, caught in an undertow we couldn't resist, I was filled with disbelief that this was really going to happen.

Patsy stormed out of the kitchen and went to the bedroom. Dripping blood from my unattended hand, I followed her.

"Now you listen to me," I commanded. I held her by the shoulders for a moment. Then I stood in front of her, blocking her way, with my arms by my sides.

"Don't you bully me," she cried. "Don't you muscle me."

She hit at me. For an instant, she put her hands around my neck as if to choke me.

"You hate me," she said. "I can see it."

"No, I adore you," I said. Overwhelmed by the impossibility of ever making myself understood, I picked up a plastic bottle of lotion—the lotion I use when I massage her—and threw it against the wall. It struck the framed poster, over our bed, of Manet's *Bar at the Folies-Bergère*.

Shattered glass filled the air and rained down on our bed. Patsy was undone. Her body heaved with sobs.

I went back to the kitchen. I kicked the cabinet door under the sink, cracking it. Then the storm passed. Quiet filled me. Stillness. The certainty that one lifetime would not be enough to undo the harm. I resumed doing the dishes.

Patsy came into the kitchen. She too was calmer now.

"I always used to be afraid of you. I can't go back to that. I won't," she said. "I'll leave."

She noticed the damaged cabinet door.

"You don't understand, do you?" she said. "It's not the destruction of property I care about. I feel as if I live in a house of straw. The only sense of home I've had since the attack is inside these walls. That's what you've destroyed. I feel like I don't have a home. It's gone. I feel shattered."

I said nothing. Silence seemed the only way forward.

"How am I going to sleep?" she asked. "I can't possibly sleep in our bed."

I went to the bedroom and cleared the glass off the bedspread. I didn't then realize that she was saying something more than that she couldn't sleep in a bed covered with broken glass.

"How could I lie down and sleep?" she explained several days later. "I knew I could find no rest anywhere in the apartment. I might as well just stand like a tree in the living room. I felt like the violence was inside the house. I had lost my ally and friend and protector. My reason for being here was gone. There was no difference between inside and outside. I might as well have been standing in the street."

Knowing she would be unable to sleep, Patsy took a sleeping pill. I came to bed and passed a sleepless night lying on the other side of the bed, light-years away from her.

I got up at dawn, put the dishes away, wiped dried blood from the floor, and cleaned shattered glass from the picture. Standing in the alley, by the Dumpster, picking glass from the frame, I studied the Manet print. Patsy had returned with it from a French Impressionist exhibition and had suggested we hang it above our bed. She had said she thought it expressed something of our relationship to the world. I understood what she meant: the conviviality of the mirrored bar at a French nightclub, the tangerines and roses among the bottles on the bar, the gaiety and wit of the green-slippered feet dangling from a

swing in the upper left corner. But there was also something mysterious about the picture—and about her feelings for it. At the center of
the scene, directly facing the viewer, stands a woman: the barmaid. She
is delicate and alluring, yet her beauty is edged by sadness. She seems
detached and reticent, unreachable, not fully present in the world
around her. The mystery is deepened by a second perspective on her:
reflected in the mirror behind the bar, she faces a man in hat and top-
coat. There seems to be more to their encounter than a request for a
drink, but the man's face is difficult to read. Seen from behind, the
woman's body—so graceful and poised at the center of the picture—
seems stolid and worn.

When Patsy got up, her eyes were swollen, her face puffy. She looked
as if she had been beaten. We talked little. As we went about our household chores, we moved through a medium of gravity and regret—at
once distant and close, estranged and immensely considerate of one
another.

The children woke up. What had they heard? Josh, it turned out,
had slept through the fight, but Betsy had not. Later in the day, I talked
with her about it.

"Yeah," she said, "I heard you fighting. I heard Mommy say, 'Don't
fist me!' What did that mean? And I heard her say, 'Stop choking me.'
What did you *do* to her?"

After two days of not touching one another, I reached out for Patsy
in the middle of the night. She turned from me. I got up and dressed.
It was 4:30 A.M. Cold and windy. I went outside and got in the car. I
wasn't sure where I was going until I got there. I drove through deserted streets to the park where we had deposited Juke the other night.
His bench was empty.

The only place open at that hour was Dunkin' Donuts. Among
cops, newspaper-truck drivers, and assorted nocturnal oddballs, I sat
over coffee. I felt immensely tired. My body seemed a hateful thing.
Familiar feelings: I had been here before. What was different was my
inability to shake off the sense that I stood accused: "That's the one.
That's the man who hurt me." Since the attack, a distinction had begun
to take hold in Patsy's mind between me and the violent men with
rough hands she feared, between me and the man who assaulted her.
Had that distinction now collapsed?

I thought about him. At that moment, he was, I assumed, like me,
out abroad in the city. Perhaps he had a lair somewhere to which he

returned to sleep, but I didn't imagine him asleep now. For all I knew, he might be close at hand. We might pass on the street or sit down next to one another at Dunkin' Donuts.

AT A reception at the university, I chatted with an acquaintance. We talked about running. He knew that Patsy and I were runners, that we ran marathons. He asked whether Patsy had "gotten over her injury." For a moment, I wasn't sure what he was referring to.

"Didn't she have terrible injuries to her face—broken bones, a long time in the hospital?" he asked.

There were broken bones, I replied, but she was released the same day, after about six hours in the emergency room. The physical injuries were the least of it, I continued. She's doing okay, but it will take a long time to heal.

"But it wasn't rape or anything . . ."

"Yes it was," I said. "That's precisely what it was—a sexual assault."

He changed the subject.

I felt as if I had been given a glimpse of the dynamic by which sexual violence is rendered invisible. Through what process of partial communication, miscommunication, muffled communication had he been left with the impression that Patsy had suffered not a sexual assault but a running injury?

STORIES, RAMAN has written, demand to be told. It's dangerous to neglect them or hoard them. "They hate it when they are not passed on to others, for they can come into being again and again only in that act of translation."

Among the Indian folktales he has collected are several that tell of stories that change form and inflict revenge on those who don't tell them. In one, a song a woman knows but never sings and a story she knows but never tells escape through her mouth while she sleeps and assume the forms of a man's coat and a pair of shoes, causing her husband to fly into a jealous rage. In another, four stories a man has carried inside him since childhood, untold, conspire to kill him so they can go live with someone else.

Of the various perils life may hold for Raman, it's unlikely he will be set upon by vengeful stories. For he is a most generous storyteller, delighting his friends and their children, his colleagues and readers with a seemingly inexhaustible fund of stories. Wherever one encounters him, in whatever situation, in whatever field or genre, he is most essentially a storyteller. Draped in titles and honors, he is, simply, a man telling stories. (He insists that his graduate students in anthropology be able to tell a given story before they analyze it.) His appetite for narrative is huge and wide-ranging: so far as I can tell, the only publication this world-class intellectual subscribes to is *People* magazine.

Each Wednesday night he joins us at our table for a meal of soup along with our neighbors Abby Brown and Dorothy Freedman. We are also joined by Karuna Bahadur, a recent additon to the building, who has long known Raman. "Wednesday night soup," as the kids have come to call it, is one of those small institutions that sweeten daily life—full of gossip, conviviality, and laughter. At the table there is an air of anticipation—the children watch Raman closely—as we await the turn in the conversation that will provide him with the occasion for a story. When he discerns an opening, he brightens. He is not histrionic as a storyteller; what fascinates is not theatricality but an effortless unfolding of language and pleasure—an almost erotic flow. He enters and inhabits the tale, savoring the subversive energies that animate it, and finally, with evident satisfaction, brings it to a close.

Raman puts himself at the service of the tale. This is, for him, a matter of principle. He is not proprietary about the tales he collects and tells. In assembling his anthology of folktales from India, he was troubled when publishers insisted on the prerogatives of copyright. The notion that someone owned a tale was alien to him. He described himself in the introduction to the collection simply as the most recent teller of the tales.

I have been reading some of his papers and talking with him about folktales. He distinguishes sharply between myths ("official") and folktales ("subversive"). It's the latter that interest him. He often returns in his writing and in conversation to the idea that in India (and elsewhere) oral traditions are a medium for countertraditions to the dominant traditions, for critiques and satires that display the underside of the reigning ideas and norms—a counterrealm in which the unsaid can be spoken, oppressive silences broken, and the most difficult subjects addressed. Such traditions, he has written, "give voice to people who are deemed voiceless and unprivileged, like women and children, the lowly, the poor, and the unlettered." Folktales are, he said to me one day as we sat in the garden, "a domain of freedom and resistance."

Raman grew up speaking four languages: "Sanskrit and English were our father tongues. Tamil and Kannada were our mother tongues." Sanskrit was the language of the Indian past; English was the language of colonial India and the West. The mother tongues belonged to the world of women and children, to the street and bazaar. They are also the vehicle for the oral traditions; they are the languages in which folktales are told—told most often in a domestic setting by a woman. Thus the voices that speak through Raman's retellings are often women's voices.

In an Indian household, according to Raman, it's usually the grandmother (and other women in the kitchen) who tell children tales, rather than the mother or some other authority figure. Were the mother to tell them, "power" would be involved and the child might experience the moral content of the story as a reproach.

In recent years, Raman has been particularly interested in exploring the counterrealm of what he calls "women-centered tales." In the tales in which men are protagonists, women figure mostly as prizes at the end of the man's quest. Such tales often end with a marriage. In women-centered tales, by contrast, men are usually "wimps," says Raman. Rather than ending with a marriage, the tales frequently start with a marriage. That's when the woman's troubles begin. For example, she must domesticate an animal husband or contend with the cruelties of her husband's family. The resolution of such tales, he says, often turns on the woman telling her story and being heard.

A BOY in Betsy's class is obsessed with her. This has become a matter of concern for the teacher, his parents, and us. He follows her around, stares at her, pleads with her to be his friend—not just friend but best friend, only friend. He is fixated on her. He seems to want to possess her. Thwarted, he harasses her and tries to turn others against her.

"If he wants to be my friend," Betsy asks, "why does he hit me?"

PATSY'S ATTACK dreams continue. For her, the nights are not a time for rest but a time for the most intense imaginative work. Again and again, she is brought by different scenarios to the moment of pure terror.

"I WAS in our apartment, in the bedroom. There was another woman there. The woman told me that she had recently been raped. Like a child, I was straining to understand her words. Suddenly the door opened. It was a nondescript white man in a trench coat. 'He's back!'

the woman screamed. He grabbed her in a hammerlock around the neck. I tried to escape. With his free hand, he grabbed me by the neck. I tried to cry out to my mother for help. (Her room was right next door.) 'She's gone,' the man said. When I woke up, I felt vast despair."

"I WAS out in public with Betsy, who was a baby. I was agitated because she needed to be changed. I found a room and was changing her diaper. Two men came into the room. They were white, well-dressed corporate types. They started talking me up, trying to persuade me to have sex with them. By this point, Betsy had dropped out of the dream. The men became more insistent. They pushed me down to the floor while arguing with me.

"'But this is rape,' I told them. 'If you go any farther, this is rape.'

"They denied that it was rape. Then one of them suggested, 'Let's call the priest.' I was relieved, thinking I would gain an ally. But when 'the priest' came into the room, he immediately assured them that it wasn't rape. I realized that he was just another man who was going to join in."

AN EVENING in November. I went up to Raman's apartment to help him get a jammed window open. He asked about my work, and we talked for a while.

As I was leaving, he said, "Sometime I'll tell you a story about a woman who can turn herself into a tree."

"Like Daphne?"

"No, not like Daphne. Daphne is saved when she turns into a tree. In this story, the woman is most vulnerable when she is a tree. It's a story about women's creativity."

PATSY EMERGED after a sleepless night. Her anguish was immediate. For the first time, she reported, she was able to take a perspective outside herself, had seen what he had done to her. During the attack, even as she fought and struggled, she had left her body, had vacated it. She didn't *feel* what he did to her.

"He could have cut my fingers off, and I wouldn't have felt it. The only thing I really felt was the choking—I couldn't breathe."

She continues to feel cut off from her body. Running in the marathon that year, she recalled, she didn't feel anything—so completely had she vacated her body. "It was all mental."

WHEN DID we begin to use the word "rape" to describe what happened to Patsy? I don't recall a particular moment. It wasn't a conscious decision. As our understanding of the nature of the injury deepened over time, the word took on a resonance and inevitability: it came to name the crime.

"Sexual assault" is a useful term. It reflects an effort in the law—and in common usage—to avoid certain confusions that attend the word "rape." Above all: the notion that the crime is defined by reference to the assailant's penis rather than the injury inflicted on the victim. Yet it lacks the power—conferred by a history of boundless human suffering—of the word "rape."

Early on, we used to say that Patsy "got away" by which we meant not only that she survived but that the rape was not completed: he ripped her out of the world, he tried to destroy her face, he forced his hand inside her, but he didn't, so far as she knows, touch her with his penis. Now when we say she "got away," we mean only that she wasn't killed.

I ENCOUNTERED Raman on the sidewalk, en route to his office. We walked together for several blocks. As we walked, he told me the story—a folktale from the Kannada-speaking region of South India where he grew up—of the woman who could turn herself into a tree.

"This tale," he said by way of introduction, "is about the question of when a woman is safe."

A poor woman has two daughters. When the girls reach puberty, the younger daughter tells her older sister that she will turn herself into a flowering tree. The sister can then pick flowers from the tree which they will sell to make money for their mother. She instructs her sister to go to the well and bring two pitchers of water.

"I'll sit under this tree and meditate on the Lord," she says. "You pour the water from the first pitcher all over my body. I'll turn into a flowering tree. Pluck as many flowers as you want, but take care not to break a sprout or tear a leaf. When you're finished, pour the water from the other pitcher over me and I'll become a person again."

The older sister poured the first pitcher of water on the girl and she was transformed into a tree. Taking care not to hurt a sprout or leaf, the sister picked flowers. They were lovely and fragrant. When she had enough, she poured the second pitcher of water over the tree, and the tree again became her sister. They gathered the flowers, wove them into garlands, and the older sister sold them at the king's palace.

The king's son, curious about the source of the beautiful flowers, followed the older sister home. Hidden from view, he watched as the girl transformed herself into a flowering tree. He went home and lay silently on his bed. The king and queen tried to find out what was the matter. Eventually, he told of the girl who could turn herself into a beautiful tree.

The king sent for the old woman and asked after her two daughters. The old woman trembled with fear in the presence of the king. When she reached home, she was furious with her daughters. She beat them with a broom and demanded to know what they had been doing. How had the king come to know of them? Finally, the frightened girls confessed. The mother was incredulous. So the girl had to demonstrate that she really could turn herself into a tree.

It was arranged that the younger daughter and the prince would marry. After the wedding ceremony, the prince was aloof from his new bride. Two nights passed in silence. On the third night, the girl asked, "It is for this bliss you married me?"

"I'll talk to you only if you do whatever I ask," he answered harshly.

"Will I not do as my husband bids me? Tell me what you want."

"You know how to turn into a flowering tree, don't you? Let's see you do it. We can then sleep on flowers and cover ourselves with them. That would be lovely."

She protested that she had no such powers. He was insistent.

"I don't like all this lying and cheating," he chided her. "I saw you the other day become a beautiful tree. If you don't become a tree for me, who else will you do it for?"

The girl yielded to his bullying. She told him to get two pitchers of water and explained the procedure.

"Remember," she warned, "pluck all the flowers you want, but take care not to break a twig or tear a leaf."

She sat in the middle of the room, meditating on God, while he poured the first pitcher of water over her, turning her into a tree. He picked all the flowers he wanted, then poured the second pitcher of water on the tree, and it turned back into his bride. They spread flowers and covered themselves with flowers and went to bed.

Each morning they threw the flowers they had slept on out the window. The growing heap of withered flowers was noticed by the king's unmarried younger daughter. She spied on her brother and sister-in-law and discovered their secret. One day she insisted that her sister-in-law join her and a group of her friends on an outing to an orchard. Once at the orchard, she pressed her sister-in-law to turn herself into a tree. At first, the girl resisted, denying she could do such a thing. The king's daughter was insistent, "Oh, I know all about you. My friends have no flowers to wear. I ask my sister-in-law to become a tree and give us some flowers and look how coy she acts. If you don't become a tree for us, will you do it for your lovers?"

Finally, the girl agreed to become a tree. She sent for two pitchers of water and instructed the girls on how and when to pour them. But the girls didn't listen. They poured the water on her carelessly, unmindful of her instructions. She turned into a tree, but only half a tree. It began to thunder and lightning. In their greed to get at the flowers, the girls tore up the sprouts and broke the branches. In a hurry to get home, they poured the second pitcher of water at random and ran away. When the princess became a person again, she had no hands and feet. She had only half a body. She was a wounded carcass. A half-human thing.

The next morning a cart driver found the thing in a gutter: a shapeless mass of flesh with the face of a beautiful woman. He lifted her into his cart and covered her with his turban cloth, ignoring the lewd remarks of his fellows. He transported the thing to the next town and left it in a public shelter at the outskirts of the town.

Meanwhile, the prince was in despair. His wife had not returned with his sister and her friends. The sister had lied about what had happened. No one knew where the princess was. Days passed. The prince sank deep into grief. He put on the robe of an ascetic and went out into the world. He just wandered. He didn't care where he went.

The cart driver had deposited the thing with the beautiful face at the outskirts of the town where the prince's elder sister and her husband lived. When the maidservants from the palace went to fetch water, they would see her. They persuaded the queen to let them bring her into the palace, where they bathed her in oils, dressed her, and applied medicine to her wounds.

The prince, having long wandered the world, ended up outside his sister's palace, bearded and unkempt, looking like a madman. The servant girls, fetching water, saw him and reported to the queen that he looked very much like her brother. The queen had him brought to the palace and realized, after studying his face, that he was indeed her brother. She had him bathed, clothed in finery, fed good food. But he remained silent. Each night she sent one of her beautiful maids to his bedroom. Seven maids in seven nights. They caressed his body, but he remained unmoved.

Finally, the servant girls, with the permission of the queen, dressed up the thing, and placed it on his bed. It massaged his legs with its stump of an arm. It moaned. He sat up and looked at it. After staring at it for a few moments, he realized it was his wife. He asked her what had happened. Silent for many months, she now spoke and told him her story.

"What shall we do now?" he asked.

She told him to get two pitchers of water. "Pour the water from this pitcher over me and I'll become a tree. Wherever there is a broken branch, set it right; wherever a leaf is torn, put it together. Then pour the water from the second pitcher."

He did as she instructed. With great care and gentleness, he set right the broken branches and torn leaves. Then he poured the second pitcher over the tree. And his wife stood before him, shaking the water from her hair.

RAMAN HAD given me something of great value—a fresh idiom, cast in images, for thinking about violence and healing, about creativity in general and sexuality in particular. One is most vulnerable, the story suggested, at the moment of greatest creativity, the moment of opening to the world, the moment of flowering. To offer one's special gift is to be exposed to danger and to be dependent on the care of others.

Raman observed that the girls in folktales are often described as being twelve years old. This is a way of saying the girl has reached puberty. He added that in Tamil and Sanskrit the word for "menstruation" and the word for "flowering" are the same.

In the story, Raman pointed out, the girl's gift is coerced in a series of encounters that culminate with the violation that leaves her a half-human thing without hands or feet. She is also without speech. It is a feature of such women-centered tales, he said, that a woman's agency—her capacity to act—is bound up with her recovery of her voice, with her telling her story and having it heard. The story of the healing of a woman is thus often also the story of the education, by way of loss and grief, of a husband.

Several weeks later, I prevailed upon Raman to tell the story, over dinner, to a group that included Patsy and Barbara. After he had finished, Barbara spoke of how pained she was when it proved to be other women who ravaged the girl/tree.

Raman said that in India the most difficult, tormenting relationships for a girl will often be with the women in her husband's family—the household she joins after marriage. He also said that he thought it was a mistake to focus too narrowly on the violence of men against women. The violence that occurs in families takes various forms. We should focus on the violence adults do to children, the violence the strong do to the weak.

Patsy observed that part of the logic of the story is that "you could avoid harm by shutting down."

"Yes," said Barbara, "you could be safe by not flowering."

It is also part of the logic of the story, said Raman, that the violated woman—the ravaged half-human thing—can only be healed by becoming a tree again, by becoming vulnerable and flowering again, by trusting another to mend her broken branches.

PART

——

IV

1991–92

TWENTY-FOUR

CHRISTMAS IN Vermont. We arrived in the evening. The air was cold, the night sky clear. Darkness and quiet enveloped us. It was like diving into another medium. Since the assault, Patsy has lost the city dweller's capacity to screen out intrusive noises. The sounds of the night—a siren, a car hurtling by, a shouted obscenity—penetrate to her core. The quiet in Vermont is a relief. There is, however, no respite from the turbulence inside her head. Almost every morning during our visit, upon awaking, she had a tale to tell.

"I WAS in a deserted airport. A man came up behind me. I turned around and glared at him. I tried to send him a message that I was determined to resist. He didn't do anything. The airport filled up with people. I felt embarrassed that I had reacted so intensely to the man. Then he walked by me. As he passed, he asked, 'How did you know?'"

"WE LIVED in a high-rise apartment. I was home alone. A man was to come and pick up a box of clothes. I was concerned because the elevator opened directly into the apartment. I was thinking about possible strategies for protecting myself when the elevator door opened. It was a bland white man in a suit. He stepped past the box of clothes and attacked me. I was struggling with him when I woke up."

"We were at a bar somewhere with a group of people. You were flirting with another woman. Suddenly I found myself alone. I didn't have a car to get home. I decided to take a cab. It was dark and ominous outside. A few cabs with male drivers drove by. I didn't wave at them. I was waiting for a woman driver. Eventually, one showed up, but she was driving a scooter rickshaw like in India. I didn't go with her. Another cab pulled up with two women in it. They got out. The cab disappeared, and one of the women offered to carry me on her back. 'But that will take so long,' I protested. The dream was about: How can you trust someone?"

Would we ever touch if I didn't do the touching? Sometimes I think what Patsy wants is for me to be present yet disembodied. She tolerates my touch but does not answer it. I feel the resistance inside her seeming passivity, the reaction inside her inaction. Her movements are so familiar to me. A sorrowful choreography. The way she curves her shoulders and draws in her elbows to her sides when I touch her breasts. The way she allows me to kiss her lips only for the briefest moment before turning away—as if I were forcing her head underwater. Her body forms a cage that keeps her in and me out.

Yet sustaining warmth does reach me. I don't doubt we are living out a great passion. When we wake in the morning, we lie together for a few minutes before rising. My chest to her back. My body nestled along the contours of hers. There is such ease in this, such deep friendliness. It's hard to believe that at other times these bodies, in this bed, suffer.

One morning we lay in bed in the cottage, wrapped around each other.

"I don't know how you've been able to stand the sexual pattern," Patsy said. "I can't imagine what it's like for you."

I began to say something in response, then checked myself and remained silent.

"For years, I've felt that my wiring was faulty, that certain switches get thrown at the wrong time and others fail to get thrown at the right time. Over our years together, the mixed signals have gotten stronger and more painful. I feel like the assault had the effect of overloading the system and blowing it."

She rearranged her legs under the sheets.

"Now I feel as if I'm resting."

AMID THE holiday commotion, I had a quiet conversation one night after dinner with Patsy's sister Betsy. She recalled a visit she had made to Chicago soon after the attack. She had accompanied Patsy on her first walk to the Lake. She felt protective. When they were children, Patsy had a certain way of grabbing the back of her coat to keep her from going into the street—she would steer her that way. This was something Patsy continued to do, sometimes to Betsy's annoyance, even when they were quite a bit older. Walking beside her older sister, Betsy had the impulse to hold on to the back of Patsy's coat—to protect her, to guide her, to keep her out of harm's way.

She also told me that in the spring following the attack, her assistant at the small preschool she runs in rural Massachusetts asked why she didn't play her guitar and sing anymore with the children. She realized she had stopped singing. Often in the past she had walked down the path from the house to the school singing at full volume. It was one of the ways she got in the mood for school. Then, later in the day, she would take out her guitar and sing with the children. She had not done so during the months following the attack.

A woman on the South Side of Chicago was sexually assaulted. A woman in the hills of western Massachusetts stopped singing.

ON NEW Year's Day, Patsy learned that the Chicago gallery had decided against doing an exhibition of the storefront church photographs. The prospect of the exhibition had given direction and purpose to her work for months.

"I really didn't expect this," she said. "I feel devastated."

We aren't yet sure about the basis of the decision, but it appears that concern about how blacks would respond to a study of a black institution done by a white was a central consideration. The letter said that five years ago they would have done an exhibition.

I'm angered by the decision. The idea that respect for the sensibilities of others is best accomplished by imposing segregation of the imagination offends me. But such questions of principle don't engage Patsy at the moment. Her reactions are more visceral.

"I feel humiliated," she said.

It's as if this professional disappointment has forced her back into the underlying body of feeling left by the assault. In one sense, it's completely unrelated to the assault, but in another sense nothing is unrelated; the assault touches every dimension of her life.

"I feel as if there's a heavy weight bearing down on me. I'm full of fear. I'm at the edge of a cliff."

I can't reach her, can't comfort her. She is enveloped in despair. Her body seems dead to my touch. It's as if she is, to herself, a worthless thing. I sense I could do anything I wanted with her body. It's alarming not to feel her resistance.

TWENTY-FIVE

SINCE OUR return from Vermont, Betsy has had trouble sleeping.
She says she doesn't feel comfortable in our apartment.

"I don't like our house," she told me. "It's too scary."

Her fears seem genuine. At the same time, it's as if she were speaking with another's voice. She has said certain things again and again:

"I'm spooked."

"I have the creeps."

"I can't take it."

When I try to talk with her about the dangers that exist in the world
and the precautions we take, she says, "Don't tell me. I don't want to
know." And she covers her ears.

Every night she asks the same question.

"Daddy," she asks, "what should I dream about?"

ON THE evening of January 16, President Bush announced to the
nation, "The liberation of Kuwait has begun."

Several days earlier, Betsy had asked, "Why is it that we don't want
war?"

We had tried to explain.

Now, as the President made his announcement, she listened intently.

"Why is he smiling?" she asked.

IN THE first days of the war, Raman came to Wednesday night soup
with a poem titled "A Young Warrior" written in Tamil in the fourth
century:

> O heart
> sorrowing
> for this lad
>
> once scared of a stick
> lifted in mock anger
> when he refused
> a drink of milk,
>
>   now
> not content with killing
> war elephants
> with spotted trunks,
>
> this son
> of the strong man who fell yesterday
>
> seems unaware of the arrow
> in his wound
>
> his head of hair is plumed
> like a horse's,
>
> he has fallen
> on his shield,
>
> his beard still soft.

In times of war, Miłosz observed, poetry becomes as essential as bread.
Those words come back to me now as public discourse about the merits of going to war yields, in words Wendell Berry wrote during the
Vietnam War, to "the arguments of power / that go blind against / what
they would destroy." We disappear those we would destroy imagina-
tively before we do so physically. Blindness is as much a condition of
violence as the presence of the weapon.

In the course of working on *A Worthy Tradition*, I spent several years
immersed in a sequence of Supreme Court decisions dealing with the
question of freedom of speech during wartime—a fundamental issue

for the First Amendment tradition. Now, as the Gulf War unfolds, I see that I never really grasped the underlying issue. What is at stake is not simply the need for information nor the need for all sides of the argument to be aired. That way of talking puts the matter in too rational a frame. It doesn't allow for the irrational and mysterious in war—for the sense in which war is something that comes over human societies. What is ultimately at stake is the need to keep visible the nature of war once we have entered a powerful gravitational field where it is most difficult to do so. What shuts down discourse is something far deeper and stronger than overbroad or self-serving government censorship. In order to go to war, it appears, we must render invisible the underlying nature of what we are doing, the reality of broken bodies and shattered societies and generations of grief.

In the case of the Gulf War, this dynamic has been particularly striking because the war was preceded by a searching national debate about the merits of going to war. We had a great deal of relevant information. Contending views were thoroughly aired in Congress, on op-ed pages, around dinner tables. Then, as the government stepped over the threshold of war, it was as if the nation had been transformed overnight. For a time, during the first days of the war, a collective hallucination took hold that we could have a war in which our marvelous weapons wreaked terrible destruction on another society and no one was killed—on either side.

The words of another poet, embodying a standard of moral seriousness in language of biblical simplicity, have come back to me in recent days. Robert Lowell, in a poem in which he reflects on the suffering he has caused in the course of his life—the injuries to others, the injuries to himself—pauses and then closes with these words:

> my eyes saw what my hand did.

SECOND WEEK of the war. Dawn.

"I have been lying here awake since four-thirty," said Patsy. "I feel like Betsy. 'What nice thing can I think about?' I can't think of anything. I wake up each morning, and all I can think about is that night is falling in the Persian Gulf, and the bombing is about to begin again. It's hard to get up these days. I'm not sure what's worse—what I dream about or what's real."

She described the dream that had wakened her.

"I was in a deserted village somewhere. Throughout the village there were carcasses and body parts of some animal. They looked like donkeys. They were being killed and used for some unknown purpose. The stench was horrible."

While others rely on CNN to give them access to the war, I rely on Patsy's raw nerve ends and inflamed imagination.

"The whole world," she said, "seemed like an abattoir."

WE WENT down to the Loop to participate in a demonstration against the war. I went with my usual ambivalence about such events. I have written in defense of demonstrations in the public forum. I believe that the freedom to take to the streets is fundamental. I love crowds and move easily through them; happiness, for me, is a congested Indian bazaar. Yet I have never felt comfortable in large demonstrations. Perhaps the issue is pride of authorship. I'm uneasy about the fluidity of the message. And I'm even more uneasy about efforts to make the crowd speak with a single voice. I'm constitutionally unable to chant slogans. Even organized singing in a political context carries hints of the authoritarian that make me uneasy.

The demonstration was, as I feared, a mess. Speakers without moral stature or insight harangued the crowd. Assorted fringe political groups seized on the opportunity to promote themselves; some carried signs declaring "Turn the Guns Around." We saw only a handful of people we knew; among them, Bill Ayers, wandering through the crowd looking for Bernardine and their three boys. There were many young people chanting "No Blood for Oil" and other slogans. There was much adolescent energy. The tone was festive. The demonstrators seemed as delighted to be chanting in the streets as the administration seems delighted to be pursuing the war.

I was overcome by a sense of personal failure—failure to work for peace on a daily basis, failure to live a life of active nonviolent resistance. I thought of Randy Kehler and Betsy Corner, risking something they love in the name of peace, and the activity swirling around me seemed like inconsequential posturing.

PATSY REPORTED a series of questions Betsy recently asked her:

"If I died, who would be sadder—you or me?"

"What would make you sadder, if a robber killed me or if I killed myself?"

"What does it mean to say 'I' or 'me'?"

PATSY AND I had a misunderstanding. There was an errand to run in the evening—a form to be filled out for Betsy's soccer league at the home of a woman who lives several blocks from us. Patsy had a meeting at seven-thirty. I had understood her to say that either she would take care of the errand en route to her meeting or I would do it at nine when she got back. It turned out that I had misunderstood. She was as uneasy going to the woman's house at seven-thirty as at nine. She was upset with me. She saw my confusion as evidence of my failure to understand her condition. When I got back, there was a note on my desk:

Jamie—
I don't think you understand the humiliation I continue to feel at not being able to be on my own—it includes running, going to meetings at night, driving—general dependency. It is not over—may never be. Every day has its own terrifying moment—every night has its dream. It's not my choice of how to be in the world moment to moment.
            P.

WATCHING A television documentary on the Civil War, I was struck by the perception that in the aftermath of a war the realities of the violence are for a time kept visible by the injured bodies of surviving combatants. This was especially true during the Civil War, when medical intervention so often took the form of amputation. But it's true in our day too: think of what the image of the wheelchair-bound Vietnam veteran represents.

The realities of sexual violence are so elusive in part because it's possible to inflict terrible wounds on the soul by way of the body without leaving scars. Imagine how we would experience the world if the effects of sexual violence were visible on the bodies of victims. What would it be like to move through a world in which every third or fourth person was missing a limb, was in a wheelchair, or was otherwise visibly disfigured? How would we regard one another, how would we approach one another, how would we touch one another?

I reported this line of thought to Barbara Engel.

"The effects of sexual violence *are* visible on women's bodies, if you have the eyes to see them," she said.

She recalled that after she was raped, she put on forty pounds.

"I *wanted* to make myself unattractive. I wanted *not* to be noticed. It was an act of self-defense."

Then she made a point so unexpected it brought on a sensation in me akin to vertigo.

"The effects of violence are often visible in the intensely sexualized bodies of women who have been abused as children."

Such women, she said, sometimes become prostitutes.

"Girls who were fucked by their father and their brothers, who were fucked again and again by a long chain of men who picked up the scent, are often extremely sexy. They've been taught that they are only sexual beings. It's as if it's the only thing they're good for."

She paused.

"If the effects of sexual violence seem invisible, it may be because we're so busy as a culture celebrating and exploiting them."

PATSY TOLD me about a conversation she had with Josh and Betsy. They were driving downtown. As they went under the viaduct at Forty-seventh Street, Josh pointed out a black teenager on the south side of the street wearing a Bulls jacket.

"If he crosses the street," Josh said, "he could get shot for wearing that jacket. He could get shot for wearing his hat in the wrong direction."

Betsy was intensely curious. "Why could he get shot, if his hat's on backwards?"

"Because of gangs," Josh replied.

"What's a gang?"

Patsy explained that there are parts of the city where only poor people live. They don't have jobs or decent housing. Almost the only business is selling drugs. Gangs of young men fight with each other for control of this business and for other reasons.

This appeared to be the first time Betsy had taken in the idea of racial and economic segregation—the idea of a separate place.

"Do a lot of bad guys live there?" Betsy asked.

Patsy was left unsure whether Betsy grasped the distinction between poor people and "bad guys."

"Imagine what it must be like," she said to me, "for young black males always to be objects of suspicion. I've often thought about the boy they brought into the emergency room that day. What was it like for him? Imagine if Josh was picked up like that."

I WAS deeply involved in the antinuclear agitation of the Reagan years. Among other things, I wrote regularly for the *Bulletin of the Atomic Scientists*. In 1984 I wrote the unsigned editorial statement for the *Bulletin* when they moved "the doomsday clock"—a symbolic measure of the editors' assessment of the risk of nuclear holocaust—closer to midnight. Nothing I have ever written has been more widely quoted—my words came back to me on editorial pages, in Japanese, on the lips of the President. (What no one could know was that the anonymous voice behind the editorial "we" had found language to evoke the chill between the superpowers in the distress of his marriage at the time. "There has been a virtual suspension of meaningful contacts and serious discussions. Every channel of communication has been constricted or shut down; every form of contact has been attenuated or cut off. . . .")

Unlike some journalists who covered the arms race, I was not fascinated by the technology of weaponry. I wrote about the subject because I found the violence threatened by nuclear weapons so elusive: I needed to bring to bear the discipline of my craft in order to think about it at all. I was aided by the fact that nuclear weapons are part of an intimate personal geography: the first controlled nuclear chain reaction occurred a block away from our apartment, under the stands of the old Stagg Field, since demolished to make way for the library, where I used to train and compete as a runner. Growing up, I knew various of the scientists who contributed to the design of the first atomic bomb. When I was born, my parents were renting a third-floor apartment in the home of Harold Urey, one of the Manhattan Project scientists who had received the Nobel Prize in chemistry in 1934. (My father used to tell an amusing story about a cold winter night when the Ureys' furnace cut out. A number of the Manhattan Project scientists, among them Enrico Fermi, conferred in the basement, unsuccessfully seeking the solution to a problem eventually solved by the Ureys' teenage son.)

Today the spot where the first nuclear chain reaction occurred is marked by a wonderful Henry Moore sculpture that manages in a single gesture to evoke a mushroom cloud and a skull, while at the same time being a thing of beauty and an inviting place for children to play. Its simplicity provokes in me an arc of perception that reaches back past the nuclear bomb, the precision guided missile, the artillery shell, the automatic weapon, the revolver, the knife, the club, and the rock to the human hand. To the possibilities we hold in our hands.

TWENTY-SIX

I N THE years since the assault, we have made a variety of changes in
the way we live. For the most part, Patsy seems to regard these as necessary but regrettable concessions to fear. But at least one adaptation has
enlarged rather than diminished our lives. Before the assault, we both
ran regularly, but more often than not separately and at different times.
It was easier that way, given the shapes of our workdays and the demands
of young children. Since the assault, we run together almost every day,
usually at lunchtime, covering a distance of about eight miles. This is
often the most private and satisfying time we have together during the
day—a chance to touch base with each other and to talk. It is, for us,
the equivalent of taking a long daily walk together. "The only difference," Patsy once remarked to friends, "is that we can't hold hands."

These midday runs put me in touch with Patsy's spirit. I am grateful we have this way of knowing each other through our bodies,
through our shared experience of the world. Running beside her, I am
moved by her physical dignity. Others, looking on, might imagine we
are motivated by vanity or the desire to remain youthful. No doubt
such motives are present, but they are faint. Far from being an effort to
hold on to youth, running, as we practice it, is a discipline of aging and
ultimately dying. I imagine us decades hence taking our daily walk
together, exerting the same degree of effort, the same push to keep

going against discomfort and fatigue and the downward pull of iner-
tia, in order to walk a few blocks. Perhaps then we'll hold hands.

This spring we have been working out on Saturday mornings with
a few local runners. The organizer of these outings is a man named
Zeus Preckwinkle. I came to know Zeus as a fellow member of the
board of a youth service organization, but I had long been aware of
him as a presence in the neighborhood—in part because of his excel-
lence as a runner and in part because we look quite similar, at least as
we run by, and so are often mistaken for one another.

Zeus's wife Toni is a Chicago alderman. Her ward embraces part of
Hyde Park–Kenwood and the impoverished black neighborhoods
north of Forty-seventh Street. Toni is black. During the election campaign, her opponent tried to use her marriage to a white man against
her. He spread rumors in the black communities within the ward that
her husband was "a Jewish developer" who had designs on their neighborhoods. The charge was awkward—it invited Toni to deny her husband was Jewish in the same breath she denied he was a developer. It
was also laughable to anyone who knows Zeus. He has, for close to
twenty years, been an elementary school teacher. His ambitions lie in a
realm far removed from real estate. He surveys the neighborhood not as
a developer but as a runner, ranging daily through its streets and parks.

Now in his mid-forties, Zeus had a solid career as a competitive
runner. As he got older, he continued to compete. He is now one of
the better runners in the city in the masters (over forty) age division.
Without apology or restraint, he loves to run. Working out with him
has put me in touch with something I have long held in check. For the
first time in twenty years, I am yielding to the great passion of my
youth.

On Saturdays we usually cover ten miles, much of it at an easy pace
that allows for conversation, but most workouts also include some
speed work—four three-minute runs, say, at a brisk pace. This is the
sort of workout a group of mixed abilities can do together. After each
"pickup," we regroup and resume our conversation.

It's been years since I have done speed work. As I got older, I settled into a pattern of long, slow runs. Now I am recovering my
strength. My legs feel lively again. It excites me to run fast.

Patsy, too, enjoys these workouts. She especially enjoys wandering
the neighborhood with Zeus, who doesn't limit his runs to the lakefront. But she is also apprehensive. As I get stronger and recover my

appetite for running hard, will I lose interest in running with her? Will she be left behind?

PATSY HAD a dream in which she and another woman eluded the men chasing them by flying. She had to convince her companion that it was possible to fly. At first, flight was exhilarating. Then it became alarming, as they were carried farther and farther away from the earth.

PATSY WENT to a meeting in Evanston. En route she picked up Bernardine at her office in the Loop. At about eleven, she phoned to tell me she was about to leave. Our usual practice is for her to call me on the car phone once she has parked outside our building. I then go out and see her in. This time, however, she had forgotten to bring the phone. So she said she would honk softly three times outside our bedroom window to alert me that she was there.

Lying on our bed, reading, I dozed off. I awoke to the sound of Patsy's key in the door.

"I must have fallen asleep and not heard the horn," I apologized.

It turned out she hadn't honked, for someone else had seen her to the door. After leaving Evanston, she had driven Bernardine back to her car in the Loop. They had said good night, then had driven back to the South Side, in sight of one another, on Lake Shore Drive. Bernardine, with a wave, had exited at Forty-seventh Street.

Patsy had immediately been overcome by panic. She felt exposed and utterly alone in an alien world. She turned off at Fifty-third Street. Bernardine pulled up next to her, having driven through the neighborhood to intercept her at the exit, and rolled down the window.

"I'm going to follow you home," she said.

Patsy felt a wild mix of emotions: surprise, gratitude, and, despite her relief, oh-you-really-shouldn't-have-bothered.

When they reached our building, Patsy got out.

"Thank you so much, Bernardine, but who will follow *you* home?"

"Your spirit will follow me home."

She waited to see that Patsy got in the door. Then she drove home.

BARBARA ENGEL told me about a woman who would only drive on one-way streets, because after being raped she couldn't trust that drivers coming from the opposite direction wouldn't hit her.

PATSY PULLED a thigh muscle and was unable to run for two weeks. She tried to compensate by walking and using a stationary bicycle at the field house but was intensely frustrated. The injury denied her the one reliable form of rest in her life, deepening her depression. When I returned from a long run or a Saturday workout with Zeus, I would be met by her suspicion and resentment. It was as if she suspected me of having an affair.

One day, soon after she had resumed running, Zeus and I went for a twenty-mile run. She and I had discussed whether she should come. She had decided not to; she was concerned she would reinjure her leg. The next day I found a note on my desk:

Dear Jay—
I have been too angry to want to talk for fear I would say things I didn't mean. And I have no energy for a fight.

Yesterday I was distraught. Though I know you are sensitive about the running and are enjoying it more with Zeus, I feel ready to leave this city if I can no longer run, ride bikes, etc. I think you think you know what it's like, but you don't feel the trap. I feel cast aside because I'm a woman, not fast enough, etc. You will have all sorts of responses, but what I feel is that we no longer do this together. I am just as serious a runner as anyone, for many years more so than you, but am untrained. Every time you opt to run without me, I have to give it up or run alone. Yesterday the track + Midway were deserted, and I had to run 8 miles in the streets, not comfortably, and feeling like a rat in a maze.

You can't solve all the problems I am having at the moment, but I truly don't think you know what this feels like. In my worst moments I feel that you have the friends, the book, the community and I have the suffering yet to be done and no one to turn to. I am totally humiliated by all of this and I would just go out there myself and run, if I could.

I think you should know that I don't talk to anyone about this, because it's 2½ years later and I don't want to be perceived as a poor victim—I don't really believe that anyone who hasn't experienced it can understand.
P.

That afternoon we went for a run together. I apologized and began to explain. As I spoke, I became aware that my explanations were beside the point.

Later, back at the apartment, I embraced her.

"I don't think I'm going to make it," she sobbed.

A SATURDAY afternoon in late April. Patsy and I went for a walk. Betsy, on roller skates, came along. Dressed in shorts and a blue shirt with a red watermelon motif on it, she was in high spirits. She sailed down the sidewalk, her ponytail bobbing behind her. The recent loss of her two top front teeth made her look at once younger and delightfully witty. Her knees and shins were embroidered with bruises and nicks and scabs. There was a dab of red paint—the residue of a school art project—on the back of one ear.

I love to watch Betsy skate: her straight back and strong body, her economy of effort, the deftness with which she maneuvers around pedestrians, the elegant flick-of-the-ankle that powers her glide. She skates with a wonderful combination of abandon and control, vigor and agility. Her movements are generous and full. Cracked and broken sidewalks are transformed by her grace.

As we walked along behind her, Patsy reported a conversation they had had that morning. They were driving on Lake Shore Drive to a park on the North Side where Betsy's soccer team was to play a game.

"Do you remember when your face was all swollen and your nose was broken?" Betsy had asked. "Where did the bad guy who did it to you come from?"

Patsy explained that he had come across the overpass from the poor neighborhood on the other side of the Drive. On the way home, after the game, Betsy resumed the conversation. She asked Patsy to point out the spot where the attack had occurred.

"It was almost as if," Patsy observed later, "she realized for the first time that there was *a place*."

THAT EVENING Patsy, Betsy, and I went to a "Take Back the Night" rally, staged by a University of Chicago student group, at which Barbara Engel was to speak. Josh didn't come with us. He was at a rehearsal of a theater group of which he is a member.

The rally was held in a park near campus. The grass was littered with yellow dandelions; the trees were furry with new buds. Spring smells, laced with auto exhaust, hung in the humid air. After a day of inter-mittent showers, the evening sky brightened as the clouds thinned, then darkened as night fell.

As we walked across the park to the site of the rally, Betsy insisted we stop for a few minutes at a playground. She climbed on one of the structures. Another child—a boy, a year or two older—had transformed the jungle gym into a balance beam and was triumphantly walking back and forth across it, some five feet above the wood chips blanket-ing the ground. Betsy was impressed.

The turnout at the rally was small; perhaps sixty people. Most were college students. A sprinkling of men. Betsy was the only child pres-ent. Patsy introduced me to a couple of women she knew and point-ed out several others.

"The black woman with the clipboard was active in the Women Against War group," she said. "The girl with the black hair holding the banner was raped on campus. She was in one of my self-defense class-es. She was in really bad shape at the time. The older woman over there with the blue waistpack on has been in every self-defense course I've taken. She teaches judo and repairs motorcycles."

The organizers passed out candles. Dixie-cup collars around the wicks shielded the flames from the wind.

Barbara was nervous. She found it hard to talk to groups that includ-ed her friends, she said; it was easier to address the anonymous audi-ence beyond the television camera. Patsy was surprised that Barbara, who is such an effective speaker, should feel nervous on an occasion like this. Barbara recalled that when she was a student at the U of C, she was afraid to speak in class. It was only when she found something she cared about so much, that she regarded as so important, that she overcame her inhibitions and found her voice.

Barbara climbed up on a bench and gathered the group around her. Her strong, clear voice carried over the noise of the traffic.

"Imagine," she began, "a woman walking down the street. Night has fallen. She hears footsteps behind her. Her breath stops in her throat. This old, deep dread and terror rise as the footsteps behind her quicken."

Betsy decided she wanted to go back to the playground. Patsy and I resisted briefly, then let her go. She set off resolutely, but her steps soon slowed. She turned and looked back at us. Reassured that we were watching, she trotted on toward the jungle gym.

"Imagine a woman rushing to get dinner on the table to feed three cranky children. The front door opens. The kids whisper, 'Uh-oh, Daddy's home.' He walks in, jaw clenched, a furious hard look in his eyes, and she knows sometime tonight he will call her a worthless piece of trash, put his strong hands around her neck, and try to choke the breath from her after he has pounded her head against the wall. She hopes the children will not see it."

Betsy, nearing the playground, about a hundred feet away, looked back at us one last time, checking in, then ran into the fenced enclosure. Patsy and I exchanged glances.

"Imagine an eleven-year-old girl, the shyest of seven children, living in the Philippines near a military base, sold by her father to a house of prostitution, and resold four or five times a night to twenty-year-old American GIs to have her body violated hour after hour in every conceivable position and orifice.

"Imagine an older Afro-American woman sexually assaulted by the young white businessman whose house she cleans. When she tries to report it to the police, they tell her he has accused her of stealing his valuables and fabricating the charge of rape to mask her theft. The cops look at him—his nice job, nice condo, fast car. They look at her—on welfare, old, worn thin from work. And they do not see her truth."

Straining to see, I could just make out a small figure, atop the jungle gym, walking back and forth. She waved. I waved back.

"Imagine a Cambodian woman living in Uptown assaulted by her husband, beaten and raped with a broom handle, unable to speak English, frightened that if she reports him she will end up deported, unable to communicate with the police because they have no one who speaks her language at 911. She has no option but to return to his savagery."

To my relief, Betsy was headed back toward us—running and skipping. A dancing figure in the darkening air.

"Imagine a ten-year-old girl curled in her bed, face to the wall, hearing her father open the door to her room yet again, feeling his hands on her body as she screams silently, 'Daddy, go away. Daddy, *please don't do this!*'"

Long past the point where one expected her to shift to generalities and argument, Barbara continued to tell the stories of particular women she had known.

"Imagine a woman who has put herself through school, the first in her family to get a college and graduate degree, in the business world now, up for her first big promotion, and the boss calls her into his office and closes the door. As he unbuttons his pants, he suggests that if she wants to really succeed in this company, she should get on her knees and open her mouth."

Betsy was now picking dandelions. She brought me a bouquet to hold—the yellow heads flopping atop limp stems—and set off to pick more.

"Imagine a young college woman at a party where she meets a young man she's noticed in her classes. She dances with him, flirts, and is pleased when he offers to walk her home. At her door, she is slightly apprehensive when he invites himself in for a beer. Two hours later, she regrets she ever laid eyes on him as she struggles to decide if she should report the rape."

I began to think that Barbara might never stop, that she might go on and on, presenting image after image of violation. "Imagine . . . Imagine . . . Imagine . . ." I had entered into the rhythm of the speech and so was surprised, and somewhat disappointed, when she finally shifted to general analysis.

She made explicit the point her examples evoked: violence against women takes many forms. Rape by a stranger is only one of them. Acquaintance rape, incest, sexual harassment in the workplace, the battery of wives or partners, and prostitution: all are violence against women.

Addressing herself to the men in the audience, she said, "I don't want to sound bitter, but my heart has ached to hear male voices join ours. Men of conscience must come forward and join us in saying, 'Enough! The violence must stop. I will not *collaborate* with the violence through my silence.'"

She closed with a call to transform power. "How we fight is critically important," she said. "We must recover a way to be powerful that isn't oppressive to others, that is power-with, not power-over. We must thoughtfully, with our eyes and hearts open, redefine power."

Barbara was followed by several other speakers. Then the candlelight march through the neighborhood began. The route was to be east on Fifty-fifth Street to Lake Park, north on Lake Park to Fifty-third Street, west on Fifty-third to University, then south on University, past fraternity row, to campus. I had to leave to pick up Josh at his rehearsal. Patsy and Betsy, candles in hand, joined the march. Their plan was to have the march deliver them home—toward the end, it would pass our building on University Avenue.

As I drove off, I was relieved that I had an excuse not to participate in the march. Was I embarrassed to be part of a demonstration of this sort? Perhaps, but more likely it was my old resistance to chanting slogans. I simply can't do it.

I picked up Josh, then drove through the neighborhood, looking for the marchers. We found them on Fifty-third Street—walking past brightly lit shops, their faces softly illuminated by the candles they carried. Patsy and Betsy were toward the end of the procession. I had expected Betsy to be tired and cranky and eager for a ride home, but she was enthusiastically adding her voice to those of the other marchers:

REAL MEN DON'T RAPE
REAL MEN DON'T RAPE

YES MEANS YES
NO MEANS NO
HOWEVER YOU DRESS
WHEREVER YOU GO

Josh and I drove home. I waited by the gate for the procession to pass. As Patsy and Betsy left the march, voices called out to them, "Good-bye." "Thanks." The march then continued on past the fraternities, which on this Saturday were quiet and dark.

Patsy reported, with a note of surprise in her voice, that it hadn't felt strange or unnatural to walk through the neighborhood chanting "Real Men Don't Rape." The response of those on the street had been positive.

"I had a sense of recognition from people. 'Right on!' they would say when we explained what we were doing. 'Okay, I'm with you.'"

Although we had often been out on these streets together at night, Patsy said, she saw them anew.

"Walking through my neighborhood at nine o'clock on a Saturday night, I had a jolt of recognition: So that's how it is. Everyone is out. There are couples and families. But I realized that I wouldn't walk alone or with Betsy on these streets. I wouldn't go out without the protection of a man. In a sense, there is no Saturday night for me. A woman alone can't participate."

TWENTY-SEVEN

FOR REASONS known only to herself, a female mallard built her nest on a small terrace that extends out from the front steps of a house up the block. The house belongs to our friends Marshall Sahlins, an anthropologist at the U of C, and his wife Barbara. The duck then proceeded to lay ten eggs. It seems an odd place to nest: on a busy street full of cats and dogs and undergraduates. Across from the library, half a block from athletic facilities, on what passes at the U of C for fraternity row. On closer examination, though, she chose well. She is out of sight, if just barely, from the sidewalk. The eaves of the house provide shelter. And her muted colors blend into her surroundings (brick, ivy, leaf refuse). When I point her out to others, it sometimes takes them a moment to see her.

The day I learned about the duck from Barbara Sahlins, I took the children to see her. Within a few minutes of returning home, Betsy wanted to go back again. The next morning, at our urging, Patsy went to take a look.

"It's the most remarkable thing I've ever seen," she said. "It would be tragic if anything happened to her."

Day by day, the duck seems to sink deeper into her nest, as leaves and down accumulate around her. She becomes more and more a part of her surroundings. The nest seems an extension of her body. She is an image of maternal care—quiet, still, immovable. The combination of her inwardness and her exposure to the world's dangers is immensely moving.

She has become a day-to-day presence in our lives, part of the daily round. Patsy and I rarely walk past the Sahlinses' house without looking in on her. When the children come home from school, they visit her. Returning from a speaking engagement in Madison, Wisconsin, I carried my bags up the Sahlinses' steps and checked on her before going home.

The gestation process, closely observed and much brooded upon by the duck's human neighbors, has thus far passed without incident—apart from one night when Marshall, hearing quacking at 4:00 A.M., rushed downstairs to shoo away a cat.

A still point in an environment full of movement, the duck seems unperturbed by the human turbulence around her. Several yards away from the nest, fraternity boys, unaware of her existence, toss footballs around and party. At the house next door to the south, workmen demolished and replaced the front walk and steps. Jackhammers pounded. The duck sat on its eggs.

A widening circle is coming to know of her. ("Do you want to see a *secret?*" Betsy asks visitors.) The Sahlinses have graciously allowed their front yard to become a sort of village common, as people they have never seen before climb their front steps to view the duck.

She has provoked much conversation. Some of it is light. Talk about the meaning of the phrase "sitting duck." Jokes about the duck's choice of an anthropologist's house as a nesting place: "Nature's revenge on culture." When I showed the duck to Raman, he told me a funny story about the revenge of a wise old monkey on an Indian village. Much of the talk, though, is undefended by irony. We are, simply, moved.

"One sees immediately what she represents," said Jean Comaroff, a South African anthropologist. "The themes she dramatizes for us, living as we do in this environment."

A recurring theme of conversation is the meaning of safety in nature and society. At first, the duck's situation seemed anomalous and unusually dangerous. But would she and her eggs be significantly safer in the wild? Perhaps, but wherever she was, her survival would depend on a set of strategies—the location of the nest, her coloration, her capacity for stillness—that, if successful, would allow her to go unnoticed in the midst of a perilous world. What a novel idea it is that people have a right to be safe. Presumably, for most human beings most of the time safety has meant something akin to what it means for the duck.

PATSY SHOWED me some of the images she has pulled together for the photo-montage. The most arresting and disturbing is a black-and-white enlargement of the Polaroid snapshot of her battered face taken by the policeman in the emergency room. The face could be that of a corpse. It *is* the face of someone who has just collided with the possibility of her own death. Her swollen eyes are closed. A broad bandage across the middle of her face covers her nostrils. The only signs of life are her hand resting on her head and her slightly parted lips, which suggest breath.

Various other images, the yield of our visits to the attack site, have strange power. If only they could be deciphered, perhaps they would hold the key to what happened. The "MEN→" sign on the rest-room building. The basketball courts on which stand eight backboards without nets—large cement rectangles amid the green, facing the Lake, like the eloquent ruins of a dead civilization. The newly planted young trees.

One of the photos Patsy has selected provides a glimpse of the depth at which she is organizing her perceptions. It's an image of Betsy, a few months old, asleep on the grass in Vermont. She is sleeping deeply. Great care has been taken to ensure her comfort. Wrapped in a receiving blanket, she lies on a folded quilt, with a pillow under her head, inside a tent of mosquito netting. A female body, at home and safe, in the green world.

THIS SPRING Patsy has found the lakefront threatening and inhospitable. Our usual workout these days is an eight-mile run in the course of which we do several pickups of two to ten minutes. I run ahead during the pickups, then wait for Patsy. There are thus stretches during which, though I may be in sight, Patsy runs alone. This has given her some bad moments. One day as she climbed the hill at Forty-seventh Street—I was out of sight, having gone over the hill—a solitary black man crossed the path. Alarmed, Patsy gave him a wide berth. When she caught up with me and we were running side by side again, we talked about it.

"The difference between a careful, prudent person alert to dangers in their environment and someone who has been attacked is the time element," she said. "Thirty seconds with no one looking and you can completely disappear. You just can't imagine how quickly it happens."

On a weekend run with Zeus, we were joined by an Englishman in his sixties, once a world-class runner. It was a long, slow, chatty run. Later Patsy told me that at one point we passed a tough-looking black man on the path. I hadn't noticed.

"He didn't look at any of you," she said. "He looked straight at me. Into my eyes. It was chilling. Imagine a man like that hitting me with all his force."

She observed recently that the feelings of "the immensity of it all" which she at first associated with black poverty she now associates with gender and male violence. Instead of lessening, she said, her sense of sex as violence, of the world as being full of violent sex, has intensified.

She made this observation as we ran on the lakefront. She had just pointed out a man at the water's edge, partially obscured by the rocks, who appeared to be masturbating. A solitary figure against Lake and sky. Part of the landscape.

JOSH HAS had a busy spring. He is the only rookie on the Yankees, the defending champions in Hyde Park–Kenwood Little League. At the same time, he is in the cast of a production by a community theater group of *I Never Saw Another Butterfly*, a play set in the Terezín concentration camp and based on children's drawings and poems that survived the war—and the children who made them.

"Between pitching and the Holocaust," Patsy observed, "Josh has lots on his mind these days."

His Little League team has some of the character of its namesake—the New York Yankees—in their heyday. During my youth, the Yankees were the dominant team in the American League. The embodiment of power and confidence and class. An aura attached to their pinstripe uniforms which somehow made them winners even when they lost.

When I was Josh's age, I used to spend Saturday mornings haunting the lobby of a hotel in the neighborhood, the Del Prado, now gone to seed, where visiting American League teams stayed. I would lie in wait outside the hotel coffee shop and collect autographs from the players when they came down for breakfast. It was a special occasion when the Yankees came to town. There was no greater thrill than to approach Mickey Mantle, as he hobbled down the stairs to the coffee shop on fragile legs, bleary-eyed from fatigue and perhaps a hangover, and ask him for his autograph.

Located outside Prague, Terezín (also known as Theresienstadt) was used by the Nazis for propaganda purposes—as a model camp they would show foreigners. In fact, it was a transit camp en route to Auschwitz. Many of those brought there were intellectuals and artists from Prague. As part of their propaganda strategy, the Nazis actively encouraged the arts. Few of those sent to Terezín survived, but some of their art did, including the material that forms the basis of *I Never Saw Another Butterfly.*

Josh played a boy named Miroslav Synkov. He was deeply invested in the enterprise, studying his lines and spending long hours at rehearsals. He was one of the two youngest members of a cast that included several adults and, mostly, teenagers. We were never altogether sure what he made of the substance of the play. He didn't talk about it much.

Using a book of photographs of Polish Jews on the eve of the Holocaust, we pieced together a costume for him from items around the house: a Greek fisherman's cap, an Indian kurta, an Irish vest. He performed barefoot. The director sewed a yellow star on the vest. When he went off to his first dress rehearsal, I was overcome by the sight of him.

One Saturday in May, Josh's two lives converged. He had a baseball game in the morning and a matinee performance of the play in the afternoon. The game went into extra innings. The time of the performance drew closer and closer. I made a sandwich for him and laid out his costume on the sofa in the living room. When he finally got home after the game, I watched as he stripped off the Yankee pinstripes, stood for a moment eating the sandwich—slender, naked, delicate—then put on the death camp uniform with the yellow star and rushed out the door.

WHAT IS going to happen when the duck's eggs hatch? Does she know what she is doing? Marshall is skeptical. He called the zoo for advice but received little help.

"They're city people," he joked. "They believe in the wisdom of nature."

When I showed the duck to Hans Zeisel, he recalled the experiments with "imprinting" conducted by his childhood friend Konrad Lorenz, conjuring up the vision of Marshall quacking in greeting to the ducklings as they emerged from the eggs, then leading them off to a more suitable environment.

Dorothy Freedman called the Audubon Society hot line and was assured that the duck *did* know what she was doing. Within twenty-four hours of the hatching, she would lead her brood off to water. She would have a definite destination. We should not intervene. Our job was to run interference for her: as in the title of the famous children's book, to make way for ducklings.

Late one afternoon, I was in the kitchen making a salad for dinner when Betsy, breathless, pushed through the back door.

"Come on, Dad, the duck eggs have hatched." She ran back to the Sahlinses'. I followed.

After picking up the children at school, Patsy had gone over to chat with Barbara and Marshall, who were outside. Betsy tagged along. Marshall was mowing the lawn.

"We think something's wrong," he said. "It looks like she's eaten one of them."

Standing on the front steps, Barbara and Patsy chatted. Barbara pointed out pieces of broken eggshell stuck to the duck's chest. Then they saw movement. The duck seemed agitated. She rose off the nest, and several little brown and yellow heads peeked out from beneath her.

A festive scene. Hugs and congratulations. Neighbors hurried over with cameras and children. Marshall uncorked a bottle of champagne and passed out glasses. We toasted the duck and joked with the Sahlinses about the adjustment they will have to make to the "empty-nest syndrome."

The duck's posture was different now. She lifted off the nest, arched her body, and partially extended her wings in order to create space for the active little ones beneath her. I had seen her daily for a month, had studied her and meditated on her, but only now did I see that there was a brilliant violet band, bordered by white, on her wings. For the first time, I understood—deeply understood—that the coloring of female birds is so often muted and dull, by contrast with that of males, because of the requirements of nesting.

We were concerned about how the ducklings would get down from the ledge. We joked about building a scaffold or a slide or lining the steps with pillows. As it turned out, reported Marshall, who witnessed the moment of their departure the next morning, the ducklings simply jumped off the ledge behind their mother.

The duck and her brood headed south to Fifty-seventh Street. Marshall and Barbara stopped traffic and got them across the street. We had expected that they would head for a small pond in the main quadrangle half a block away, but they turned east instead and proceeded, past the faculty club, toward the Lake. Their destination, it appeared, was Wooded Island, a mile and a half away. A slender spit of land about half a mile long in the Jackson Park lagoon, Wooded Island is a bit of domesticated wildness in the shadow of the Museum of Science and Industry. Its inhabitants include various birds—among them, ducks and a large population of Canadian geese—as well as muskrats, feral dogs, and the like.

Patsy and I joined the procession several blocks into the journey. The duck led the way. I was struck by her grace, authority, and stature, now that she had stepped away from the nest. She was followed by the ducklings in uncertain formation. They, in turn, were followed by a human phalanx: Barbara and Marshall, Jamie Redfield and his seven-year-old son, Patsy and me.

We had a role to play. At intersections, in the absence of curbs designed to accommodate wheelchairs, the ducklings would tumble over the curb on one side, then try to hop the curb on the other. There were always a few who couldn't make it and needed a boost from a human hand.

At Fifty-eighth and Kimbark, one of the ducklings fell through the grates in a manhole cover. Someone from a nearby house brought us a butterfly net which we used to fish the duckling out of the sewer. Wet and oily, it rejoined the brood.

The duck, whose forward movement had been arrested by the "peep-peep-peep" of the lost duckling, set off again. Almost immediately, other perils threatened. The duck quacked and spread her wings in alarm: a cat. We shooed it away. Then a more serious danger presented itself: an overbearing woman with a cardboard box determined to scoop up the ducklings and take them to Wooded Island, where, she said, they would be reunited with the mother. We resisted her.

"My father was an ornithologist," she said, pulling rank on us. She clearly regarded us as sentimental amateurs.

"It will be a *miracle* if they make it to Wooded Island," she said.

"Yes," said Barbara Sahlins serenely, "it will be a miracle."

We continued east on Fifty-eighth Street. The duck led the way. She knew where she wanted to go. Most of the time we deferred, but when she started toward an elementary school playground during recess, we deflected her back onto Fifty-eighth, then up Dorchester to the Midway.

Once on the Midway, the duck followed the runners' path toward the Lake. We were now confronted with the problem of how to get the ducks across the heavy traffic on Stony Island Avenue and Cornell Drive. The solution—prescribed by both common sense and the literary precedent of *Make Way for Ducklings*—was to summon the police. A campus policeman drove by. We waved him down, and he joined our procession.

With the policeman's help, we stopped traffic and made way for ducklings. Once they reached Wooded Island, the duck and her brood headed straight for the water and swam off in formation. When they hit the water, we felt a sense of deliverance. We stood on the banks and applauded.

"She really did know what she was doing," said Patsy. "She had a plan."

"Yeah," said Marshall, "and we were part of that plan."

The next day Patsy and I ran through Wooded Island. It's a strange place. Those who go there are generally hunting for something. Bird-watchers. Fishermen. Gay men, mostly black, seeking each other. We had come in search of the duck and her brood. We stopped running and stood at the water's edge. We could see several groups of Canadian geese—adult pairs, followed by goslings in tight formation. There was a female mallard, attended by a drake, with half a dozen ducklings in tow. At first, we assumed this was her. Then we saw another female, no male in sight, followed by three ducklings, swimming close to the bank. Three ducklings! Three left out of ten? They swam so close to the bank and were so oblivious to us that I could easily imagine predators picking them off. We couldn't be sure it was her, but neither could we be sure it wasn't. Confronted with a perception I didn't want to have—resisting the possibility that *Make Way for Ducklings* might in reality end this way—I felt a familiar tension: the allure of sentimentality—the impulse to tell a story that pleases and coheres by denying the true conditions of life—contended with the claims of fidelity to what happened. I recognized this tension. It's the undertow I move against daily as I try to find ways of telling Patsy's story, our story, without falsifying it.

TWENTY-EIGHT

I T's AS if I've been storing up fatigue in every available space, in every corner of my being, and now it's seeping out," Patsy said recently. "I feel like I'm disappearing into fatigue."

Close to three years after the assault, this appears to mark another phase in her recovery of her body from terror: the capacity, simply, to feel tired. She compares it to the point, about six months after the attack, when the fog of shock lifted and her fears became sharp and immediate. Fatigue is now present throughout her day, as if gravity is bearing down on her with added weight. It's the medium through which she moves. Perhaps this is a good sign—a necessary prelude to rest—but for the moment it only deepens her distress.

"I feel angry all the time, and I feel like crying all the time. I hate myself for being so weak."

Her anxieties have come to center on a photo assignment she has taken on for the U of C's School of Social Service Administration—the graduate school of social work. The project will involve traveling to several cities to do portraits of SSA graduates. She worries about flying—an old fear experienced now with renewed force. She worries about staying in motels and moving around unfamiliar cities on her own. She worries that there will be times when no one will know where she is. And she worries that her worries will absorb the energy she needs to execute the assignment.

As she frets about the logistical requirements of the SSA project, she seems unaware of the degree to which she has recovered the capacity to function out in the world. She once again moves widely through the city. Recently, on assignments, she has made several trips to the Cabrini-Green public housing development on the North Side and to the Cambodian enclave in Uptown. When we are unable to run together, she often goes out on her own. She runs around the track or the Midway, and recently, on a day when the lakefront was being heavily used, ran around the Point and down toward (but not past) Forty-seventh Street.

When we have tried to discuss her anxieties about the project, she has quickly become angry with me for making practical suggestions, for treating her fears as a problem to be solved.

PATSY RECOUNTED a dream. "A group of people are diving off a pier into the water. It's dangerous. There are rocks in the water. Several people dive in at the same time. I see that one girl hasn't come to the surface. She is unconscious under the water. So I dive in and bring the girl to the pier. Two men—they're like doctors or scientists, but not really—attend to her. They say that when the girl wakes up, she'll be utterly devoted to them. As we wait for the girl to regain consciousness, she gets smaller and smaller like in a fairy tale. By the time she comes to, she is tiny. And she does looks up at the men with childlike devotion. They put her in a locket. Then they say that they're going to conduct an experiment. They leave the locket hanging on the pier and walk some distance away. The shrunken girl in the locket becomes fierce in her efforts to get out and follow them. The locket jumps and swings around. She is desperate. They laugh."

IN A quiet moment in the midst of her anxious turbulence, Patsy recalled standing by the road, bleeding, in the moments after the assault and thinking, The good part is that I'll never be unhappy again.

PATSY SPENT four days in Washington, D.C.—the first of several trips she will make for the SSA project. Alone, in our bed, I slept deeply for the first time in months. As often happens when we are apart, I yielded to fatigue. An almost luxurious sensation: to be deeply tired without having to mobilize to deal with moment-to-moment tensions.

Something similar seemed to happen with the children. There was a decrease in the level of agitation and conflict in the household. They were accommodating and tolerant of my efforts, in Patsy's absence, to manage the household and meet their needs.

Patsy sounded good when she called. She was full of news. Her visit coincided with a huge celebration of Desert Storm. The capital was full of troops and military hardware and tourists having their pictures taken with tanks.

She also reported that she had lunch with an old college friend, who is married to a State Department official. Once close, they had stayed intermittently in touch via the occasional postcard and phone call but had not really talked in many years. Her friend, Patsy discovered, had recently been "reborn" as a Christian. When the woman heard the story of the assault, she informed Patsy that Satan exists and is abroad in the world. In her struggle on the lakefront that day, she said, Patsy had not been alone.

"Jesus was with you."

THERE IS a woman we often see running alone on the lakefront north of Forty-seventh Street. A student at the university. Tall and pretty, she runs hard and carries herself well, with an erect posture and long-legged grace. Her expression is focused; her eyes look straight ahead. She fully inhabits her effort; no Sony Walkman for her. I have admired her and worry about her safety.

While Patsy was in Washington, I saw this woman twice on my solitary runs. Each time, as I overtook her, I felt a tension. Should I warn her about the dangers of running alone on the lakefront? I might have found it easier to do so if our eyes had ever met, but she always looked past me. I didn't speak to her, then berated myself. Maybe she doesn't have a clear sense of where she is. What if she is assaulted for lack of a cautionary word from me? I thought of how her self-possession would shatter, of how deep the hurt would go.

One afternoon, after I had seen her out running, we passed in the aisles of the Hyde Park Co-op supermarket. Fresh from her shower, wearing shorts, her hair falling free rather than pulled back in a pony-tail as when she runs, she looked terrific. Those long legs! I was confused. Perhaps I should approach her in this setting and warn her? I didn't want to alarm her, didn't want to take away her pleasure in running on the lakefront, didn't want to tell her the freedom she thought she possessed was illusory. There was too much to say—more than a simple warning could convey.

There was also something else: I didn't want to appear to be coming on to her. I thought of the pattern Barbara Engel once described of the predator who traps women by purporting to be concerned about their safety. I was confused by the stirrings of desire in me. I see many women running alone on the lakefront. Why my particular concern for this one? Is it because I find her attractive? Having looked at her and wondered for an instant what it would be like to have those long legs wrapped around me, it felt like bad faith to approach her and warn her of men lying in wait for her. I said nothing.

WHILE WE were running, Patsy told me of a nightmare:

"I was in a dilapidated house in a shantytown. The house was full of women, black and white. The atmosphere was tense. There was an ominous sense that something terrible was about to happen—but what? Outside, through the window, I could see you and another man. You were searching the area around the building for bombs. Then you disappeared into the night. Several cars converged outside the house. Men with machine guns and dogs stormed out of the cars. At this point, I knew what was going to happen. They had come to kill the women in the house. I had to get out of the house. I ran into the backyard. There were quilts lying on the ground. I heard shooting and screams from inside the house. I crawled under one of the quilts to hide, but as soon as I got under it, I realized that I had made a mistake. When one of the men came to the back door, he would see the lump under the quilt and shoot me. That's when I woke up. I was terrified."

Most of her dreams, as she understands them, explore some aspect of the attack. In this case, she speculated, the dream was exploring the condition of being sightless in the midst of violence.

"When I was under the quilt, he could see me but I couldn't see him."

AT A picnic in the backyard of a journalist friend, I talked with Cleo Wilson, the Playboy executive who had shepherded us through the award occasion in California. She asked me what I was working on. I told her.

"I was raped," she said.

It was a date rape. Her mother and sister were staying with her when it happened. "My mother knew immediately. The moment I walked through the door, she shouted, 'Take off those clothes!'"

Cleo had a history of abuse. As a child, she had been sexually abused by her foster father. Only after she was raped did she learn that her sister had also been raped. She hadn't known.

"Does your wife have flashbacks?" she asked.

Her dreams, I said, have again and again returned to the rape.

"I don't have dreams," said Cleo. "But sometimes suddenly I'll *smell* him."

"When did it happen?" I asked.

"About eight years ago, I think," she replied. "But it always seems much more recent. Like two or three years ago."

She recalled times in the year after the attack when she was afraid to leave the office and embarrassed to ask the security guard for help.

"I don't know how your wife can stand to talk about it with you all the time. I could never do that."

Until recently she dealt with the rape by not dealing with it, she said, by not talking about it, by trying to get on with her life.

"That worked for a long time, it worked well, but now it's not working anymore."

Betsy, on top of a doghouse with another child, drinking a Coke, called out to me. I had my back to her and wasn't aware. Cleo directed my attention to her.

"Hey, Dad, look," she called out. "We're having drinks-on-the-house!"

We laughed.

"I've never told my kids," said Cleo. "They know about the abuse by my foster father but not about the rape." She said, in effect, she didn't want to darken their sense of the world, to make them fearful, by adding this to that.

"If I were as frightened to walk the streets of the city because I'm Jewish or because I'm a certain sort of writer as you are because you're a woman," I said, "I wouldn't be living in a free society."

"We don't know what it would be like to be free," said Cleo, so softly I wasn't sure at first that I had heard her correctly. "It's always been like this—for millions of years. It's never been different. We don't know what it would be like to be free."

"How are you doing?" a friend recently asked Patsy. An answer occurred to her later. "What I might have said is that I rarely have a day when it doesn't affect me, when there are not intersections with the world that plunge me back into my fear, but it's not moment-to-moment now."

Patsy, Zeus, and I celebrated the Fourth of July by taking a long run. The lakefront was densely populated and alive with activity. It was like a cheerful refugee camp. Family groups took refuge from the heat in the shade of trees, under umbrellas, canopies, and tents. People picnicked and played ball. There were small children everywhere. As we passed, we heard snatches of music—sustaining rhythms—from a hundred radios. The air was thick with the mixed aromas of hamburger and ribs, chicken and starter fluid, arising from barbecue kettles and grills, from hibachis and converted oil drums. By the end of a twelve-mile run, I felt full—as if I had inhaled a meal en route.

A couple of days later, as Patsy and I ran together, she recalled our run on the Fourth.

"Running over the hill at Forty-third Street with you and Zeus," she said, "I imagined I had been killed there. Now, two and a half years later, you and Zeus were running over that hill. I wondered what it would have been like for you. Would the world be transformed for you as it's been for me?"

The day before we were to leave for Vermont, Betsy came to me, upon waking.

"Daddy," she said, "I had a bad dream last night. There was a bad guy who was trying to get Mommy. We were on a plane. The bad guy was in disguise. When we landed, he ran after Mommy. She went into a bookstore and hided. Then the bad guy went after me. I ran to Mommy. He chased me and found Mommy and killed her."

That night Patsy and I made love. I was aware of arousal and distress building within her. By the end, it was as if her soul had come unmoored and was rattling around inside her body.

TWENTY-NINE

Vermont. Betsy climbed Mount Mansfield with Patsy and her sister Betsy Evans. Patsy descended, while Betsy and her Aunt Bets went up to the Chin. When they reached the Chin, Patsy was still in sight. They waved.

"I love my mom," said Betsy Rose, full of emotion. Then, after a pause, "Are there bad guys in the woods?"

On the trail, Betsy and Aunt Betsy met a man carrying a three-year-old in a backpack. He was strong and fit, moving at a good pace. He proved to be a veteran of the Persian Gulf War—a recon man who had spent six months in Saudi Arabia. After he had passed on, Betsy and Aunt Betsy talked about him and about the war.

"His mother must have been shot when he was born," said Betsy, "because if she was alive, she wouldn't have let him go to war."

A brief wire-service story on page 3 of *The New York Times*. The facts were simply stated and incomprehensible: at a co-ed boarding school in Kenya, the boys had attacked the girls' dormitory. They had raped seventy-one of the girls. Nineteen girls had been killed in the attack.

Some days later, the *Times* published a follow-up story by Jane Perlez. The boys and girls involved ranged in age from fourteen to eighteen. The episode began with a protest by the boys over the fail-

ure of the school to pay fees required for their participation in an athletic event with other schools. The boys "complained they had been
humiliated" by the school's dereliction and wanted to have a strike. The
girls refused to join in the strike.

"The boys," writes Perlez, "decided to take their anger out against
the girls." They stormed the dormitory, knocking down the doors with
large stones. "In the stampede to escape, the police said, 19 of the girls
were crushed to death or suffocated when beds collapsed on them."
Seventy-one of the girls "were raped in the tall grass alongside the dormitory building."

The episode has provoked much public discussion in Kenya of the
low status of women. It appears that there have been other episodes of
rape at the boarding school and at other, similar schools elsewhere in
Kenya. A local probation officer observed, "If girls hadn't died in this,
we wouldn't have known about it."

The deputy principal of the school was a woman. She spoke with
the President of Kenya, Daniel arap Moi, when he visited the site of
the incident.

"The boys never meant any harm against the girls," she is reported
to have said. "They just wanted to rape."

THE OTHER night I looked up at the sky and saw a falling star. I was
reminded, for the first time in years, of my sexual initiation, gently
administered during the summer after high school by a girl from the
University of California, several years older than me, in the High
Sierra. After we made love, with our sleeping bags draped over us, I
would look up at the sky. The falling stars were distant reflections of
the dizzying sensations unfurling inside my body. How long ago that
now seems.

PATSY AWOKE in the middle of the night, fleeing a nightmare. It took
a while to calm her, for she had dreamt that someone was trying to get
into the cottage: the threat was in the world into which she awoke. As
I held her and rubbed her back, I heard Josh in the next room moan-
ing in his sleep. In pleasure or distress? I wasn't sure. What, I wonder,
does my son dream about?

During our time in Vermont, he has been delightful. Cheerful and
at ease. Skinny-dipping. Playing in the water with Betsy. Hitting rocks
from the porch of the cottage with a splintered baseball bat. Playing

croquet. Doing chores with his grandfather. Playing tennis and baking pies with Patsy. Talking with me.

Several times, after days at once full and relaxed, he has declared, "I had a *great* day today." And: "Today's been a *perfect* day."

Since Betsy Evans arrived several days ago with her twelve-year-old son Sorell and a friend of his, Josh has been remote and volatile. His face is a grimace of irritation and prepubescent world-weariness: the blasé, oh-God-this-is-so-dopey expression of an eleven-year-old boy who has seen it all.

To what degree does his behavior reflect his vision of what it means to be a big boy—his understanding of how such exalted beings behave—and how much does it reflect the strain of trying to hold his own with the older kids?

WHILE JOSH's friend Taylor Chrisman was visiting, we climbed Mount Mansfield. We had planned to climb Camel's Hump, but the weather was ominous. It was overcast; rain threatened. So we decided to stay close to home and to go as far up the Butler Lodge Trail as the conditions and the children's level of enthusiasm would allow.

The climb to the ridge was pleasant. The kids were a bit balky at first, but they picked up as we got higher. It drizzled intermittently but didn't rain heavily. Hiking out in front, I saw a deer. Josh and I hiked together much of the way. It pleased me to see him testing his strength.

When we got to the top, the weather began to worsen: it looked as if we would get wet before the day was over. Josh wanted to descend via the trail we had come up. There had been lots of scrambling up rocks which he had enjoyed and wanted to repeat going down. But we were concerned that stretches of the trail would be hard-going once wet. We decided instead to descend via the Sunset Ridge Trail, a relatively direct and moderate route. We made our way across the ridge and picked up the trail.

As we descended the stretch of exposed and rocky ridge between the summit and tree line, conditions deteriorated: rain and hail and, worst of all, high winds—gusts of about sixty miles per hour. At times the winds threatened to blow the children off the ridge. The gusts were strong enough to blow rocks off the cairns marking the trail. Patsy held hands with Taylor and Josh. When an intense gust started, she got them down low—sometimes crouching, sometimes flat on the ground.

I carried Betsy in my arms. She was frightened. The driving rain and hail hurt her and the force of the wind scared her. I took off my shirt and wrapped it around her head like a shawl. She buried her head in the crook of my neck, talking and crying continuously.

"Daddy, are we going to die? I wish I was in my bed asleep. Why is your neck so scratchy? I don't want to die. I'm never going to climb a mountain again. I wish I was asleep and this was a dream."

Riding a surge of adrenaline down the mountain, bare-chested, lashed by wind and hail, with my weeping daughter in my arms, I felt exhilarated. I roared into the wind. I live for this, I thought, I live for moments like this.

When we got down into the trees, the kids were giddy with relief. They chattered and laughed as they bounded down the trail. Once it was clear that conditions on the trail were safe, I ran down the mountain to the house, got Lew's truck, and drove up to the campground to collect Patsy and the children.

The next day Patsy said to Betsy, "You're lucky to have a Daddy who's strong enough to carry you down the mountain."

Betsy wasn't impressed. "Michael Jordan could've done it," she said. "Mike Tyson could've done it."

ON THE afternoon of Patsy's forty-eighth birthday, we did a hard workout on the high school track in Essex Junction. When we arrived, a group of girls was using the track under the direction of an older woman. The girls' track team, we assumed. While we warmed up, the girls stopped jogging and regrouped in rows on the track, facing the stands where the older woman sat, clipboard in hand, chain-smoking cigarettes. This wasn't a track workout, we realized. It was cheerleader tryouts.

While we ran our 400-meter intervals, they went through their drills and cheers. Strong and beautiful at forty-eight, in touch with her physical powers, Patsy became more and more deeply offended by the spectacle as our workout progressed.

"I'm really appalled," she said during one of our rest laps. "Why don't they do something for themselves instead of standing on the sidelines and cheering the boys?"

Fueled by indignation, she ran harder and harder.

"This really offends me. It's like being a whore. What a terrible use of these strong, young bodies."

PATSY HAS been feeling tense and ragged. Every irritation, every act of inattention, every sharp word—from her parents, the children, me— seems to go to her core. She is volatile and unsettled. She no longer seems grounded in herself and in this place.

One night her restlessness woke me. I rubbed her back and held her. She released the feelings that have been building in her for days.

"I've been trying to tell you how bad I feel, but you're not listening to me. I'm not getting any support from you. Why don't you understand?"

I began to say something about the impact of this place on her, about the way she gets drawn into her role in her parents' household, about how we lose our bearings.

She cut me off.

"That's not it at all. It's not really my family. The pain just takes on the coloration of this place. Somewhere else it would take on another coloration. Next month it'll be three years, and I feel as if nothing's happening. I can see now how it works, how the feelings left by the attack become part of whatever is most problematic in your life—your marriage, or sex, or whatever. It comes to be seen as *who* you are."

Abruptly, wanting to make sure I wouldn't discount what she was saying, she said, "I'm *not* having my period."

For several days, she said, she had been feeling good—at home in the world, close to me. "I was feeling *light.*" That's why the upsurge of terrible feelings was so distressing.

"I can see clearly now what will happen," she said. "You won't understand, and I'll be completely alone."

Tears pooled inside me. I lay beside her, silent, feeling the dead weight of my body. Had someone said a comforting word to me at that moment, I would have wept. For whom, I'm not sure.

Several days later, while running, we had a conversation that helped me better understand what she had been trying to say in the middle of the night.

Since the assault, she said, a pattern has repeated itself each time we have left Chicago and come to Vermont for an extended visit. She arrives full of expectation and hungry for respite. She delights in the environment and savors the freedom it allows. She is relieved of the moment-to-moment vigilance she must practice in Chicago, relieved of those moments each day when she is startled, when her alarm system goes off. The internal process of coming to terms with the assault, however, continues; it's unrelenting. Over time, pressure builds inside her. It's a relief to be away from Chicago, but it's also disorienting: the feelings generated by the assault no longer have objects. There is no framework for making sense of them. So, as she had put it, they tend to take on "the coloration" of this environment—they attach to inappropriate objects.

"After feeling dreadful for several days," she said, "I was relieved when I recognized the source."

"What are the feelings?" I asked. "How would you characterize them?"

"Pure pain," she said. Pain before it has assumed the forms by which we name and understand it.

"I now understand how people's lives get ruined by something like this," she said. "Like water flowing into channels that are already there, the pain will flow into the most difficult areas of your life."

OUR WEDDING anniversary. Bill and Suzan Pinsof and their nine-year-old daughter were visiting from Chicago. We spent the day shepherding them up Mount Mansfield. That night they took us out to a French restaurant in Jeffersonville. It was a pleasant evening. The food was excellent, and everyone was in good spirits.

Once Patsy and I were back at the cottage, I was full of feeling. It was a mild night. There was a full moon. I had the impulse to make love outside. On our wedding night, she had led me down to the pond, and we had lain together there.

We sat on the porch. When I touched her, she tensed.

"I feel guilty," she said. "I know I'll disappoint you."

"I want your affection, not your guilt."

She became distraught. Damn my quick tongue.

"You should leave me," she sobbed.

She got up and left the porch. My spirit collapsed into familiar pain.

I heard the screen door close. Patsy had gone outside. I went upstairs and lay on our bed. The physical afterglow of the day on the mountain was extinguished. Soul pain radiated through my body.

I dozed and drifted. Where was she? I imagined her, in despair, under the stars. Then that image was displaced by something else: the pain that had taken over my body assumed a form—pointed, burning—as I imagined a knife being driven into my back and shoulders. I didn't fight back. I didn't resist. I yielded myself up to the pain.

THIRTY

THE DAY after our return from Vermont, we took a run on the lake-front. Patsy was in distress. Her breathing was shallow, her body tense. We passed the spot where she was attacked.

"I can't tell you how it fills me with grief to see this place."

A young black with hard eyes was walking on the path. Patsy shuddered.

"Imagine me in the control of such a person. Imagine him hitting me in the face again and again."

We ran on in silence.

"The thing I feel most when I think about it now is the *anger* behind his fists—how angry you would have to be to treat another person that way."

She speculated on why a rapist would strike first at one's face, at one's eyes.

"I think maybe it's not so much so that you can't identify him as so that he can't identify you," she said.

That night I was awakened by the familiar sound of Patsy, inside a nightmare, whimpering with fear. I woke her and held her.

"I was at a funeral," she said. "I returned to my sister's house alone. I was in a small, narrow, closetlike room with a window, waiting for the others to return. I heard someone come in. He attacked me through the clothes. Wrapped me up and bound me in the clothes. I couldn't breathe. I couldn't get free. I couldn't scream. I was terrified."

The two most terrible moments of the assault, she said, were the first—the moment of intersection when she realized what was going to happen—and the choking. Her dreams have again and again returned to the moment of ambush, but this was the first dream to explore the sensation of being strangled, of suffocating.

"The dreams are so real. They take me back into the emotions I felt."

As we talked, lying together in the dark, Patsy was struck by a new perception.

"Imagine if I had died," she said. "I would have been buried with my face like that. It never would have healed."

NIGHT AFTER night, in her dreams, Patsy returns to the scene of the crime. The fierce vitality of this story-making process is extraordinary. ("That's why," she once remarked, "the nights are so exhausting for me.") Advancing along various paths, her imagination seeks the narratives, the images, the metaphors to render the experience of violation—stories through which to take into consciousness the terror that enveloped her during those moments on the lakefront.

ON SATURDAY afternoon, Patsy took Betsy and her friend Andrew to his house. Betsy was on roller skates and Andrew on his bike. Patsy jogged along with them. She was wearing her running clothes; we were planning to run together when she returned. They cut through Nichols Park and then the Murray lot. At one point, they passed a group of black youths—teenage boys and girls, horsing around in the park. Betsy skated over to Patsy and squeezed her hand.

"How are you going to get home?" she asked.

"I'll run," said Patsy.

"I don't want you to run, Mommy. Somebody might hurt you."

Then, a few minutes later, she asked, "How old was that white guy who tried to kill you?" Patsy did not respond.

At the corner of Fifty-third and Kenwood, they passed a group of Hispanic youths outside a fast-food joint who frankly looked Patsy over. This was not lost on Betsy.

"I don't want you to run home," she said. "You're going to get hurt."

"It'll be safe," Patsy reassured her. "It's the middle of the day, and there are lots of people around."

"But there were people around the day you were hurt, weren't there?"

YESTERDAY, RUNNING ahead of Patsy on the lakefront, I stopped as I approached the hill at Forty-seventh Street and waited for her to catch up. There was a middle-aged black man sprawled on the grass under a tree. He had broad features, and his round belly showed through his unbuttoned shirt. To my eye, he looked like a genial drunk.

When he saw me slow down, he called out, "Gotta match?"

And then, "Are you a fisherman?"

I laughed.

Patsy caught up and thanked me for stopping. When she looked at the man on the grass, she said, she saw a male lion in menacing repose on the African savanna.

Later in the run, we stopped for water at the fountain beside the rest rooms near where she was attacked.

"This is such a wild place for me," she said. "I feel like an animal approaching a water hole—looking around for predators before putting my head down to drink."

"I WENT to therapy yesterday and just wept. I sat down and immediately started to cry."

LYING IN bed at the end of the day, Patsy spoke of an article that had appeared in *The New York Times* earlier in the week on the arrival of crack cocaine in Chicago. It had focused on the impact of the drug and the violence that accompanies it on the neighborhood of Englewood. As we turned out the lights, Patsy spoke of her horror at the idea that some pathetic soul, his humanity emptied out by the drug, would hurt us or the children and not even know or feel what he was doing.

The next morning she reported that she had dreamt of a wonderful horse that enabled her to go anywhere safely.

"I FEEL that you and the children have a home here and I don't. There's nowhere I feel at home. I'm so exhausted, so depleted. I don't feel anger. I feel disgust and humiliation. I feel removed from my work. Sex has become more painful rather than less. I'm depressed about what's happened to my life. And I'm depressed about what I'm doing to your life. I don't have any sense of process anymore. It feels as if it'll be permanent, and that terrifies me."

WE WERE lying in bed. Dawn light, seeping through the shutter slats and pooling in the corners of the room, was diluting the darkness. Patsy reported a dream she'd had that night.

"I was running on Lake Shore Drive. I came upon a crowd of people standing near the edge of the road. I pushed my way through to see what was happening. There were a whole bunch of dogs lying in the road. It was confusing. There was a black dog and lots of light-colored dogs. The black dog was ugly and frightening. It looked terrible— mangy and matted, covered with caked blood. It was dead. The other dogs were alive. They were collie-like and had sweet faces. They were lined up in a row and were tied together. It was so sad. Their eyes were open.

"It turned out that the black dog had attacked the light-colored dogs and bitten them. The black dog had rabies. Someone had killed it. The other dogs had been tranquilized, while tests were run to confirm that they had been infected with rabies. When the results came back, they would be killed.

"When I woke up, I realized what a racist dream it was."

I AWOKE to the sound of Patsy, in a dream, whimpering with fear. I woke her and held her. The next day, as we ran on the lakefront, she recounted the dream.

"It was one of those dreams where you aren't sure whether you're awake or not. We were in bed in the dark. The ceiling fan was making a racket. We got up to adjust it. You were on the other side of the room by the window. I realized that there was another person in the room. He was sitting on the bed.

"'Jamie, who's that?' I asked.

"'I don't know,' you said. 'It looks like me.'

"I rushed toward the person, trying to feel his face. You were there, and at last we could find out who the dreaded man was. He grabbed my arm.

"I cried out to you. 'Help me, help me.'

"But you—the you I was talking to—were gone. And I was alone, in the bedroom, struggling with this stranger who looked like you."

PATSY'S DREAMS advance ever deeper. This is the first one to yield an image for how her fears of sexual violence shadow our relationship. And it's a precise image: the two Jamies. That is how I often experience our lovemaking. At the beginning, she embraces the Jamie she loves and trusts, but as we proceed she finds herself in the grasp of a threatening stranger.

Are there, for me as well as for her, two Jamies?

LATE AFTERNOON on the third anniversary of the assault.

"At about this time three years ago, you were just arriving at the emergency room," Patsy said. "I had no idea what had happened to me. I didn't know whether I was dreaming or what."

IN THE midst of an anxious dream—I had forgotten my luggage in a public men's room and was rushing back to reclaim it—I was awakened by Patsy's moans. I woke her and held her. She trembled and wept for several minutes. Then she told me her nightmare.

"I was out in a city with Barbara Engel. We were organizing an exhibition. I went off to get some supplies. I found myself alone on a staircase in a large public building like a railroad station. Four black men were coming down the steps toward me. They didn't rush at me. They didn't say anything. It was in their eyes—what they were going to do to me. I knew I would never be able to get away."

It was different, she said, from the other attack dreams she has had. "It was so stark. There were no embellishments. It was just me and them—looking at me."

She broke down again. I stroked her hair.

"This is the dream I will have for the rest of my life," she sobbed. "I know now it will never go away. It's so deeply imprinted. It's a kind of absolute knowledge."

The dream was still a presence in her mind the following afternoon.

"I woke up last night feeling that it was going to happen again," she said. "It's hard to imagine how I'll avoid it happening again. When you start breaking down the day into minutes and seconds, when you know what it's like. . . . It's not less likely because it happened.

"I didn't feel any relief when I woke up. It didn't matter that it was a dream. The reality of the feelings and what they are connected to in the world is inside me. The terrible thing is that I know that any dream I have has actually happened to some woman. Whatever dream I come up with won't be a fantasy. I wake up, but for some woman somewhere it's not a dream, and she doesn't wake up."

PART

———

V

1992

THIRTY-ONE

Hans is dying.

He called on a Saturday morning last November. We spoke for a few minutes about an essay he is writing, in German, on the future of socialism. Then he changed the subject.

"I have some bad news, my friend."

"What is it?"

"I have terminal cancer. Liver cancer."

"What's the prognosis?"

"At worst, months. At best, a year."

"Oh, Hans, I hope you know how much . . . "

"So, my friend . . ."

Unable to talk, both in tears, we hung up. Later in the day, Patsy called him.

"You know," he told her, "I could have died fifty years ago in the Holocaust. I'm eighty-six years old. I've had a full life. The awkward thing is *knowing*."

On Sunday afternoon we visited Hans and Eva. The apartment was hot. Hans was dressed as if for tennis. We stayed for an hour, talking as always about politics and law, trading stories and gossip, reporting on the progress of our respective work. We didn't so much avoid the topic of his condition as refuse to make any concessions to it. I told him I would work with him in the coming months on whatever projects he most wanted to finish. He seemed delicate and wide awake, as if he had just seen something surprising. Throughout our conversation, Eva watched him intently.

It was dark when we left. As we walked to our car, a black woman with a boy about Betsy's age in tow called to us from across the street.

"Excuse me."

My first thought was that she was a panhandler. She walked over to us.

"Where are you going?" she asked. "Could you give us a ride to Ashland Avenue?"

I said we were only going a few blocks. Polite and well-spoken, she explained that her car had broken down. She and her son were trying to figure out how to get back to their home at Eighty-seventh and Ashland.

"Do you have bus fare?" I asked. "The number 55 Garfield bus will take you to Ashland."

No, she replied, she didn't have enough money for the bus. I took out my wallet to give her a few dollars and discovered I only had a twenty-dollar bill.

Patsy had drifted away. She was standing by the car. I asked her if she had change. She shook her head emphatically.

"Come with us," I suggested to the woman. "We'll get change and take you to the bus stop."

Patsy got in the driver's seat. I got in the passenger seat. The woman began to get in the back, but her son balked.

"No," he cried, "no, no!" His voice was at once plaintive and insistent.

"Come on, it's all right," she reassured him. But the child refused to get in the car.

Patsy looked over at me in the darkening light and mouthed the words, "I'm afraid."

"A child at his school was kidnapped and disappeared," the woman explained. "The children have been told over and over again never to get in cars with strangers."

She finally managed to persuade him to get in the backseat beside her. He sat huddled next to the door, as if ready at any moment to make his escape.

We drove to Fifty-seventh Street. I got out and went into University

Market to get change. Patsy got out too. She stood on the sidewalk, some distance from the car, while I was in the store. When I returned, I could see that she was agitated.

"I'll walk home from here," she said. Before I could respond, she set off.

I gave the woman several dollars and gave the boy a chocolate bar. Then I drove them to the bus stop. The woman and I chatted en route. In the midst of our conversation, the child, unbidden, said, "Thank you."

As they got out of the car, I said that it was good he was so cautious about getting in cars with strangers.

"Yes," she said, "I was glad to see that."

She thanked me.

"Take care," I said.

When I got home, Patsy was in the kitchen preparing dinner. She seemed at once embarrassed and angry. She told me she had been frightened that the woman was a crack addict working some sort of scam, that she would pull a gun or a knife on us, or that a man would burst out of the bushes and attack us. The way the boy had resisted getting in the car had deepened rather than allayed her alarm; she feared it might be part of a trap being laid for us.

"I just couldn't assess the situation," she said.

THIS MIGHT be told as a story about race, and in a sense it is, but at a deeper level it is an instance of how violence shapes the world. An encounter between two souls wounded by violence. Patsy's native generosity had been displaced by her fear. At the same time, the little boy, frightened by the disappearance of his classmate, his fear perhaps sharpened by the fact that we were white, had been unable to trust even his mother when she told him it was all right to get in our car.

Since the assault, Patsy has been giving me an account, made ever more compelling by accumulating detail, of how her ordeal on the lakefront has altered the lens through which she takes in the world. Her lucidity has kept visible the ways in which those moments of terror have entered into her relationship to the world, affecting everything—the quality of light, the taste of bread, the feel of skin upon skin. Everything.

Her reaction to the mother and child outside the Zeisels' was not an expression of her values. That was part of what upset her: her values had been overridden by her exposed nerve ends. It occurred to me that the way people injured by violence react to those they identify with their tormentors is not, at least initially, a matter of choice.

Extend the logic. Think of the racial divide in America not as a matter of broad attitudes and values but as a history of specific blows and wounds, a history of particular violent acts, the effects of which reside in people's nerve ends, change their brain chemistry, and pass so directly between generations they might as well be genetically encoded. History inscribed on the nervous system.

PATSY AND I next saw the Zeisels after we returned from Christmas in Vermont. We called on them on a Sunday afternoon. We hadn't seen them for several weeks and were unsure what to expect. Hans seemed frailer, more delicate. He complained that he had less energy each day and so could only work for ever shorter periods.

Jean, their daughter, an actress in New York, was there. A visiting nurse had also joined the household. Together with Eva, they ministered to Hans's needs.

Over the holidays, Jean reported, a steady stream of visitors had called on Hans. It sounded like a cross between a death watch and a salon.

I asked Hans if he was in pain. No, he replied, he was not. Apart from the ebbing of his energy, the most disturbing manifestation of the disease was his loss of appetite. In the absence of a desire for food, he must force himself to eat.

Yet his other appetites remain keen. When the conversation engages his interest, he becomes animated and joins in. Nor has he lost his sense of humor. Of those who wrote him in response to a memo from the dean informing law school faculty that he is dying from a terminal disease, he said, "It's awkward for them. They can't send a Get Well card." And he described an article on the death penalty he is working on as "a quasi-posthumous work."

He asked about Vermont. Patsy described Betsy skiing—her vigor and lack of fear.

"Fearlessness," said Hans, "that's a good thing to have in life."

"Especially in a female," added Patsy.

The next morning, as dawn light filtered through the slats in the shutters, Patsy and I lay in bed, entwined, for a few minutes before rising.

"I wonder what it's like for Hans in the night," she said, "when he wakes up alone in the dark and knows he's dying. Is he afraid?"

WHEN WE next visited the Zeisels, Hans was in bed. Before we went back to see him, Eva showed us a catalog that had just arrived in the mail from Russia. An exhibition of her work, which has been making its way around the world over the last few years, had recently opened in St. Petersburg. Simply and inexpensively produced, the catalog contained beautiful photographs of Eva's work taken by an unnamed photographer who had a strong feeling for her designs and visual wit. It was delightful. Patsy especially appreciated it, for she knows how hard it is to photograph art objects in such a way as to reveal their shapes and not to flatten them.

The catalog also included a striking photographic portrait of Eva, taken in Berlin in 1931. The perspective of the photograph and the play of light on Eva's face emphasized the broad, gentle lines of her jaw and cheekbones. Those lines, Patsy observed, resemble the lines—so distinctive, so recognizable—that recur in her work. Eva's designs are, she said with rising excitement, a kind of self-portraiture.

This delighted Eva. It had long been a thesis of hers, she said, that "designs are extensions of their designer's movements projected into lines and forms."

WE SOMETIMES joke that living in our small apartment is like living on a boat; every square inch is articulated. The space summons forth a sort of dance, requiring qualities of attention, consideration, accommodation that wouldn't be necessary if we could put more distance between us. I sometimes think of the apartment as a literary form, as the form in which our household is cast. It's very much a work in progress. We live for years with the questions and impasses that fidelity to form gives rise to. We are patient. To hit upon a solution to a design puzzle we have long lived with is an intimate pleasure—a shared delight. Finding the right piece of furniture or the right arrangement of space can be like coming back years later to an unfinished poem and completing the rhyme.

A few days ago we moved the dining room table a few feet. Its placement had always been governed by unexamined notions about symmetry. It was equidistant from two walls. When we moved it closer to one wall than to the other, a number of other possibilities were released. It was liberating.

It was also disorienting. Vacuuming in the living room on a Saturday morning, Patsy reflexively took her bearings from the table, turned abruptly, and caught her nose on the edge of the door frame. She called out to me in a voice of the purest alarm.

"I think my nose is broken," she wept. Her hands were over her face. "I heard it crack."

She later told me that she had immediately been flooded by darkness.

"I knew I hadn't been hit," she said, "but the moment I struck my nose it was as if a chemical reaction took place in my brain."

Had she heard something crack in her face when he hit her?

"He hit me again and again. I was so amazed. I didn't feel any pain. Maybe I heard something crack."

When Patsy cried out, Betsy, too, had come running. She was standing as close to Patsy as she possibly could. I was annoyed with her.

"Don't cling to her, Betsy. Give her a little space."

Betsy didn't move. She said nothing. Her resistance was absolute.

Patsy sat on the sofa with her head back. I brought her an ice pack to put over her nose. Betsy lay, completely still, her eyes open, across her mother's chest.

"I felt," Patsy said later, "as if she was telling me she would never let it happen again."

THIRTY-TWO

ALAN SHAPIRO came by for a visit. A poet who used to teach at Northwestern, Alan and his wife Della had moved to Chapel Hill, North Carolina, several years earlier. It was good to see him; I had missed him. He had been on the road for a week, giving a series of poetry readings. The final reading had been the night before at the Art Institute. Among the poems he had read were some from a work in progress with the working title "The Voices of Women: An Autobiography." He seemed gratified by the response but also tired and a bit let-down. He was, he said, eager to get home to Della and his two young children.

It pleased me to think of Alan as a householder with small children clamoring for his attention. During the years we had seen each other regularly, he had been a solitary; charming and gregarious in company, yet somehow isolated. I had attributed this to his sense of vocation as a writer. Although well under six feet tall, he had played basketball in high school and college. I imagined him as a scrappy guard who could be counted on to hurl his body after loose balls. That was the sort of headlong intensity he had brought to the process of becoming a poet.

I enjoyed Alan's company. His wit gave frequent pleasure, but what I valued most was his seriousness. Fiercely honest and unsentimental, he embodied, for me, stringent standards of responsible speech—a fidelity to language of almost desperate force. Despite his frequent complaints about the time and energy teaching took away from his writing, I was sure he was an excellent teacher. When I gave him a manuscript to read, I knew he would engage it at the depth at which the choices had been made. Whether his reactions were critical or celebratory, it was satisfying to be read so deeply, to have that quality of attention brought to bear on one's words.

Often we would talk, over glasses of whiskey, late into the night. Then Alan, declining my offer to sleep on our sofa, would make his way back to Evanston, to one of a succession of apartments he rented during those years, back to the refuge of his books and manuscripts.

Among the things I knew about Alan was something I hadn't known how to incorporate into my sense of him. Once, years earlier, he had mentioned that he had been raped. It was a seemingly offhand remark. He hadn't volunteered more, and I hadn't known how to ask. So I had carried this piece of information for years—bracketed, suspended, unassimilated—in my mind. I didn't know where to put it.

Now, after the assault on Patsy, there was a context that hadn't been present before. When I had last seen Alan—the previous spring he had given a reading at the U of C—we had spoken of what Patsy was going through. I had asked if we might talk sometime about his experience.

"Sure," he had said, "we can talk about it sometime."

Had he, I wondered, expected to do so when he came to see us?

Patsy made a pot of tea and joined us at the dining room table.

We chatted for a while and exchanged literary gossip. Alan reported on the soon-to-be-published issue of the literary journal *TriQuarterly* which he had guest-edited. He had included a series of Patsy's storefront church photographs. He described for her the one he had chosen for the cover. She was clearly pleased.

I asked if he would mind talking with us about the experience of being sexually assaulted.

"Yes," he said, "we can talk about it." He added that he had never really discussed it with anyone. "Not even Della knows."

It had happened in 1970. He was a student at Brandeis. He had been visiting his girlfriend at Connecticut College in New London. Hitchhiking back to Brandeis, he got a ride in a truck. A big rig. He rode in the cab. The trucker drove him back to the outskirts of the campus, then assaulted him.

Alan didn't describe the specifics of the rape, and I didn't ask.

At the time, he told no one. He didn't seek counseling or therapy. During his college years, he was so often depressed and withdrawn, he said with a shadow of a smile, that others weren't aware of any change in his behavior. His parents lived in Boston and he saw them frequently, but they didn't notice anything.

"Did you think during the assault that you were going to die?" I asked.

"No. And I wasn't physically hurt. What I felt was completely disoriented. It was unintelligible, as if someone you'd been having a conversation with suddenly started talking in tongues."

Patsy observed how different this was from what women so often describe: the recognition that "this thing I've always feared, always known, is happening."

"For me," said Alan, "there was no history, no context for making sense of it." This was especially so in 1970, for he knew nothing about homosexual rape.

"Afterward I felt shattered and ashamed. I felt that I had disappeared as a person. I felt that I could no longer be a man."

He still couldn't, he said, bring himself to describe precisely what had happened.

The expression on his face was familiar: an upwelling of unmastered emotion I had often seen in the faces of women when they spoke of rape. Patsy looked on intently.

Alan returned several times to the same image. "I felt like an object," he said. "An inanimate thing conscious of itself as an inanimate thing." "A pure object totally at the mercy of the world's forces." "An object that can feel."

"Our identities are composed of our relations with others," he said. "To be treated like an object wholly subject to another's will is to have the relations that constitute one nullified."

He spoke slowly, trying to find the words to evoke the isolation and shame inflicted on him, twenty years earlier, by a violent man.

"It was," he said, "like being pushed aside on the street by someone for whom you're just an obstacle in their way—not Alan Shapiro, who has these friends and family, who has written these poems, and so on, but just an object."

A surprising image. It took me a moment to grasp the point. Alan was not equating the gravity of the two situations but rather was evoking the fragility of human identities: even such a small rudeness is enough, for a moment, to obliterate one's identity.

I asked him about the impact of the assault on his development as a writer, on the themes that animate his work. He said he hadn't written about it directly, that "The Lesson," a poem about a pedophile who used to hang around the playground when he was ten, was the closest he had come to addressing it.

"But isn't there," I asked, "a sense in which you've written about it again and again, a sense in which your work has been centrally concerned with the experience of victimization?"

Alan pondered this assessment for a moment.

"One thing it has affected," he said, "is my sense of history. My sense of the fragility of civilization before the forces of history, of how easily and completely it can be obliterated. Do you remember 'The Sweepers'?"

The poem opens his book *Covenant*. It describes the clearing and leveling of a path for a Roman army to pass through the rubble of a city it has destroyed. The sweepers—"nameless, stateless" individuals (were they, before the fall of the city, slaves? masters?)—clear the debris and use the bodies of the dead and dying to fill potholes and ditches. Alan writes of ". . . the dumb animal / persistence that so easily and thoroughly turned friend and relation, / the whole rich tapestry of customary feeling, law, memory and lore / into mere fill for gullies." Of the sweepers, he asks:

> Did they resent the half-dead
> for their clumsy fit, their ineffectual resistances,
> the ones stuffed head down, legs above the surface
> writhing pathetically to get away, like giant insects,
> or the ones feet first, their heads above the surface
> unable even to flinch as the horses trampled over face and skull?

"That's my view of history," he said. "Human beings unable even to flinch as horses trample over their faces."

It was time for Alan to go. He and Patsy embraced. I walked him to his car. Unable to find a parking place on campus, he had parked several blocks away. Walking beside my friend, I felt a tenderness I didn't know how to express. It was good to know he was returning not only to books and manuscripts, his nest of texts, but to his wife and children.

The previous spring at his reading at the University of Chicago, in introducing a poem dealing with victims of the Holocaust, Alan had spoken dismissively, almost contemptuously, of the famous lines from Ezra Pound's Canto LXXXI:

> What thou lovest well remains,
> the rest is dross
> What thou lov'st well shall not be reft from thee
> What thou lov'st well is thy true heritage.

Considered in light of those who lost everything they "lov'st well," Alan had said, the Pound lines were—no more damning word in his vocabulary—"sentimental."

The remark had provoked a surge of resistance in me. I had to make an effort not to take it personally, for I had used those lines in dedicating *A Worthy Tradition* to my mother ("To my mother, from my father, by way of their son"). They expressed for me an understanding, nurtured by the years of work on my father's book, of the passions that sustain a living tradition—of what, surviving death, lives on. This was not, I felt, a sentimental delusion. I had earned it with my life. It was inseparable in my mind from the hard knowledge of all that was irretrievably lost to death, of all that no amount of loving effort could redeem. For me, the Pound lines spoke of resistance, through memory and language, to surrendering any more to death than is absolutely necessary.

Alan, I knew, shared such a view of the ongoing work of culture. Our conversations, over the years, had deepened my understanding. (A favorite image of his, from a poem by Henry Vaughan, for the act of reading: "the dead *alive* and *busie*.") Yet the achievements of civilization, he insisted, were fragile: under violent assault, they became "mere fill for gullies." He refused the consolation offered by Pound. What thou lov'st well, he insisted, *can* be reft from thee. Utterly and for all time.

Sitting over tea at our table, listening to Alan talk of being an object endowed with feelings and to Patsy talk of having her ties to the world cut, I was aware of myself as being uninjured by violence and, at the same time, impaired, as if I lacked a sense they both possessed. There is a word for this mix of robustness and obliviousness: privilege. Not the privilege of gender, race, or class (though not altogether unrelated either). Rather, while Patsy and Alan bear the weight of the knowledge inflicted on them by violent men, I remain in a world where people enjoy, in Nadezhda Mandelstam's words, "the privilege of ordinary heartbreaks." The Pound lines, my father's book, the strenuous recoveries of meaning through grief belong to that world. It is a world that, embracing tragedy and loss, is rich in meaning. What Patsy and Alan are aware of, what they perhaps cannot *not* be aware of, is a larger darkness that can, in an instant, swallow that world whole.

THIRTY-THREE

WHAT I know of the isolating power of violence I know not from the inside out but from the perspective of one end of a connection that was torn when Patsy was ripped out of the world: the end that remains embedded. Alan evoked the fragility of civilized life with the image of "the whole rich tapestry of customary feeling, law, memory and lore" that can with appalling ease be turned into "mere fill for gullies." As if compelled to take every opportunity to build or repair connections between people, I find it almost impossible to refuse to participate in a community initiative or decline to attend a meeting to address a neighborhood issue. I feel driven but don't fully comprehend why: do I imagine that it's possible to stitch, stitch, stitch away at the fabric of human connectedness and produce a weave dense enough to resist brute force?

In any case, I now find myself, with vague embarrassment, at the center of a neighborhood controversy over *parking*. The issue was precipitated by a proposal to create a residential-permit parking zone near campus. Under the proposed plan, parking on several blocks would be restricted to residents and their guests during certain hours. This proposal is being advocated by a small group of residents, led by the wife of a senior faculty member, who feel they are entitled to park in front of their houses. They resent having to compete for parking places with university students and the customers of the shops on Fifty-seventh Street.

I was drawn into the controversy by Jonathan Kleinbard, vice president of the University of Chicago for news and community affairs. A former newspaper man who joined the university administration some twenty years ago, Jonathan is a major player in the curious politics of the neighborhood. He is, by virtue of his role and personal style, something of a lightning rod. A rapid-fire mumbler out of the side of his mouth, he has an abrupt, telegraphic manner that some find abrasive. Those with grievances against the university usually end up dealing with him, and all too often the issues become personalized: he is seen as the enemy.

We have always found him deeply considerate. After Patsy was assaulted, one of the first calls we received was from Jonathan; and he was frequently in touch thereafter. The fact that this was his job didn't make it any less welcome. I admire his institutional loyalty. At the same time, I sometimes wonder if he hasn't lost the capacity to distinguish between the interests of the community and those of the university. From his perspective, they seem inevitably and in all situations to be the same. In this respect, he is the most recent embodiment of a long-standing tradition.

That tradition dates back to the 1950s, when the university responded to the great surge of population out of the Black Belt and into surrounding areas by "stabilizing" the neighborhood through massive urban renewal and the deployment of a large security force. While congratulating itself on preserving Hyde Park–Kenwood as a "stable, integrated, middle-class community," it erected barricades against the rest of the South Side. And it eliminated much of the commercial space that had housed assorted clubs, shops, bars, and dives. The loss of such convivial public space appears to have been less an unintended by-product of redevelopment than one of its objectives: a way of removing attractions that drew "outsiders" into the neighborhood.

The principal vehicle for the university's campaign to shape and secure its environment was the South East Chicago Commission. This organization ostensibly grew out of a mass meeting called in 1952 to discuss crime in the neighborhood—a meeting prompted by an abduction and attempted rape—but it appears already to have been in the works. Under the direction of Julian Levi (the brother of Edward Levi, my father's colleague and friend, who was to become president of the university), the commission aggressively pursued the university's interests. Julian Levi was blunt. Referring to the "noble experiment" of racial integration, he once remarked that the "perpetual discussion of the joys of interracial activities will cause men and women of good will . . . to applaud the 'noble experiment' while at the same time they caution their daughters not to go to the University of Chicago lest they be raped on the streets."

Today the commission is a less aggressive presence. At first impression, it might look like a community organization, but it remains the university's tool for achieving its ends in the neighborhood. (Its letterhead is adorned with a long list of board members drawn from the neighborhood—I'm among them—but there are no meetings.) Its present executive director, Bob Mason, is a friend. A former policeman who served in the sex crimes division on the South Side, Bob conducts his business in a mild, soft-spoken style very different from that of Julian Levi. Yet the premise underlying the university's relationship to the neighborhood remains the same. "Of course," Bob once remarked to me with the matter-of-fact realism of a cop, "this is a *managed* community."

By eliminating so much commercial space, the university's urban renewal strategies largely destroyed the ecology of the neighborhood and hence its capacity to regenerate itself. In the case of Fifty-seventh Street, the commercial street nearest campus, the university—in the person of Kleinbard—takes pains to nurture and protect the handful of businesses that have survived. (I had first gotten to know Jonathan several years earlier, when a secondhand bookstore on Fifty-seventh Street was threatened with eviction, and I had helped mobilize public pressure on the landlords.)

The situation brings to mind an image used by the leaders of Solidarity in Poland. The Communists, they said, had taken the aquarium of Polish economic life and turned it into fish soup. The challenge facing Solidarity was to figure out how to turn the fish soup back into an aquarium. Such has been the impact of urban renewal on the local economy in Hyde Park–Kenwood. And Jonathan, in his efforts to manage that which by its nature cannot be managed, embodies the contradictions in the university's relationship to the neighborhood. While carrying forward the tradition that produced the fish soup, he is moved by his genuine affection for the place and his feel for urban life to try to reinvent the aquarium.

He thus responds with alarm to any threat to the handful of businesses that have taken hold on Fifty-seventh Street. And the proposed parking restrictions would affect several restaurants and bookstores. At a meeting convened by Jonathan, I agreed to draft a petition opposing the plan which was then circulated by businesses and concerned individuals. For weeks, coverage of the controversy—articles, editorials, letters to the editor—filled the pages of the *Hyde Park Herald*. So it was that I found myself the spokesperson for the opposition to residential-permit parking.

MY MIND keeps circling back to Alan's words:"Our identities are composed of our relations with others."This way of talking about the self is at odds with the modern conception of the individual as sovereign and autonomous. It's at once postmodern and archaic. To say we are members one of another is, from this perspective, quite exact: not just a moral ideal but an existential fact.

Seen in this light, torture and rape—the torture that is rape—can be said to *dismember* the self by destroying the web of relations that define and sustain it. "It's as though the moment I was hit," Patsy said, "I was cut off from myself—as though all my connections to the world were slashed."

Her phrasing suggests that she was, in the same moment, cut off from the world and cut off from herself—that these were not two different things. Is this what torturers know about the self? Is this the expertise they bring to bear on their victims: the knowledge that if you sever a person's ties to the world, her identity will collapse?

On the evidence of reports by Amnesty International and other human rights groups, torturers routinely assault their victims by way of their relations. Women are tortured in front of their husbands, men in front of their wives; parents are forced to watch their children being tortured, children to watch their parents. Every human connection supporting civilized life is ravaged. It's almost as though the torturers, in their hellish laboratory, were conducting experiments in the nature of the self. What happens to the soul of a person who is powerless to intervene, to protect, to comfort those she loves as they scream out in terror? Or to the soul of one whose children look on as he is swallowed and consumed by pain?

Patsy's account of the assault—a narrative that deepens with each telling—is a story of such *loneliness*. She often returns to the question of precisely what it was that terrified her.

"I was very afraid of this person, but I wasn't afraid of what he was doing. I wasn't afraid of—Oh my God, he's going to rape me and it's going to hurt and he's going to do this awful stuff. I was afraid it meant the end of me. I couldn't feel anything. I had no pain. I didn't even think what he might do to me. I just knew that whatever it was, each thing seemed to be worse than the last. And I knew I was incapable of physically getting rid of him, of overpowering him.

"My fear was that I would never see the children again. I kept thinking, I can't let it happen. When I said to him, 'I have a baby at home,' that was a way of saying, 'I'm connected to dependents, and I can't leave them. You can't take me away.' I wasn't afraid of pain. I wasn't afraid of death. I was afraid of the *aloneness* of it. That terrified me. The world just disappeared. I'm not afraid of death if I don't know about it. The problem is the *knowing*—that period of time when you *know* you're going to be separated, and you *know* that you'll never see them again, and they will suffer. The isolation was what was so terrifying. Certainly this is what torture is all about. It's why people's children and parents are killed in front of them or raped in the next room when you know. It isolates you. You've lost all control over any way to make those connections in your life—any kind of meaningful connections. That's what I'm afraid to ever experience again, to be so utterly alone and still alive."

Among the various names for torture techniques, the most telling perhaps is what torturers in the Philippines call the mock executions they inflict: "the process of dying." A name that could be applied to torture in general. And to rape.

"There was," Patsy reported, "only death."

ON FEBRUARY 14 the *University of Chicago Maroon* reported that a student had been abducted and raped ten days earlier. She had been walking on Fifty-seventh Street, between Woodlawn and University Avenues, at about midnight. As she passed the mouth of our alley, a man grabbed her and forced her into a car. There were two other men in the car. They took her to an abandoned building west of Hyde Park and raped her. They held her for about an hour and a half, then released her. She made her way back to campus on the number 55 Garfield bus.

The young woman was seized a block from our home. At the center of campus. A block from the library. On a street students pass back and forth on all day. Some expressed shock that such a thing could happen at the heart of the most secure area in Hyde Park. Not Patsy.

"It's completely consistent with my sense of the world," she said.

The university administration was slow to report the rape to the student body. The only communication about the incident, circulated almost a week after it occurred, was a memo from a deputy dean of students to other administrators, housing staff, and advisers. Marked "Confidential," it described the incident as an "assault." The word "rape" was not used. It was unclear what those who received the memo were supposed to do with it—whether and by what means they were to communicate the information to students. A reasonable inference was that they were to hold the information and not to share it.

The incident was first made public by members of a campus feminist group who distributed flyers on campus. They had learned of it via an overheard conversation among library staff. Then, ten days after the incident, the *Maroon* story appeared.

Students were critical of the university's handling of the issue. They charged that the administration's failure to circulate the information earlier and more widely constituted "a cover-up." Kleinbard and other university spokesmen responded that they had withheld the information at the request of the victim and in the interest of the ongoing investigation. Students asked why protection of the privacy of the victim and the pursuit of the investigation required suppressing information about the assault. Kleinbard conceded that the university could have handled the matter better. "It was," he said, "a judgment call." The police had had two suspects in custody. "We made a decision to try to help the police by not releasing the information right away. Maybe in hindsight we should not have done that."

I later learned that the victim had been reluctant to identify the suspects and bring charges. The reason she gave, I was told by a friend close to the case, was that she didn't want her parents to know. She wanted, she said, to spare her family pain and grief. The police were unable to persuade her to bring charges.

In addition to stressing the victim's desire for privacy, spokesmen defended the university's silence by stressing that the rape was an *isolated* episode, that it didn't appear to be part of a pattern, and that hence there was no pressing need to inform the community about the modus operandi of criminals who might strike again.

In the absence of criminal proceedings, the public vehicle for addressing what had happened was the controversy over the university's response. Students pressed two demands: improved procedures for notifying students about crime; and better resources for victims of sexual assault. They cited programs elsewhere and argued that the U of C fell far short of the standards set by various other universities.

The leaders of the student protest proved effective publicists. They held rallies at the flagpole in the main quadrangle. They contacted the media and gave many interviews. Local television stations, unlike the deputy dean of students, were not reticent about using the word "rape."

It was a public relations debacle for the university. An avalanche of negative publicity over several days. The students' grievances clearly had merit. At the same time, as I watched Jonathan during a rally in the main quadrangle rush with his odd bounding stride from reporter to reporter, trying to counter student interviews, I felt a measure of sympathy. His aim was clearly to protect the university's interests. That entailed seeking to correct distorted perceptions of the neighborhood which the convergence of race, sex, and violence, as refracted through the mass media, inevitably gave rise to. When I thought of parents deciding not to send their daughter to the University of Chicago for fear she would be raped by a black man, I identified with his efforts to provide a larger context.

Yet I could also see how infuriating this sort of response was for the students. The administration sought to meet the students' narrow grievances by appointing a task force on crime notification "to review and recommend guidelines for making information about criminal activity public." It did not, however, address the concerns underlying those grievances. The students were searching for ways to explore and give expression to the sense in which *the community* was a rape victim. They were trying to create a space in which certain conversations were possible, in which certain questions could form, in which it was possible to be actively confused about these matters. The university's insistence that the rape was "an isolated event" and assurances from the South East Chicago Commission that the incidence of violent crime in the neighborhood was down seemed self-serving and dissembling to students who were trying to come to terms with the nature and extent of sexual violence in the world through which they moved. *An isolated event?*

I spoke with several high-level officers of the university, beginning with the provost, and urged them to fashion a broader, less defensive response—to engage the grief and fear and confusion of the students.

These were friends who knew what had happened to Patsy. They received me politely.

"I hear you," said the provost.

Always a bad sign.

I didn't doubt that the administration was full of individuals who were appalled by the rape and sympathetic to the victim, but in their official roles they had institutional agendas to attend to. Other considerations overrode their human responses. I was reminded of my friends at Playboy, individuals capable of humane responses to individual victims of sexual violence who submitted to institutional imperatives that demanded that the larger realities of violence against women be pushed into invisibility. Yet it was easier to see how this served the purposes of an institution like Playboy than those of an institution dedicated to the development and exercise of critical intelligence.

How UNSPEAKABLY sad that it is the *victims* of torture who experience "shame." In the case of rape, this is often said to be due to benighted social attitudes, to a stigma society attaches to rape victims. But I wonder whether the condition the word "shame" refers to might still be present even if those around the victim were infinitely sensitive. Is "shame" perhaps among the names we give to the response of human beings when their ties to the world are severed and their identities dismembered? More precisely, is it perhaps the name for what it feels like to struggle against dismemberment, to struggle to stay connected?

For Patsy, ripped out of the world and rendered powerless, the ultimate horror was "to be so alone and still alive." "There was," she said, "only death." And Alan evoked the flooding of his identity by shame by saying he felt he "had disappeared as a person." The forced entry of the torturer—into one's life, one's body, one's story—reveals that one is not the subject of one's unfolding life but only, as Alan put it, "an object that can feel." And what that object feels is shame.

In *The Drowned and the Saved,* Primo Levi quotes the terrible words of Jean Améry, an Austrian philosopher active in the Resistance who had been tortured by the Nazis and sent to Auschwitz:

> Anyone who has been tortured remains tortured. . . . Anyone who has suffered torture never again will be able to be at ease in the world, the abomination of the annihilation is never extinguished.

Faith in humanity, already cracked by the first slap in the face, then demolished by torture, is never acquired again.

Torture is not simply an event in the life of the victim; it alters the terms of existence. The violence done to the body enters the soul. It's a continuing assault on the victim's identity. Améry writes of the enduring humiliation of having been reduced under torture to "flesh and death." To have been rendered powerless by one who wants only to hurt and humiliate you, to have suffered annihilation (all but the final loss of consciousness) by cruel hands is to carry deep within the terrible knowledge that you can be reduced, in Améry's words, to nothing more than "a prey of death."

My lovely Patsy contains this knowledge.

THE DAY after the *Maroon* story appeared, Patsy had an assignment photographing a conference at the Divinity School. It was dark when she finished, so she called and asked me to walk up University Avenue to meet her.

Walking home, we passed the spot where the girl had been abducted. On one side of the mouth of the alley where the men had lain in wait is a Unitarian church, containing a preschool and the headquarters of the Chicago Children's Choir. On the other side is University Church, which houses the Blue Gargoyle Youth Service Center, an agency that offers, among other programs, a highly regarded adult literacy program. Directly across the street is the Quadrangle Club, where much of the faculty gathers for lunch and conversation each day.

We talked of how terrifying it must have been for the girl, in the midst of this dense mesh of human connections, to have been so suddenly and absolutely isolated by violence.

"I can't imagine anything worse than being pulled into a car like that," Patsy said. Then, after a pause, "No, that's not right. You can always imagine something worse. It's like my dream. Whatever you might imagine, it's happened to some woman somewhere."

"Yes," I said, "in a sense, you're always taken to the same place, aren't you?"

Patsy was silent.

The next morning she reported that she had been awakened in the night by the sound of a woman weeping as she walked past our apartment.

"I thought of the girl who had been abducted. There was a pain in my stomach. It spread and filled my whole body. I began to think about Betsy. I could see how terrible it's going to be to have her out on those streets. I don't think I'm going to be able to bear it."

I AM unsettled now when I encounter the word "rape" used metaphorically. For example: "the rape of the land" or "I feel raped." In many instances, it's an effective image. Yet even as it illuminates, such usage runs the risk of depleting the core meaning of the word. A dangerous magic.

I RECEIVED a call from Nina Helstein. A social worker in her late forties, Nina grew up in Hyde Park. Her father, Ralph Helstein, was a celebrated labor leader who played a key role in building the United Packinghouse Workers of America and ultimately served as president of the union. He was also a civil rights activist—one of the handful of labor leaders who, early on, supported and marched alongside Dr. Martin Luther King, Jr.

Nina and I were nodding acquaintances but didn't know each other well. She was moved to call me by an article that mentioned I was working on a book about sexual violence. She had a story, she said, that might interest me—a story about how the university had responded to a series of rapes in the neighborhood some years earlier. We made a date to talk over coffee at the Medici, a restaurant on Fifty-seventh Street.

"No need for small talk," she said as we sat down.

A person of considerable warmth, she spoke with clarity and narrative tact. The proper telling of her story clearly mattered to her.

It happened about ten years ago. At the time, she was a graduate student at the University of Chicago. Then as now, she lived in a town house on Dorchester Avenue. One night she heard what sounded like someone trying to break in. She called the police. They came promptly but found nothing. Two weeks later, she returned home in the evening and found her living room full of people—neighbors, the police, her parents (who lived a few blocks away). They discovered that a ground-floor window had been broken.

"Is there something going on in the neighborhood I should know about?" she asked the police. "Should I move out for a while?"

They shrugged her off. "They treated me like a hysterical female. They patronized me."

She had the glass in the window replaced. A week later, a man removed the windowpane and broke into her house. He choked her and told her that if she cried out he would kill her. Then he raped her in her bed. Her account of the rape was telegraphic; there was no need for details for the purposes of the story she had to tell. For a moment, her face flooded with emotion. Then she composed herself and moved on.

After he left, she called the police and went to the emergency room. When she returned home, there were several messages on her answering machine. Among them were a call from a television producer and a call from someone associated with the "victim assistance program" of the South East Chicago Commission.

She was angered by the call from the producer. She returned it immediately. She intended to tell the woman off but was disarmed by her sympathetic response.

"I'm terribly sorry to bother you at such a time, but I'm so mad I could spit," the producer said. She told Nina that there had been several other rapes in the neighborhood which followed the same pattern. The victims were white women in their thirties, living alone. In each instance, the rapist broke a window, then returned several weeks later, when the glazing compound was still soft, and pushed the pane of glass out. The police and the university were aware of this pattern but had not informed the community about these episodes, about the danger. Would she be willing to be interviewed by ABC News? The producer assured Nina that it wouldn't be necessary to reveal her identity, if she didn't want to. They could show her in blacked-out silhouette, alter her voice electronically, and so on. Nina said she would think about it.

She then called the South East Chicago Commission. She didn't know what the commission was. She assumed that it was a community organization and that its victim assistance program was designed to assist victims. She didn't recall the name of the first person she dealt with at the commission. She told him that they had to get word out to the community: they had to warn women. He was resistant. "We can't do that," he said. "We'd have a circus on our hands."

In the days that followed, she had several conversations with Michael Murphy, the executive director of the commission. His job, she said, was clearly "to handle me." Her request was simple: that a story appear in the *Hyde Park Herald* informing residents of the pattern and warning them of the danger. Otherwise, she told them, she would agree to be interviewed by the local ABC station.

After much resistance and maneuvering, Murphy finally agreed to prepare a press release for the *Herald*. He called his secretary into the office and dictated a statement. In it he referred to the crime as "a home invasion."

"What do you mean 'a home invasion'?" Nina challenged him. "I was *raped*."

"When I first came to the commission," Murphy replied, "Julian Levi told me, 'We never use the word "rape" here.' And I have never found it necessary to do so."

"If I can live it," Nina shot back, "you can say it."

Murphy rewrote the press release, using the word "rape," but then a few days later he called to say that the police had requested that they withhold the story. The initial rationale for not informing the community—that it would "upset" residents—now gave way to another: the demands of law enforcement. An article in the *Herald* might make it harder to catch the rapist.

Nina kept pressure on the university. She met repeatedly with the head of campus security, with Murphy, with friends on the faculty, with Kleinbard. She told everyone she spoke with that she didn't want to do the television interview but that she would if they didn't place a story in the *Herald*. Eventually, a story did appear—a story that used the word "rape" rather than "home invasion."

"The rape itself I would have recovered from more easily than this," said Nina. "I felt that they cared more about real estate values and about attracting students and faculty than they did about the safety of women in the neighborhood. They didn't care enough to warn women, when they had the information to do so."

She paused, her story finished.

"What was so terrible was their refusal to acknowledge what had happened. The fact that they didn't care about what happened to the next woman," she said, "meant they didn't care about what had happened to me."

WHEN I reported Nina's story to Patsy, she recalled being troubled after she was assaulted by the lack of any reporting of the crime to the community. Despite the fact that there was an obvious group in danger—women who run on the lakefront—no effort was made by the South East Chicago Commission or the university to warn them. How strange to think that Patsy, as she struggled for her life, envisioned a newspaper article telling of the rape and murder of a jogger on the lakefront: that was how she saw the fate she was resisting. It was also, it seems, something others were resisting. The newspaper article, that is.

WHAT, I wonder, is happening in the soul of the young woman who was abducted and raped? What is she going through? What is it like for her to have the controversy provoked by her ordeal swirl around her without participating in it? The reason she gave for not bringing charges was that she wanted to spare her parents pain and grief. She explained her decision in terms of the relations that constitute her. Does this happen often? Is it possible that when a rape victim doesn't tell her husband ("He'd die if he knew") or others close to her, this not only reflects her concern about how they will react but is also a bid to stay connected, to preserve the relations that define her? By assuming the role of protecting others, does she seek relief from the experience of being rendered utterly powerless?

TWO WEEKS after the abduction-rape, I woke up angry. A story had formed in my mind: a star male professor—Cass Sunstein, say, or Rashid Khalidi, or William Julius Wilson—leaves his office after dark, or perhaps steps out of the faculty club after dinner. A car is waiting in the alley. Three men jump out and grab him. They quickly subdue him and force him into the car. They take him to an abandoned building, beat him, strip off his clothes, inflict agony on his soul by way of his genitals, heap abuse on him. They have singled him out for assault because he is white or black, Jewish or Palestinian. After abusing him and threatening him, they leave him to make his way back to campus on the number 55 bus.

Such an incident would be seen as striking at the core of the university, wouldn't it? It wouldn't be treated as a marginal episode (however terrible), as a distraction from the central business of the university. We wouldn't take comfort in the proposition that it was "an isolated event" or that the incidence of torture of black or Palestinian or Jewish intellectuals was down somewhat relative to last year. Or would we? I'm not sure how the university would, in fact, respond. Waking up angry, in the clarity of early-morning light, I had little doubt, however, about how it *should* respond, in view of the standards of intellectual integrity it purports to uphold. The fundamental mission of a university has everything to do with making and maintaining connections—connecting us to one another through open inquiry and discourse, connecting us to the past through language and narrative, drawing us deeper into the traditions that flow through and sustain us. Surely my imagined abduction and torture of a male professor must be seen as a grave injury to this civilizing enterprise, as a direct threat to the central business of the university. And unless we are to make distinctions, in the realm of torture, among members of this community of learning on the basis of gender, age, and status, then the abduction and gang rape of a young female student is no less grave an injury to the university.

PATSY AND I attended a candlelight vigil for the student who was abducted and raped. A group gathered in front of Regenstein Library. About 150 people. Almost all were students. A number of males. Few adults besides us.

After several statements by students, the group moved to the corner of Fifty-seventh and Woodlawn where a flower was planted on the grounds of the Unitarian Church. Many of the students had candles. They placed them around the plant. The ceremony felt spontaneous, as if a ritual was being invented on the spot.

A male student, holding a candle, was distraught. He clearly knew her. He was comforted by a female student.

Surveying the gathering of students, I didn't see Patsy and myself, I saw Josh and Betsy. It occurred to me that college students are, in some respects, a rootless population, akin to those populations—runaways, prostitutes, the homeless—that are disproportionately preyed upon by urban predators. In most instances, students have moved away from home. They are between families—between the families they were born into and the families they will form. They are, for the most part, shallowly rooted in the place where they have come to study. And they are at a moment in their lives at which they are inclined to assert their freedom and independence in ways that expose them to risk.

What does the university tell them about this place when they first alight here? Much is made during "orientation week" of boundaries. Dinner at the Chinese restaurant on Sixty-third Street where my family used to dine occasionally is, I am told, cited as a reckless expedition; stories are told of students seeking Tai Sam Yon's egg rolls who end up getting mugged. Advice on how to navigate in the neighborhood is dispensed by residence heads in the dorms. In one dorm, a friend reported, new students were told that they shouldn't make eye contact with black males on the street. The person offering this advice drew an analogy to a hostage situation in which one doesn't want to do any-thing that would call attention to oneself and so make one a target of violence. What an image for one's relation to the place where one lives and to one's neighbors: hostages!

At the outskirts of the crowd, I noticed a girl with an artificial leg. The sight of her recalled my conversation with Barbara about how people would see each other, move among each other, touch each other, if the injuries from sexual violence were visible on the body. As I watched the students gropingly seek forms to represent the injury to the community, a kindred thought came to me. What if the history of violence in a place were visible? What if it were somehow present in the physical setting? I found this a comforting thought. For victims, it would aid the movement from an interior event flooding one with shame to something that happened in the world. For the uninjured, it would help bring into focus the true conditions of life around them. And it would provide ground on which to resist those who believe they have an interest in the crime *not* being visible in the world and who seek in various ways to push it back into invisibility.

I used to think the outrage of victims toward the police, the crim-inal justice system—or, in this case, a university—was disproportionate and displaced. After all, I thought to myself, *they* didn't rape her. But now I am beginning to see that when others fail to acknowledge the reality and gravity of what has happened, when their patterns of denial and evasion deepen the isolation of the victim, they compound the injury of the rape. It is indecent that the victim, as she struggles to fash-ion a narrative that moves the cruelties inflicted upon her from the interior regions of her soul into the world, must contend not only with the weight of her knowledge and the undertow of her shame but also with the counterforce of institutions and individuals who resist the telling of her story. The men who, as a matter of policy, never find it necessary to use the word "rape," are convinced, I am quite sure, that they are acting with hard-headed realism in defense of a great institu-tion dedicated to the life of the mind. But there is another perspective. And from that perspective, they collaborate with the rapist in denying the victim her voice and her story.

THIRTY-FOUR

I VISITED Hans and Eva in the late afternoon. Eva was alone in the living room. Hans, she said, was just rising from a nap and would be out in a few minutes. She was working on her current design project—small round tables supported by bases that recalled the compassionate birds on the china of my childhood. Several prototypes of different designs stood in various nooks and crannies of the overstuffed room. They had been prepared for her by a carpenter. In designing the tables, she worked in the medium of paper rather than wood. The floor was covered with paper cutouts.

So far as I knew, Eva had not left the apartment for weeks. In the course of their marriage, she and Hans had often been apart but now she was with him from moment to moment. She saw that he was never alone. And while he slept or was otherwise engaged, she worked on her designs.

Hans emerged from the back of the apartment, wearing a bathrobe and assisted by the nurse. Watching him shuffle across the room to his chair, I was struck by his economy of movement. No wasted energy. He had always been vigorous and athletic. When I was a boy, he had been the first person to encourage me to run. He had told me stories of seeing Paavo Nurmi in the 1928 Olympics in Amsterdam, and he had timed me as I ran around the block. He had continued to play tennis, at every opportunity, until the last few months. He was, I realized, dying like an athlete—practicing careful husbandry of his energy, concentrating his efforts.

He'd had a good day. Several hours of work. A nap. Now he was hungry for conversation.

"I'm excluding people now. I'm giving priority to work. I have so little time in the day to work, so little strength," he said. "Anyway, except for you, it's hard for me to see people now. It breaks me up."

Perhaps the difference is that he knows I'll come back again and again until the end. When others leave, especially those who have come from afar, he must assume that he'll never see them again.

His work now takes the form of dictating letters. He writes colleagues and collaborators on various projects to give them his final thoughts and suggestions. He writes friends to tell them what they have meant to him and to take his leave.

"I think when I finish this last writing, I will have no more joy of living," he said. Then, moments later, he described a new research project that had just occurred to him: a content analysis of media coverage which he expected would show that coverage of crime has increased more sharply than the crime rate has.

"I must dictate a memo on that," he said.

He reported a protracted episode of vomiting the night before. I imagined the heaving of his fragile body.

"What was it like?"

"What can I say? It's all new to me."

He spoke again, as he has before, about his lack of appetite. Together with his loss of energy for work, he seems to find this the most alarming expression of the disease consuming him. At best, food does not interest him; at worst, it revolts him. A bowl of strawberries holds no appeal. He speaks of this as a wholly new experience.

"You must not have been depressed much in your life," I suggested. "People often describe depression in just such terms: 'It's as if someone put my favorite meal in front of me and I had no appetite for it.'"

"Really?" The observation seemed to please him. "You're right. I haven't been depressed much in my life."

I began to rise to leave. Hans indicated he had more to say. I sat down.

"Eva's so strong. She can override anything." Tears and tremulous speech. Turbulence in a delicate vessel. "But the most wonderful thing she has done for us . . . " He paused, summoning the composure to get the words out. "The most wonderful thing is to have surrounded us every day with never-ending beauty."

"And what's so marvelous," I added, "is that it doesn't belong to the world of museums, though it's in museums now. It's been part of your daily life."

"Precisely."

THE CONTROVERSY over residential-permit parking came to a head with a community meeting held in the social hall of the Unitarian Church. As I entered, I checked on the condition of the flower students had planted in honor of the young woman who had been abducted as she walked past the church. It was struggling.

The meeting had been called by Alderman Lawrence Bloom. The issue was whether or not he should go forward in the City Council with the permit parking proposal he had introduced. More than 150 people showed up. Some were students; most were older. Bloom said it was "by far the best-attended meeting" he had ever called during his years as alderman and joked that "it was the largest public meeting held in Hyde Park since the Vietnam War."

The meeting lasted for two hours. After opening remarks by Bloom, a succession of speakers spoke for or against the plan. I was the first speaker. When I characterized the plan as "an unneighborly solution to a neighborhood problem," I got an ovation. From that moment on, it was clear who had been moved to come to the meeting.

Supporters of the parking plan later accused opponents of "packing" the meeting, but we could take no such credit. The truth was that the issue struck a chord. Speaker after speaker condemned the "elitism" of a plan that would serve the privileged few and adversely affect others. People spoke with passion and moral clarity. They were offended as a matter of principle. That which could not find voice in response to the abduction-rape found eloquent expression in the controversy over residential-permit parking: the injury to the community.

Soon after the meeting, Alderman Bloom withdrew the proposal.

I was uncertain what to make of the contrast between people's muffled response to the rape and their fluent outrage over the parking plan. Somehow it seemed too easy to write it off as denial. Might it also be, at least in some cases, an expression of moral tact? Sometimes I wonder if we don't misread as insensitivity the reticence that arises from finding something *unspeakable*. It's as if our deepest intuitions about the sanctity of life remain as interior and inarticulate—and hence unshareable with one another—as the isolation that terror inflicts.

A PHOTOGRAPH in the newspaper draws my eye and at the same time deflects it. It shows peasant women in Bangladesh grieving over the dead after monsoon floods destroyed their village. The women sit on their haunches, keening under the open sky. One holds her hand up as if warding away death; another reaches out as if to pull back to life the corpses that lie on the ground. The faces of the women testify to the bedrock of human existence: the marrow of life is grief.

I look away. Why do I avert my eyes? Am I withdrawing my sympathies? Do I feel that the photographer invaded the privacy of the grieving women and that in looking at the photo I become complicit in that invasion? I don't think so. When I encounter images of refugees whom disasters, natural or man-made, have left unhoused, something else seems to be going on. They *have* no privacy. That is an essential aspect of the disaster that has befallen them. Extreme circumstances—war, flood, epidemic, famine—have left them exposed. Their suffering, their dying, their grieving are done out in the open. Hence my fascination and my unease. The impulse to look away arises not out of insensitivity but out of fellow feeling. It's an impulse to restore to them some small part of what they have lost.

In "The Exposed Nest," Robert Frost describes finding a nest full of young birds on the ground in a field that a hay-cutting tractor rig has just passed over ("Miraculously without tasting flesh"):

> You wanted to restore them to their right
> Of something interposed between their sight
> And too much world at once—could means be found.

Violence isolates. It also *exposes*.

When Patsy was assaulted, the boundaries between private and public in our lives collapsed. The rape was at once the most interior of experiences and a public event. No less than a flood that sweeps away one's village, it laid waste to her privacy, leaving her with nothing interposed between her sight and "too much world at once." From the start, she recognized it as part of a larger pattern of violence against women that she would somehow have to engage in order to recover her life and her sense of the world.

"It's not just you and your assailant. You get pushed into this river, moving much too fast, of so many women raped and tortured over so many years. It's so much bigger than you ever thought."

LAST NIGHT I massaged Patsy. When she turned over, her eyes filled with tears. We didn't go forward and make love. I felt calm.

"This may seem like a strange thing for a man to say, but there is a place inside me waiting to be entered and filled by you."

She said nothing, but I sensed she had heard me.

HANS'S DYING is a presence in our lives, a pressure bearing down on us. Moment to moment, it's always there. Patsy now wakes in the night, flooded with fear, wondering what it's like for him as death approaches. Does he lie alone in the dark, in the middle of the night, knowing he is dying? I, too, wonder. Does the prospect of death, now before him—"the awkward thing," he said, "is *knowing*"— make him feel alone in the way Patsy felt alone on the lakefront, surrounded on all sides by a rapist's fury, believing she would die at his hands? How much is the terror she experienced due to the ultimate solitude of human beings before death?

Each morning, as I walk to my office, I check the American flag in the main quadrangle. When someone in the university community dies, the flag is flown at half-mast and the name of the individual is posted on the flagpole. When I see that the flag is at half-mast, I walk over and check it. Dread rises inside me as I strain to read from afar the name on the pole. I'm relieved when I discover that someone else has died, not my friend.

From my office—when the trees are bare—I can see Hans's apartment building several blocks away. It's known as Nobel Towers because of the concentration of Nobel Prize winners who live there. Saul Bellow lives on the top floor. George Stigler, who won the economics prize in 1982, resided there until his recent death. And two winners of the physics prize live there: James Cronin, who won the prize in 1980, and Subrahmanyan Chandrasekhar, an astrophysicist, awarded the prize in 1983.

Chandrasekhar was honored, in part, for work he had done as a young man in the 1930s on the question of what happens to stars when they burn themselves out. The prevailing theory at the time was that they collapse into a body about the size of the earth and stabilize into what are called "white dwarf stars." On the basis of mathematical calculations, Chandrasekhar determined that there was a limit to the mass of a white dwarf star and that larger stars would have a different fate. The gravitational force in a collapsing star of a certain size, he theorized, would cause the compressing electrons in the star's gases to move faster and faster until they approached the speed of light. Because of this state of "relativistic degeneracy," Chandrasekhar concluded, a large dying star would not stabilize but would continue to compress, to become smaller and smaller. This was derided as an absurd notion by the dominant astronomer of the time. Twenty years later, it had come to be regarded as a fundamental insight—now known as the Chandrasekhar Limit—essential to one of the great discoveries in the history of science. Those large dying stars Chandrasekhar speculated about in the 1930s are today known as black holes—regions of space-time from which nothing, not even light, can escape, because gravity is so strong.

Chandrasekhar—universally known as Chandra—is a legendary figure on campus. A Brahman, educated in Madras and Cambridge, he is a reserved and formal man, who always wears a dark suit, tie, and white shirt. He has spent virtually every day of his adult life sitting at a desk searching, in the medium of mathematical formulae, for order in the universe. His work habits and acute shyness have left little space in his life for friendship. Yet he and Hans have, in recent years, become close. Although they seem, in some respects, an improbable pair—the imperious, volatile Austrian Jew and the shy, formal Brahman—they are deeply at home in one another's presence. Chandra now comes downstairs to visit almost every day. Often when I call on Hans in the afternoon, he recounts their most recent conversation.

One day he told me that Chandra had brought down a 1713 edition of Newton's *Principia* and shown it to him. This had clearly given him great pleasure. They had discussed the question of whether intensive study of a masterpiece can enable one to enter into the movements of a great mind.

Hans's talks with Chandra seem to fortify him. A vehement atheist, he refers to notions of an afterlife as "that god-awful nonsense." He finds it more consoling to talk with Chandra.

"Listening to Chandra talk about Newton and the universe," he told me, "that's my church."

We were in his bedroom. Late-afternoon light filtered in through the windows. Shadows played across the wall of books opposite his bed. Hans, his head propped up with pillows, seemed very small and delicate.

How is it I had never before fully appreciated his physical beauty? Somehow, as his strength has ebbed and the surface turbulence of his life has calmed, it has been possible to see him more clearly—as if death were an artist and dying a refining process by which human essences are revealed.

He spoke of his death as something immediate.

"My only regret is that it comes a week too soon," he said. "I have a few more letters I want to write."

I was moved by his oft expressed wish to somehow, at the end of eight and a half decades, "eke out a few more days of work." Why, Eva asked, can't he simply *be*? Why must he always *do*? I could see her point. Yet there was something noble about the way he carried the active principle that had governed his life to its ultimate conclusion.

"I'm at peace," he said, in tears. "One shouldn't say it crying."

I took his hand. His grip was firm.

"I'm not scared of dying itself."

"Is there any part of it you're scared of?"

"No."

The moment had come for my question. I didn't doubt what his answer would be, yet felt the need to ask.

"I want to ask you something, Hans. When Patsy talks about the rape, she speaks of the terrible isolation she felt—an aloneness beyond loneliness. I'm trying to understand whether that feeling is a product of terror or is something one feels when death draws near."

I realized I had been gripping his hand more tightly as I spoke. I loosened my grip.

Hans replied with a sweet smile and a shake of his head. He seemed tired.

"It's just the body," he said. "Something happening to the body."

I stood, then leaned forward. He took my head in his hands. His kiss was passionate. Hungry.

SEVERAL DAYS later, Hans asked, through Jean, that I come over. He was lying on the sofa in the living room when I arrived. With the nurse's help, he was urinating. I chatted with Eva and Jean in the dining room until he was done. Then I went and sat with him. He sent Jean and Eva away. He wanted, he said, to be alone with me.

"I want you to take down my last letter," he said. "To my family."

With long pauses and through tears, he dictated words of love and asked forgiveness for his failings. "I love you more than anything else in the world," he wrote. "I embrace you all."

"It's hard to say good-bye," he sobbed, "after such a rich life."

Having finished his work, he was ready to die. But one more task remained, one final effort: to get to his last breath.

When Patsy and I next visited two days later, Hans seemed beyond speech. He lay on his left side, curled up, waiting. It was as if he had turned away from life, toward death. There was something childlike about his posture. I almost expected to see him suck his fingers like Betsy.

While Patsy talked with Jean, I spent a few minutes alone with him. I held his hand and felt, faintly, his answering squeeze.

Patsy then spent some time alone with him. She later told me that as she left, he opened his eyes and pursed his lips. A kiss.

WHEN PATSY telephoned the following afternoon, Eva told her, "There's no point in coming anymore, except to see Jean and me."

When we arrived at the door, we found that the emotional tenor of the household had changed. Jean, in tears, embraced us. Eva, as if to reassure herself, several times repeated words the doctor had told them, "You will suffer more than he will."

Hans had been in great pain that morning. He had screamed and vomited. The doctor had come immediately. Since then, at two-hour intervals, they had given him morphine suppositories.

He was in the same position as the night before—curled on his left side, waiting to receive death. Eva sat in a chair beside the bed. The nurse was rubbing his back. He was panting. His eyes, mostly closed during the last few days, were open and had a filmy quality. He looked like a mortally wounded animal, lying by the side of the road. "Something happening to the body," he had said.

A tape recorder, brought down by Chandra, played Bach. Did Hans hear the music? I couldn't tell. His world, so wide and rich, now seemed to have contracted down to his labored breathing, to the events unfolding deep inside his body. It was possible, too, that his remoteness was due as much to the morphine blunting his pain as to the death blooming inside him.

On the far side of the bed, under the window, stood one of Eva's tables. A semicircular glass surface resting on an interlocking base of gentle bird forms. It supported a vase full of tulips.

Patsy sat on the bed and held his hand. I relieved the nurse and rubbed his back. He moved his arm.

"Take his hand," suggested Patsy.

I cradled his hand in mine. There was no answering pressure from him.

We left the bedroom and sat for a while with Eva and Jean in the living room. Eva recalled the words of a friend after her mother died. "At least you know where your mother is buried," her friend had written.

"For those of my generation," said Eva, "that's something."

We returned home, entering through the garden. As we stepped into the apartment, Patsy said, "We'll never see Hans again at the back door."

There were fresh flowers on the dining room table in one of Eva's vases.

"I knew we needed flowers today, even though we can't afford them," she said.

The call came later that evening.

"It's over," Jean said. "He's gone."

I returned to the Zeisels' and helped the nurse coordinate the removal of the body. Eva and Jean stayed at the other end of the apartment during this operation. When I arrived, the funeral home attendants had wrapped Hans's corpse in a tarp and were strapping it onto a dolly. I helped them negotiate the doors and elevator. It was like moving a piece of furniture. They took care not to bump their load, but I sensed that this was more out of concern for our sensibilities than for the object they were carting away.

Once the corpse was gone, Eva and Jean emerged. We sat in the living room and talked. At first, Eva was agitated by a swarm of practical concerns: the obituary? the memorial service? the apartment? Hans's papers? After a while, she became calm— almost serene—and spoke of Hans's last hours. She described the final moment. She was lying beside him, holding his hand. He was breathing easily. "And then the next breath didn't come."

She brightened.

"Hans had a wonderful dream last night," she said. "In the middle of the night, he reached for my hand and squeezed it in a strong, affirming way. He put his hand inside my shirt. Then, at four in the morning, he opened his eyes and said distinctly, in German, 'How is it that we're not dead yet?'"

For Eva, those words were a gift. Over the last several months, she had seen that he was never alone, that there was always someone close at hand, always someone to hold his hand. She had made a nest for him to die in. And as death came to him, he had said *we*.

THE NEXT day was a Sunday. In the morning, I called various of Hans's friends and colleagues with the news. Throughout the afternoon, the Zeisel apartment was full of people coming to pay their respects. Flowers and food. Sobs and laughter. The release of narrative energy in the afterglow of a life. I overheard Eva, in conversation with a succession of people, recount again and again the story of Hans's final moments. "And then the next breath didn't come."

Chandra looked lost. He told me about one of his final conversations with Hans. Lying in his bed opposite the full bookshelves that ran the length of the room, Hans had said, "All those books are in my mind, but they will die with me." Chandra recalled a famous mathematician who on his deathbed had converted to Catholicism. He couldn't accept that all that was in his head would simply be lost.

"Hans accepted this," said Chandra. Then, as if completing a proof, he added, "That shows his character was more noble than that of the mathematician."

Despite fatigue and grief, there was for me, as always on such occasions, a heightening and a lightening. A quickening of my sense of life. Familiar feelings in the presence of death. I associate them with climbing in the Yukon and the Himalayas. High on a glaciated mountain, in a world of rock and snow and ice, I have seen my companions as concentrations of vitality in the vastness of the universe. Moving through the Zeisels' crowded living room, alert to the bodies around me, I tasted that bracing air. I glimpsed Patsy in conversation on the other side of the room and was pierced by her beauty. The sensation of life was immediate. I felt alive with every breath.

"I HAVE something I need to tell you," Patsy said. "It's difficult to talk about."

We were running on the lakefront at noon. It had rained earlier in the day. There were puddles on the path, and the breeze carried the smell of wet earth. The world was mud-soft and budding.

"Something very strange has been happening. When Hans died, I thought I'd feel sadness and a kind of happiness—a sense of release. I expected to feel grief. I didn't expect what I've been feeling."

When she woke up on Sunday morning, she said, she had felt disoriented. Eva had asked her to pick up some food for the occasion that afternoon. She also had to prepare a large pot of beans for an International Women's Day event that evening. As she went about these tasks, she had felt dislocated.

"Then, yesterday afternoon at the Zeisels', I couldn't connect with anyone. I looked around at the other people there. They were highlighted. They were vivid in a way that pointed up my paleness. It was as if I was disappearing as a person."

The image came into my mind of a figure fading out of a photograph.

"I couldn't talk about this with anyone but you. Who would ever understand what I was feeling? I'd be afraid they'd think I was so self-involved that I could only think about myself and not about Hans. It's humiliating. There's something degrading about it."

After leaving the Zeisels', she had gone to the International Women's Day event.

"I couldn't stay at the Women's Day dinner. I had to leave. I felt as if I had completely lost my identity, as if I had evaporated. All day long, I hadn't been able to connect with anybody. By the time I got out of the dinner, I might as well have been invisible. I had disappeared."

How could I have failed to see it? As Hans's death approached— each time we visited, she said, "he had disappeared a little more"— something had been happening inside her. Was it possible that there was no clear distinction for her between death and terror? Surrounded by love and kindness, Hans hadn't felt he was dying alone. He had remained connected, to the very end, to that which gave his life meaning. It was Patsy, living in the gravitational field of his death, who had suffered a loosening of her ties to the world and now, unmoored, was drifting toward the annihilating darkness where the tortured are disappeared by a force so strong it imprisons all light.

"I DON'T think I'm going to make it. The attack was shattering. I'm like a broken vase. I've put the pieces back together with glue—that's progress—but the glue is still curing and the pieces don't fit together quite right. I'm still so fragile. Under pressure, I'll just come apart. I can feel myself crumbling."

We were sitting together on the sofa, after the children had gone to bed. I put my arms around her. She released a sob.

"Shattering" is a word she has used before to describe the impact of the assault. It evokes not only the pain of her condition but also the *effort* required to reconstitute herself.

Victims of torture and rape often use this word. The image is not obvious or inevitable. What shatters? Our bodies are soft and supple, able to absorb blows and possessed of great recuperative powers. It's our identities that are fragile and difficult to repair. They don't simply break; they shatter.

The word is used so often it could be a cliché. Not having experienced "shattering" violence, I don't have a sense of my self as prone to shattering, but I've come to recognize, by way of the testimony of others, that this word names something real. Far from being a cliché empty of meaning, it's an instance of the power of words to illuminate. The last outpost of language at the edge of darkness.

I recall Barbara, minutes after being raped, throwing the dishes made by her potter roommate to the floor in an effort, as she understands it now, to convey to her friends what had been done to her. What makes the gesture so expressive is not simply that the plates were breakable but that they were the products of human effort and care. They had been designed and crafted; they were human artifacts. What shatters under assault is not simply something breakable. It is something made.

BETSY WANTED to roller-skate around the block. Patsy said she was too busy preparing dinner to take her.

"Why can't I go alone?" she asked.

"You're not old enough."

"When will I be old enough?"

"We started letting Josh go around the block by himself when he was nine."

"You're such a scaredy-cat," Betsy said. "You can't go from the car to the house without calling Daddy on the telephone and having him come get you."

PATSY DREAMT that she and Betsy were taken in a strange vehicle, a sort of hovercraft, to an arctic environment. It was an exciting, anxiety-provoking expedition. They were given a limited amount of food—Patsy was concerned there might not be enough for Betsy to eat—and left there. There was a hut for them to stay in; it was made of glass. Looking past the structure, she realized that they were not alone. On the other side of a barricade, there was a city. It was full of black people milling around. She awoke feeling exposed and vulnerable.

That evening, at dinner, Josh described a dream he'd had the night before. He and Betsy were competing in a road race. It was a race to the top of a mountain. Running together, they won. When they reached the finish line, they couldn't find us. Then they heard someone talking about "Ramachandra Ramanujan," and they saw Raman at the center of a large group of people. He brought them home, and Suzan Pinsof made hot chocolate for them.

Patsy said she used to have a recurring dream in which she was running in a race. The racecourse went through a big house. She had to make her way around and over furniture, to run through rooms full of people.

"When I was five or six," Josh said, "I used to have the same dream again and again. I'd be in a dark alley. It was a dead end. This guy was coming after me. Then I'd wake up."

"In *my* dream," said Betsy, "the guy has a gun."

THERE HAS been another rape of a U of C student. Walking on Ellis Avenue at night, she was grabbed by a man who forced her to the loading dock of the Court Theatre, where he assaulted her. This occurred a block and a half from our apartment and half a block from the headquarters of the campus police.

WE MADE love at dawn. Afterward I brought my face close to Patsy's and felt the cool wetness of her tears.

FROM THE start, we recognized the *force* of the process unfolding in Patsy's life. We knew she would necessarily be changed by that process. We recognized, too, the danger that I might remain unchanged, might learn nothing. In a sense, the decision to write this book was an act of companionship—a way of joining her on the journey. She had no choice but to subject herself to the process a cruel man set in motion in her life; the denial of choice was essential to the cruelty. I freely chose to undertake the book. Yet now, having adopted a form for telling this story and having worked within it every day for two years, I sometimes feel as if the literary process, too, has taken on the force of necessity.

As I understand my craft, the effort to illuminate with words is not a matter of large, blinding insights but of patiently gathering small particles of perception. Collecting fireflies and massing their glow. As particles join to form larger perspectives and fragments find their proper arrangement, some light may, with luck and grace, be cast.

The intensity of this process is cumulative. I am carried forward by a gathering momentum of inquiry. The essence of good reporting is subjecting oneself to one's subject, discerning the requirements of the story, following the inquiry where it leads. Practicing my craft at the emotional center of my life, I find myself writing about things that I have never discussed with my closest friends—the intimate marrow of our lives. I recoil from the television talk show phenomenon, from the spectacle of people turning their injuries and griefs into marketable commodities. I tell myself that I am engaged in something different. I am a journalist reporting on the world by way of our experience, a writer bringing to bear the mediating disciplines of art on difficult common experience.

Reflecting on the avalanche of bad poetry he saw as poetry editor of *The Nation*, Randall Jarrell once wrote that "it is as if the writers had sent you their ripped-out arms and legs, with 'This is a poem' scrawled on them in lipstick." Such poets "have never *made* anything," he wrote. "They have suffered their poetry as helplessly as they have anything else." What is missing from such works is the distance and technique required to awaken perception and render experience for others. Yet as I practice my vocation in the innermost circle of my life, it is precisely the distance and technique demanded by craft that sometimes unnerve me. As his wife or child cries out to him in distress, what kind of man reserves some part of himself to observe and shape and begin to *make* a representation of the moment?

I try to take my bearings from Patsy. The book is, as a friend once put it, my thinking illuminated by her imagination and experience. From the start of our relationship, I have been drawn to (and frustrated by) her singular pitch—the note given off by the tension between her reticence and her truth-telling. After the assault, this note grew stronger and more resonant. As if she knew beyond any doubt what her psychic survival demanded, she insisted on sharing her unfolding story. As in Raman's Indian folktales in which resolution of a woman's ordeal turns on her telling her story and being heard, the largest contribution of this book to Patsy's healing may prove to be the deep listening it has required of me.

And yet. Do I perhaps have more in common than I care to acknowledge with those who strip-mine their lives on the tabloid talk shows? As I write, I frequently come up against inhibitions of privacy and propriety. It's hard to know how to think about this. Are these barriers to be broken down in order to bring to light that which has been pushed into invisibility? Or are they to be honored and reinforced as protectors of that which is precious and fragile? My deep intuition is that in telling our story, we are restoring rather than invading our privacy.

But I could be wrong.

THE YOUNG woman in the flowering tree story, reduced by violence to a mutilated half-human thing without hands or feet, is also voiceless. Only when she recovers her voice and tells her story to her husband, who has been deepened by grief and so is capable of hearing her, is she restored.

Again and again, Patsy has spoken of the dark, inward, enveloping character of the assault as if it were a purely interior event. Something that happened in her soul. "A nightmare in a bubble." The terrible knowledge that one can be reduced, in Améry's words, to "flesh and death" shadows her life. It contends with, and in bad moments swallows, her identity.

The violent one rips the victim out of the world. He forces her deep inside to the loneliest possible place—the place where self and world disappear and "there is only death." He transforms her from the author of her own narrative, free to plot her life, into the object of his will, a prop in his grim story. A thing that suffers. And he leaves her sealed in silence.

Recovery from torture (to the extent that anyone can be said to recover) is thus, among other things, a *narrative* process. The victim must somehow place the dark, enveloping, annihilating interior events within her soul *in the world*. She must fashion a story that converts the nightmare in the bubble into an event in the world. It's not her essence. It's something that happened to her.

AT BARBARA Brodley's suggestion, Patsy tried a new therapeutic technique for treating post-traumatic stress called "eye movement desensitization." When I picked her up after her first session, she looked spent. Something had clearly happened.

As we drove home, she described the session. The basic technique is this: the subject holds in mind a distressing image associated with the trauma, while the therapist moves her hand rapidly back and forth in front of the subject's eyes.

The therapist had asked Patsy to think about something that had distressed her in recent weeks. She focused on the image of Hans lying in bed, at the edge of the black hole, like an animal waiting to die. At first, the hand moving in front of her face was distracting, difficult to follow. As the session progressed, she noticed it less and less. Soon she found herself weeping.

Unlike her therapy sessions with Barbara Brodley, which have moments of great intensity but move at their own pace, this form of therapy was unrelenting in its intensity.

"It's exhausting. We were face-to-face the whole time. I could see tears come into her eyes."

The therapist asked Patsy to try to visualize the attack.

"I was flooded by feelings of helplessness. I can function in the world now. I'm not disabled in the way I was right after the attack. But just below the surface I have this sense of helplessness and vulnerability. The eye exercises immersed me in those feelings."

The therapist stressed Patsy's resourcefulness in getting away. She observed that the fact that she was able to get free, when circumstances presented an opening, is perhaps related to her being a runner: someone conditioned to reach deep inside, even when spent, to make an effort. Patsy seemed to find this notion interesting, but she continued to resist the idea that she had escaped through her own efforts.

I admired the strength she displayed in insisting on her helplessness. It would be comforting to adopt a story that turned on her effectiveness in contending with difficult circumstances. But she seems determined not to let anything obscure her knowledge of the speed and absoluteness with which a violent man rendered her powerless.

"I felt that all was lost. I was a dead person. The fact that I got away was just a lucky break."

Trying to visualize the attack, she found she could see the scene *before* (she is running; there is a man beside the path) and *after* (she is running toward the woman cyclist), but she couldn't visualize the assault itself. She couldn't see it as something that happened to her in the world.

"I never saw him. After he hit me in the eyes, I was in darkness. It could have been a purely psychological event. I could have been persuaded I had dreamt it. It all happened in the dark. I couldn't see out. Even though I run by the spot every day, it could have been a nightmare."

When she realized he was going to rape her, she recalled thinking, "This is a good thing. By the time he got me on the ground, I think I had given up. But when he said he was going to rape me, he gave me a new sense of time. I came to life again. When I saw the woman on the bike path, I thought, Oh God, I'm not dead yet. The world is still out there."

She tried to describe for the therapist what it was like to escape from the darkness of the assault into the shining world. As she ran toward her, the young woman cyclist was bathed in light. She compared the moment, as she often has, to the experience of giving birth.

"Perhaps," the therapist suggested, "it wasn't you giving birth to a child. Perhaps it was your own birth. Your *rebirth*."

SEVERAL NIGHTS later, unable to sleep, I got up in the middle of the night and read for a while. The next day Patsy reported that she had been disoriented and alarmed by my absence.

"I wasn't sure whether or not you'd left the apartment. If you were gone, if you were dead, what would I do? You're the life. I'm connected to you. I'm like one of the children. I felt utterly vulnerable. If you were gone, I wouldn't be able to live here, I wouldn't be able to support the family, I wouldn't be able to take care of the children. If *I* died, nothing would change. You would go on living in the same place, doing the same work, living the same life. But if you died, everything would change."

A chilling equation: she simply subtracts herself from the world.

ON THE day Patsy had her second session of eye desensitization therapy, we went out to dinner at Café du Midi. Among our favorite restaurants, it is a French café in what was once a corner Laundromat.

Patsy was luminous with perception. She reported that she had begun the therapy session by focusing on the image of herself alone in bed after I had gotten up in the night several days ago. Swept by feelings of vulnerability and homelessness, she had had a hard time holding the image in her mind.

She found herself talking with the therapist about her "feelings of loneliness and loss while making love." Another kind of homelessness. She recalled how prior to the assault—and our efforts to make sense of our sexual patterns—she used to deal with sex by vacating her body. She withheld her self from the act. Only her body was involved. She noted that rape victims often describe something similar: they leave their bodies during the rape.

She tried to describe for the therapist "the barrier" to full participation and pleasure which she experiences during sex. Over the years, we had made progress in loosening the hold of that pattern. She had developed ways of getting over or around the barrier. As we deepened our understanding and sympathies, it had become more permeable, but the assault had confirmed her worst fears and had recharged her conditioned reflexes.

"Now," she said, "the barrier is absolute. I can't see over it. It reaches to the limit in all directions."

She described "the struggle" during sex in intensely physical terms. "When the bad feelings come, it feels like my head is going to explode. I respond by asserting *control*."

Because erotic pleasure requires yielding up a measure of control, it's threatening and must be resisted. Her struggle for control displaces all else.

"The desire to hold off the bad things is so strong I can't remember anything else."

As during the first session, when she tried to visualize the assault from the outside—to see it as an event in the world—she was overcome by emotion.

"If I try to visualize the attack from the outside, I burst into tears. I can't bear to watch it. What comes up is my face afterwards. An unrecognizable face. The fact that a man turned me into a bloody mess, then wanted to have sex with me—I find it incomprehensible. It just doesn't make sense to me."

OVER DINNER with friends, Patsy observed that she would have stopped talking about the effects of the assault long ago, were I not writing this book.

"My natural impulse would have been to suffer in silence—and to suffer the consequences of suffering in silence. But the fact that he's writing the book allows me to keep talking." She smiled at me. "He *has* to listen."

Her point, as I understood it, was not that the rape would have silenced her. After all, the book was born of her telling, not the other way around; from the first moments after the assault, she had responded with fierce eloquence, seeking words and images to make sense of what had happened. The point was rather that silence would have *overtaken* her. She would have been silenced not by something unspeakable in the nature of the assault but by the unrelenting character of its effects over time. At times, she almost seems to think of herself as being in the grip of a shameful obsession. She assumes that others, however sympathetic they were at first, would now be inattentive, uncomprehending, even bored by her inability years later to find release from the fears and questions that entered her life when she was raped.

The process of writing this book creates a space, maintained by my attention, to which she can return at will to voice those fears and engage those questions. This seems necessary, essential, the least a victim of terror might ask of those who love her. Yet were I in another line of work, could I have been as available to her as I have been? Could I have summoned and sustained this quality of attention?

RUNNING ON the lakefront at twilight, we approached a young woman walking alone.

"I really feel I should warn her," Patsy said.

"Why don't you?"

We stopped.

"I don't want to alarm you," Patsy said to the girl, "but it really isn't safe to walk out here alone, especially at night. I was assaulted here in the middle of the afternoon. When it happened, I was closer to the highway than you are right now."

"Sorry to be the bearers of such grim news," I interjected.

"It's an illusion," Patsy continued, "to think the highway is any protection. You'd be better off imagining that it's not there."

The girl listened attentively and thanked Patsy graciously. It seemed quite possible that she simply didn't know where she was.

We ran on.

Patsy was clearly relieved. She had acted on the impulse she had felt many times without acting on it. Often when she had seen women alone on the lakefront, she had felt she should warn them but had been brought up short by concern about how she would be perceived. "I imagine them thinking, Who *is* this crazy woman? I worry they would dismiss me as paranoid or timid."

What made her uneasy about warning strangers, it seemed, was not a matter of finding the right words but the absence of a context that would make those words intelligible. In such an isolated encounter, how could one establish one's character and evoke one's world? There is a sense, it occurred to me, in which this book is an effort to convey a simple warning—a sense in which it has proved necessary to evoke a world in order, credibly and resonantly, to say, "Take care."

PATSY HAS received a grant to support the photo-montage project. She has a new idea for the montage: to blow up the police photograph of her battered face, cut it into pieces, then place various images—the place, Betsy as a baby, etc.—on a background formed by fragments of her face.

She called her parents to tell them about the grant. They asked her what the montage would be like, and she tried to describe it. The next morning her mother called.

"I woke up this morning with a broken heart," she said, "thinking about you cutting up your face."

As the fourth anniversary of the assault approached, Patsy seemed bent under the weight of the years. Each autumn after we return from Vermont, she observed, the approaching anniversary contributes to her difficulty making the transition back to Chicago.

"I feel that I can't really resume my life here, can't get back to work, until it's over."

After the anniversary passed, she began to work with renewed energy on the montage. On a bright September afternoon, we went to the attack site so she could take some photos. She wanted to try to capture what the light was like on the day she was raped.

"One thing it's important for this piece to convey," she said, "is that the most terrifying place on earth can be a green field with the sun shining."

It was a beautiful day. The world shimmered with color. Green grass. Blue water. Red berries on the hawthorn trees at the spot where she had been brought down. Monarch butterflies en route to Mexico. Raucous gulls at play on the wind.

Again, I was struck by how much of the city one can see from the perspective of this ribbon of green between Lake Shore Drive and Lake Michigan. A few steps beyond the spot where Patsy was assaulted, you can see the entire downtown skyline.

Cars flowed by on Lake Shore Drive. "You'd be better off imagining that it's not there," Patsy had said to the girl she had warned against walking alone on the lakefront. Most of the cars contained a single person. Isolated bubbles, each a little domain of privacy. Turn on the radio, and it becomes a time-travel machine. A vehicle for memory, dream, reflection, but not for being present in the world one is passing through. Standing on the spot where Patsy was tortured as cars streamed past, I had a vision of nonconnection: individuals, encased in steel, divorced from their surroundings by speed, aware of each other's reality only when they collide.

While Patsy took pictures, I walked over to the rocky confusion of the lake shore. Several days after she was attacked, she had received a note from a writer friend. "There are people who essentially aren't people at all," the friend had written. "They are so crazy it's more like they are a part of nature, like lightning or a tidal wave." I had resisted this formulation; it seemed essential to reject the view that the violence human beings do is a natural phenomenon, like a tidal wave. Yet the image had stayed with me. Standing by the water's edge, I wondered what it would have been like if Patsy had drowned. How would that have been different from the death she had barely escaped?

I recalled a conversation I had recently had with Mary Hynes-Berry. Some years ago one of Mary's brothers drowned; more recently, her son Geb had been seriously wounded in a stabbing in Venezuela. Had Geb died, she said, it would have been an event absolutely different in character from the death of her brother. The drowning of a youth in an indifferent body of water is tragic and heartbreaking, but life is like that. Gratuitous human violence, by contrast, doesn't belong to the underlying nature of things. The random street killing nullifies all meaning.

"If Geb had died," Mary had said, "I wouldn't have been able to bear the *meaninglessness* of it."

Patsy was finished. We began to walk back to the car. I carried her tripod.

She spoke again of her plan to blow up the police photograph of her battered face, cut it into pieces, then place various images on a background formed by the fragments of her face.

"The first thing he did was make me faceless. That made him faceless too. I couldn't see him."

Somehow the blows to her face were as essential to the character of the assault as the sexual intrusion.

"I think that's what rape does. It turns you into Woman. Any woman."

That night, in bed, holding her in my arms, I suggested we make love. She immediately became upset.

"I have no erotic desires," she said. "None."

She got out of bed. When she didn't return after a few minutes, I went to look for her. I found her in the living room, sitting on the window seat, in the dark, looking out at the garden. She was sobbing. I stroked her hair.

"The thing is," she said, "you're writing a book, and what I feel can't be described in words."

PART

—

VI

1993

THIRTY-FIVE

LITERATURE DEALS uncertainly with endurance. Matters of sustained effort, of staying put and standing fast. Daily efforts that build into weeks, months, years, lifetimes. The conventions by which we recognize and understand stories—dramatic conflicts and defining moments, reversals of expectation and denouements—are poorly adapted to the task of rendering that which is strenuously ongoing.

Yet nothing moves me more than dramas of endurance. A long-distance race may touch me at the same depth as Shakespeare; and this is as likely at a high school track meet as at the Olympics. What stirs me about mountaineering is not just the moment-brought-to-a-point-by-danger but the one-foot-after-the-other-trudge up the mountain. During the years of work on my father's book, I could never convey to others, looking on and imagining how tedious my task was, the sheer day-to-day excitement of that decade-long effort.

The point is not that literature is without strategies in this respect; some have been inspired. Think of Faulkner's "They endured." Or Beckett's "I can't go on. I will go on." Perhaps I'm misreading as limitations of narrative what are in truth limitations of this narrator. Yet there is, I think, more to it than that. As I try to make my way truthfully from sentence to sentence, I'm aware of a tension between fidelity to our experience and the temptations of plot, aware of a danger that I will falsify our experience by overplotting it. The big scene—the violent confrontation, the devastating exchange of words—is tempting in part because it can be rendered in real time. The years of a life cannot be. These limitations, in turn, form our sensibilities; they shape how we take the world in through stories. Thus we are disposed to find anger more interesting than patience, betrayal more interesting than loyalty, a promise broken more interesting than a promise kept. And a violent act fascinates us in a way that the lifetime of grieving and healing (or failing to heal) it sets in motion does not.

I have been speaking of sensibilities formed by literature, but what of those whose imaginations have been baptized in other narrative streams? Watching Josh and Betsy stare into the sickly light emanating from the television screen, I worry less about the substance of the programs they watch than about the habits of perception—the rhythms of distraction—they may be developing. Television invites us to inhabit a world of isolated moments: this moment is not connected to the moment before it or the moment after it. Certain stories simply cannot be told in this mode. For suffering has everything to do with time.

When Patsy speaks of being "humiliated," she refers not to the particulars of the assault but to the persistence of the injury over time. She has kept the process open and unresolved. She has refused easy answers. She hasn't gotten a divorce. She hasn't bought a gun. She hasn't been born again. Her inability to falsify allows her no escape. True to her grief, she can't forget what she has come to know. And so she must suffer through what she must suffer through. She describes herself as weak and fearful, yet displays courage and strength. Her refusal to shut the process down, even as she wearies of it and despairs of finding rest, is a gift to others. It has created, among other things, the space in which I am writing this book.

Yet can I do justice to this aspect of our experience? How can I describe effortful things without imposing undue effort on the reader, describe repetitive things without being repetitive, describe tedious things without making weary those who reside (as it feels to the writer) on the other side of the page?

Imagine Patsy waking each morning, day after day, month after month, to the same sensations and fears, to the same gray light. So many indistinguishable days. So much effort, working against an undertow of panic, to get through the day. The fear that life will always be like this. *"I need for it to be over."* How many times has she said this or something similar? Day after day, week after week, month after month, year after year, what can it have been like for her? I must strain to imagine it, to glimpse the sweep of it, and I have been here beside her every day.

ARCTIC CONDITIONS. We were running, in early-evening light, on the lakefront. Suddenly a large white bird appeared beside us, gliding close to the ground on silent wings. A snowy owl, a naturalist friend later told us; he had heard that it had adopted our stretch of lakefront as its hunting ground. What was astonishing—apart from the owl's wingspan, which was easily more than a yard—was its silence. No whoosh of wings. All at once it was beside us. Pity the dark little rabbits we often see scurrying across the snow-covered ground.

REPORTS OF mass rape are emerging from the war in Bosnia. According to journalists and human rights groups, the Serbs are systematically using rape as a weapon in their campaign to drive Muslims and Croats from Bosnia. Estimates of the number of victims, as of the first of the year, range from twenty thousand to fifty thousand. Many women and children are thought to have died during or after rape.

This is not rape as a crime of opportunity in the midst of the chaos of war. It's a strategy as deliberate as the dropping of bombs. Rape is being used to drive people from their homes, to drive a people from their homeland. It's being used to annihilate, by way of the cruelties inflicted on women's bodies, the very idea of *home*. A society could sooner rebuild its cities after saturation bombing than rebuild the lives and sense of security of the masses of women and children who have been raped.

Among the horrifying refinements in the Serbian use of rape as a weapon of war are forced pregnancies. There are reports of concentration camps where women are raped again and again until they become pregnant. This seems intended as the ultimate subjugation: occupation of the womb. A wedge driven into the soul. Reporters quote Muslim women impregnated by their Serbian captors as saying that they will have nothing to do with the babies born of the violence done to them. They say they will kill or abandon these enemies within.

BARBARA ENGEL dropped by on her way to pick up her children at school. We chatted over tea for half an hour. She could talk about nothing else but Bosnia. She had spent the day working the phone, talking with other antirape activists around the country and with the United Nations High Commission for Refugees, searching out avenues to get training materials translated and into the hands of rape counselors in Bosnia. But now, sitting in the darkening light of a wintry afternoon, she seemed uncertain how to proceed. She confided to me that for several weeks she had been carrying around a *Newsweek* cover story on the Bosnia rapes, unable to read beyond the first paragraph for fear that if she fully opened herself to what was happening in Bosnia, she would "implode."

As we talked, it became apparent that what makes the reports from Bosnia so hard for her to take in is not only the scale of the suffering but also the questions that mass rape as an instrument of genocide poses about men.

"If this is a military strategy, then men really *know* this about rape. What's so horrifying to me is the idea that some men can order that this be done and other men will carry it out. It's so clearly about destroying a culture. The anger and hate are so obvious. Still, somehow, on a personal level, it can be eroticized—men's penises will get hard and they will do this to nine-year-old girls. What complex connection is there between hatred and destruction and entering a woman's body? This is not just a few aberrant individuals. When there are twenty thousand or thirty thousand or forty thousand women being raped, think of the number of men who must be raping. How can that be possible? What do they think about women, when you scratch the surface, to be capable of this? It scares me to the marrow."

I WAS working at my desk. At about 11:00 P.M., Betsy appeared at my elbow.

"I had a bad dream."

She climbed into my lap. She didn't tell me the substance of the dream.

"I don't want to grow up," she said. "I want to stay eight years old. I don't want to be a big kid. I don't want to be thirteen."

AMONG ALL the reports of atrocities in Bosnia, one story has taken possession of me. I came upon it in a *New York Times* article by the Croatian journalist Slavenka Drakulic:

Once a young woman with a baby was taken in the middle of the hall. . . . They ordered her to take off her clothes. She put the baby on the floor next to her. Four Chetniks raped her; she was silent, looking at her crying child.

When she was left alone she asked if she could breast-feed the baby. Then a Chetnik cut the child's head off with a knife. He gave the bloody head to the mother. The poor woman screamed. They took her outside and she never came back.

Can we bear to look at what is being revealed about rape in Bosnia? "You can't kill me. I have a baby at home," Patsy pleaded as she fought for her life. How unbearable those words now seem. They speak to the hope of some human measure in the rapist. He answers with annihilating fury. An assault on life itself.

THIRTY-SIX

<hr>

D ADDY, WHAT should I dream about?" has evolved into what Betsy calls our "chapter dream." When she can't sleep, she comes to me. I tuck her in and, sitting on her bed, tell her an installment of an ongoing story that I make up on the spot.

The story begins with the family boarding a plane for Paris. With great relish, Betsy contributes details—what we were wearing, the meal the airline served, the movie they showed. We arrive in Paris late at night and go to our hotel. When we awake in the morning, we are delighted to discover how beautiful the city is. After a breakfast at a sidewalk café of orange juice, coffee, and croissants—a chocolate crois- sant for her—we set out to climb the Eiffel Tower.

"It's like climbing Mount Mansfield," I say. That reminds her of something.

"Dad, do you remember the time you carried me down the moun- tain in the storm and then you ran down the rest of the way to get the truck?"

"Yes, I remember."

"You really *like* hard things, don't you?"

I laugh and resume the story. By the time we descend the Eiffel Tower, we're tired and hungry. Just then we hear music headed our way. It turns out to be a circus parade. We decide to follow it for a while as it proceeds through narrow, winding streets. A mime who is part of the parade takes an interest in us. He is charming. ("Not scary," I reassure Betsy.) At a fork in the road, the parade goes one way and the mime goes the other. He beckons to us to follow him. We exchange looks and decide, Why not? He leads us to the Seine and ushers us on to an elegant houseboat, then disappears. On the mantelpiece, resting against the mirror, is a note addressed to the Kalven family. It's from the mysterious Monsieur Pierre, inviting us to dinner that night at a four-star restaurant. . . . And then . . . and then . . .

Betsy delights in this exercise. It excites her imagination. She gives herself to the process, collaborating on details and suggesting plot turns. She is so open; her hunger for narrative is so immediate. As she helps shape the story, it is shaping her.

One night, in the midst of our story-making, she asks, "Do you *like* this as much as I do?"

She is mindful of certain dangers. We sometimes negotiate chapter endings. Before I kiss her good night, she wants me to leave things at a point that is suspenseful but not ominous.

And so it is that late at night when the rest of the household is asleep, I come into my daughter's bedroom, dressed in my bathrobe or with a towel wrapped around my waist, sit on her bed, and enter her imagination.

LAST FALL the Hyde Park Bank sponsored a contest titled "My Neighborhood." Students between the ages of five and fourteen at South Side elementary schools were invited to submit entries in which they described their neighborhoods in words or pictures. Cash prizes were offered for the best submissions. The bank hoped to get some appealing material it could use in a promotional brochure on its "community reinvestment" program; in the words of the bank president, "brightly colored, childish drawings of trees and houses, and funny little stories about the postman and the people on the block." Under federal law, banks are required to make loans within a particular geographic area. In the case of the Hyde Park Bank, its "community reinvestment area" takes in the much of the inner city, including the massive concentration of public housing on South State Street—the Robert Taylor Homes and Stateway Gardens. For the purposes of the contest, the bank defined as "our neighborhood" an area of the city that is so divided against itself that it can plausibly be described as a form of apartheid. Most of the submissions to the contest came from children living in places that the vast majority of Hyde Parkers fear and have never visited. Bank officials were genuinely stunned by what the children said about *their* neighborhoods:

> I don't like my neighborhood, because they shoot too much. They might shoot me. So, I stay in the house. I think it's safe there. One time, some bullets hit our window. I was afraid. My house doesn't seem safe anymore. Maybe, I should hide under my bed. Then I won't get shot. [Sean Williams, six years old]

> Leaving for school is scary. You never know when you might get shot. You never know when someone might shoot at you out of a window. [Demetrius Jones, thirteen years old]

> We are not bad people, we are good people, so why do we have to live like this. [Lazinnia Wright, nine years old]

The contest proved a publicity coup for the bank—a way for it to be seen as concerned about the welfare of children in neighborhoods beyond Hyde Park not by making loans to the children's parents but by publishing their words and pictures. Yet however sentimental and self-serving, the bankers' response conveyed genuine surprise at the children's reports of how violence and fear of violence color their worlds.

The Joyce Foundation, having recently launched a funding initiative directed at gun violence, decided to use the children's words and drawings as a motif running through their annual report. They hired Patsy to photograph the child artists and to do a photo essay on children of the inner city—particularly children living in public housing.

She responded to this assignment with a combination of excitement and anxiety. Not the least of the challenges was logistical. In order to photograph in various public housing developments, she needed to make arrangements for someone to meet and accompany her. Sometimes her contact would be a member of a community organization; sometimes the police.

She put great energy into making arrangements. She worked the phone. She mined the contacts of friends. Each day she set out for one or another of the housing developments that for Chicagoans represent the innermost inner city—the Robert Taylor Homes, Henry Horner, Cabrini-Green, etc.

"It's another world," she said after returning from the Robert Taylor Homes. "A dirty, ugly world. There's nothing for the eye or soul to feed on. Yet it's so compelling."

She would return home like a traveler, awash in fresh perceptions, and would report to me on what she had seen. I was stirred to see her so intensely engaged, so interested, so alive to the world. Her energy, her resourcefulness, her hunger to *see* recalled the period in our lives when we had traveled together in South Asia and elsewhere.

"Some of the little kids are so raggedy and dirty. At the same time, there are so many nice-looking kids—the teenage gang members too. I haven't seen anything like it since India. The squalor and the beauty in the same place."

She was surprised by the degree to which public housing proved to be a world of women and children.

"It's so poignant. I keep wondering, Where are the men?"

The most visible males were the members of the street gangs who conduct their drug business on the development grounds, in the lobbies of the high-rises, on nearby street corners. What struck her was less the phenomenon of the drug trade or the fratricidal violence of the gangs than the family drama—the way males at a certain point in adolescence seemed to segregate themselves. She spoke again and again of the fearful world the adolescent boys enter when they reach the age of gang membership.

"The little children play freely. The adolescents move through a dark world. The difference between being eleven and fourteen is the difference between being on earth and on Mars."

PATSY NOW moves more widely through the city than she did prior to the assault. She has gradually expanded the boundaries of her world rather than drawn them in around her. This process has been protracted and hard-won. It has also been extraordinary. The idiom of *healing*—the image of a wound that closes and scars over—is not adequate to describe her struggle to reconstitute the world after violence. I think rather of her efforts as a photographer to draw light out of darkness in order to see the world as it is. Working with available light, she is recovering the world image by image.

"Natural light is what enables you to see things as they are, to see the texture of the world," she once said to me of her craft. "It's like making a sculpture out of the dark."

THE MORE I write the closer I come to locating the themes and impulses that moved me to become a writer in the first place. A mysterious process. It's as if one's purposes can be disclosed only through the unfolding of one's passion. Marriage, too, has been like that for me. My love for this woman, whom I have found so attractive, so frustrating, so compelling for so many years is like a vessel carrying me (forever en route, never arriving) toward the center of my life. Even as I long for erotic surrender and a melding of identities, I rediscover again and again, with deepening clarity, that what moves me about her— what moved me when we first met years ago in the Rockies, what moved me a moment ago when she walked through the room—is her fierce autonomy, her insistence on being *someone else*. I love her separateness, her not-me-ness, her refusal to yield.

A BRIGHT afternoon. I was at my desk. Patsy came in from outside.

"Want to see something amazing?"

I followed her outside.

"Do you hear that?"

There was much cawing. A commotion of crows. We followed the noise to a tree on Fifty-seventh Street between Woodlawn and Kimbark. Dozens of crows were trying to drive off an owl that had alighted high in the tree.

The owl was well camouflaged—it took me a while to locate it— but to no avail. Crows swirled around the tree. They landed on branches near the owl and shrieked at it. The owl seemed impassive and oddly catlike. I recalled the regal owl we had seen last winter on the lakefront. Could it be? No, this one was smaller and darker. Apart from an occasional swiveling of its head, it was motionless. It seemed imperturbable. Or was it helpless due to its relative blindness in daylight?

Raucous and excited, the crows swooped close to the owl, then veered away. There was a jeering and taunting quality to their display. Roles had been reversed. Prey had become predator. Owls do to crows what crows do to other species: raid their nests. Having caught a glimpse on the lakefront of the silent efficiency of owls as predators, I could see that it made sense for crows to take advantage of the owl's daytime blindness to drive it away. Yet the spectacle left an impression of an enmity that went beyond adaptive strategies for survival. It looked like an outpouring of hatred. The phenomenon, I learned later, is called "mobbing."

THE SIEGE of ghosts has relented. Patsy reports occasional dreams, but the nightly immersion in stories and images of violence has eased. When we lie together now in the morning before rising, it's no longer as if she has returned to my arms from a perilous journey. She has been there beside me all night.

AFTER PHOTOGRAPHING a family in Cabrini-Green, a North Side public housing development, Patsy stopped on the way home at a trendy bakery to pick up some bread for dinner. She put her camera bag on the counter while she surveyed the contents of the glass display case. When she looked up, she saw several cockroaches scuttling across the counter.

"I was mortified. They must have crawled into my bag at Cabrini. I knocked them on the floor and removed my bag, hoping no one had seen. I felt so strange. Implicated. Almost ashamed."

"IT'S LIKE a war zone," Patsy said. "You see all the clichéd pictures. The challenge is to see with your own eyes."

She was showing me some of the work prints she had generated for the Joyce Foundation project. The photographs included some of the best work she had done in years, the best work she had done since the assault. It was remarkable, given the subject matter and context, how she avoided any sentimentality in her representation of the children. She allows them their autonomy, their full dignity. She doesn't present them as victims or as objects for our pity. Especially in her pictures of groups of boys, there is an ardor of inquiry. She is looking very hard.

MY ATTENTION is arrested by a beautiful woman. How lovely, I think to myself. Then I realize I'm married to her. Amid the dailiness and narrowing preoccupations of marriage, there are moments when I am struck, as if for the first time, by Patsy's beauty and am amazed by her presence in my life. It's like emerging from a tunnel into the light.

The years have burnished her beauty. Or perhaps, finally shedding the self-consciousness that lends a comic awkwardness to almost every photo ever taken of her, she is coming to fully inhabit that beauty. Her face has become more delicate and her body more graceful, as if aging were a process of refinement rather than loss.

The wonder is how passion has stayed alive between us during our long spell of endurance. This need for touch, for connection, that every few days brings us into each other's arms, despite the chance of pain and unmastered fear, has been our lifeline. Our lovemaking remains restricted and careful. Yet there is a quickening of feeling between us. An easing.

I SOMETIMES wonder if we aren't in danger of becoming so habituated to the effort of endurance that we will lose ourselves inside that effort and fail to recognize change when it comes. Recently over dinner with the Pinsofs, Bill asked Patsy what the effects of the assault are now more than four years later. She spoke of the assault as "the moment when everything changed" and said she can't really remember "what it was like before." For a long time, she observed, she had struggled with the presence of fear in her life. Now the struggle is less unrelenting, less moment-to-moment. She is able to function better.

"What I experience now is a dark sort of undertow," she said. "I don't expect things to ever get much better than this."

I responded to her words with a mix of alarm and relief. I don't feel any sense of resolution or completion or closure. Nor do I feel that we have recovered our lives-before-the-assault. Patsy remains intermittently depressed and anxious. Yet it's been a while since she last had a nightmare or was overcome by panic during sex. Is it possible that the siege is finally lifting? If so, where will we find ourselves?

IF VIOLENCE is blind—the eye disengaged from the hand—then perhaps the opposite of violence is attention and care. Does it follow that countless small acts of inattention and disregard might over time do large violence?

I'm brooding about a conversation I recently had with Patsy. I asked her whether she now thinks, in light of all she has felt and learned and articulated since the assault, that she was sexually violated as a child. For years, we have entertained the possibility that an early trauma might explain the sexual fears that shadowed her life prior to the assault. Now I'm not so sure. Having witnessed her honesty and creative energy in response to the rape, I find it hard to believe she could have kept hidden from herself a large injury to the core of her being.

Yet when I think of her struggle to escape from the dark "bubble" into which the rapist forced her, I can see that for many victims, especially children, essential parts of themselves may remain forever sealed inside that bubble, never to be recovered. Then again, perhaps Patsy's particular strengths of character formed *around* the injury. That may be the basis of her resistance and her lucidity, the spring from which these qualities issue. What a strange thought. Could her capacity to see deeply into the world have its roots in an experience that she can't remember, that she can't bring herself to look at? Could vision arise from blindness?

"I still think it's likely something happened to me when I was a child that frightened me—something I associated with sex," Patsy observed. "But it may not have been a big deal in itself. The injury may have had less to do with any single terrible incident than with the lack of resources around me to make sense of what happened and the way all sorts of other experiences reinforced the message. All I know is that by the time I started dating in high school, as attracted as I was to boys, I had a strong animal sense that this was something dangerous. Part of it was fear of pregnancy in those days, but there was something beyond that, and I don't know where it came from."

As we talked, it became apparent that the question mattered less than it used to. Or that it mattered in a different way. If we are in truth members one of another, then the injury to one pulses through the web of attachments to others, and the effects of violence, multiplied ad infinitum, are woven into the weave of the world. To grow up in such a world, especially to grow up female in such a world, is to be exposed to the possibility that a large injury might be inflicted by many small acts of inattention and disregard over time. Surely if one were lucid about the extent of sexual violence and attendant falsehood in the world, one would have reason to be wary and afraid.

We are shaped by mysterious forces. The notion that deep injuries can result from many small acts of carelessness and inattention is a difficult story to tell; it requires evoking a world into which the effects of violence and fear are tightly woven. By contrast, the traumatic event from which all else follows satisfies our hunger for a story with explanatory power; and some are prepared to indulge that hunger in the absence of evidence. A great deal turns on the quality of the stories we make. Perhaps, in the end, the stories we choose *not* to tell are as important as those we do.

AFTER MUCH discussion and negotiation, we agreed this spring to let Josh walk home from school. So I now pick up Betsy alone. I enjoy this. It's a break in my day, and I sometimes get to share a quiet, reflective moment in her day.

For example, one day she broke an extended silence.

"Dad," she asked, "is life hard?"

And on another occasion: "You know, Dad, this morning? When I woke up, it was just getting light. My door was open a crack. I lay in bed, listening to the birds singing and the police sirens and the sound of you in the kitchen making coffee, and I felt so happy."

RUNNING AFTER dark, I came up behind a woman walking alone. I stepped out into the street to avoid startling her.

A DREAM. I step out the back door into the garden. To my surprise, I encounter Alan Shapiro. One of his arms is a stump; he has lost his hand and forearm.

"Alan," I ask, "what happened?"

"I was raped," he sobs.

Weeping, we embrace.

PATSY SPENT the afternoon at the Ida B. Wells housing development. She returned flushed with perception.

Wells was one of the first public housing developments constructed in Chicago. Built in the late 1930s, the brick row houses that predominate at Wells more resemble the company towns of an earlier era than they do high-rise ghettos like the Robert Taylor Homes or Stateway Gardens. Wells is older, sturdier, dilapidated in more recognizable ways; it has the feel of a "traditional" slum.

Expansion of Wells in the 1960s followed the high-rise model. So there are a few high-rises in what is called the Wells Extension. It was to one of these fourteen-story buildings that Patsy was led by the policeman who was her guide. Black and beefy, he was made yet bulkier by the bulletproof vest that he was wearing.

She was to photograph a child who had participated in the bank contest. The family lived on the thirteenth floor. Although it was midafternoon, the apartment was dark. The blinds were drawn. There was not enough light to photograph. This is a problem she often encountered in public housing. In virtually every apartment she went into, the blinds were drawn. At first, she had thought that perhaps people were concerned about snipers and crossfire. Then it occurred to her that in every apartment no matter how bare, there was a television, and that television was on. The blinds were closed against the light in order to keep reflections from bleaching out the television picture. When she realized this, she asked that the blinds be opened to let in natural light.

While she focused her attention on the child and set up the shot, the policeman observed, loitered, looked out the windows. When she was finished, he called her over to the window.

"Come take a look at this."

He wanted her to see the view from the thirteenth floor. She looked out, over the desolation of blocks laid waste by abandonment and demolition, to the green and blue of the lakefront. In the distance, sailboats sliced through the water.

"It looked so beautiful, so inviting. I had a sense of what it must mean for people who live in places like Wells to go to the lakefront. Just to have some grass to lie on."

To the north, she could see the downtown skyline. To the south, the green of tree-lined Hyde Park–Kenwood. And directly below her: the lakefront running path where she was assaulted.

"I was stunned. I almost told the policeman what I saw, then caught myself. Looking down at the running path on the other side of the Drive, I kept thinking, We live in the same place. It's one place."

AT THE dinner table we talked about smells we like. Betsy reported that, among other things, she loved the smell of gasoline. Then, recalling the smell of the basement in her grandparents' house in Vermont, she said, "And I love the smell of . . ."

She paused, searching unsuccessfully for the word "mothballs."

". . . And I love the smell of *butterfly thighs* in Grammy Dot's basement."

"HEY, DAD, look!"

As we entered the yard, Josh and Betsy pointed to a second-floor window of the fraternity. It took me a moment to see what they were pointing at. Silhouetted against the play of light on a wide-screen TV showing a pornographic video, four young men, beer cans in hand, were dancing to the hard rhythms of rap. They laughed and shouted and thrust their hips toward the flickering images of women's body parts on the screen.

PATSY REPORTED the following conversation with Betsy:

Betsy told her that it was crucially important that she kiss her good-bye each day before she left for school.

"My kiss will keep you safe. It'll be like a wall around you. It'll give you good luck. On the day you were hurt, we had a fight and I didn't kiss you."

"How do you know?"

"I remember."

"I don't remember that."

"How could you with what happened to you that day?"

"But you were only four."

"I remember. I've always felt like it was my fault because I didn't kiss you."

A few days later, Patsy and Betsy had an argument over breakfast. I drove the children to school. Betsy was quiet in the backseat. As she got out of the car, she said, "Kiss Mommy for me."

THIRTY-SEVEN

F OR MONTHS, Raman has been suffering from mysterious pains in his right leg. He underwent test after test, but his doctors weren't able to determine the cause. Although he was stoical, it was clear that the pain disrupted his sleep, his work, his life. At times, it appeared acute; at other times, he seemed distracted less by the pain than by the uncertainty of its source. Then, finally, a test revealed a "soft tumor" on his spinal column which was putting pressure on his nerves. The doctors assured him that the surgical procedure required was routine and that the tumor was almost surely benign. They promptly scheduled surgery within a few days of the diagnosis.

Raman's reaction appeared to be a mix of relief and apprehension— relief that the source of the pain had been identified and apprehension about the surgery and what it might disclose. The day before he was to go into the hospital, I dropped off a prescription he had asked me to pick up for him. Standing at his door, we chatted for a few minutes. He was wearing white Indian pajamas. As he talked of his fear of hospitals, my cosmopolitan friend seemed for a passing moment an unworldly Indian villager.

The next day I had a lunch date with a friend at a local trattoria. When I saw Patsy at the door of the restaurant, I knew something terrible had happened. The children? One of our parents? I went over to her. We stepped outside.

"What's wrong?"

"Raman died."

The sentence was incomprehensible. I understood both words but not the statement they formed.

They never operated. When they began to administer the anesthesia, Raman's heart raced wildly. The doctors were unable to restore normal functioning. He went into cardiac arrest and died.

Patsy and I embraced on the sidewalk as if clutching at each other to keep from falling off a cliff that had opened at our feet.

She had to leave for an appointment. I cut short my lunch and spent the afternoon walking the streets. Movement was necessary. The sensation of vertigo kept returning. Raman was such a magical presence, so otherworldly; it never occurred to me he would do something so prosaic as die.

I tried to steady myself with the thought that if he were here, Raman would have a story for the occasion. He always did. The story would be wonderfully apt. It would almost surely make me laugh. And its effect would be to place the matter at hand in a different light, illuminating it not through broad generalizations but through the particulars of a narrative. The thought warmed me, then left me chilled, for I had no story that could help make sense of Raman's death.

When I returned home, I encountered Molly, Krittika, and Krishna. They were sitting in a car, so I couldn't act on my impulse to embrace them. I don't remember what words passed between us. All I remember are their stunned expressions. Their beautiful eyes looking out at me.

I sought out Dorothy, Abby, and Karuna and told each of Raman's death. Somehow it was important that they learn of it from me. Later that afternoon, I observed Dorothy, walking around the block, clutching Raman's book of Indian folktales in her hands, as if seeking solace in the embrace of his words, in the inexhaustible yet now exhausted flow of stories from his lips.

When I entered our apartment, I found an envelope Raman had pushed under the door on his way to the hospital. It contained a check to reimburse me for the medicine I had picked up for him. On the envelope he had written:

Jamie
            Thanks
                Raman

Patsy returned, and we went out for a walk together. As we wandered through the radiant remains of the day, she said, "The terrible thing is not just that we won't see Raman again. It's that he won't see the world again. Think how sad that would make him."

Our first impulse was to blame the doctors. They must have screwed up. How could they have neglected to test whether he was allergic to the anesthetic? But within a day the autopsy disclosed that he had advanced heart disease. The primary artery in his heart was 95 percent blocked. This was a small source of relief and perspective. Death can be heartbreaking and infinitely regrettable without being somebody's fault. Raman who had seemed so ageless, who seemed to be made of a substance finer than flesh, proved to have a bruised, rotten heart. He was sixty-four when he died—the same age at which his father had died of a heart attack.

KARUNA AND I sat together in the garden. Insulated by shock, it was as if we were suspended between the blow and its reverberations.

"If we felt the full force of grief all at once," she observed, "our bodies would die."

I recalled reading somewhere about Cambodian women who after witnessing atrocities committed against their families by the Khmer Rouge had gone completely blind without any physical basis for blindness. (A line from one of Raman's poems: "Sight may strike you blind.")

THE DAY after Raman's death, the flag in the main quadrangle flew at half-mast to mark his passing. As I drew close, I saw that one of his poems had been affixed to the flagpole by loving hands. His voice spoke:

A Hindu to His Body

Dear pursuing presence,
dear body:
        you brought me
do not leave me
behind. When you leave all else,

my garrulous face, my alien mind,
when you muffle
and put away my pulse

to rise in the sap of trees
let me go with you and feel the weight
of honey-hives in my branching
and the burlap weave of weaver-birds
in my hair.

RAMAN DIED on Tuesday. Patsy and the children were to leave for Vermont the following Monday; I was to follow two weeks later. As the day approached, Patsy plunged into despair. Raman's death, like Hans's, left her unmoored. Again, the proximity of death seemed to draw her back into the gravitational field of the black hole. It was as if Raman's *disappearance* had been the result of an act of terror that had sucked him out of the world.

Lying in bed on Sunday morning, we talked.

"I feel as if I'm an island. No one in the world is close to me. Not you. Not my mother. I wish I had died instead of Raman. He had so much more to offer the world than I do."

When I tried to comfort her, she exploded.

"I've never felt so sad. I'm heartbroken. I don't feel like I have a home anymore. If I didn't have children, I think I'd commit suicide."

She had a brunch meeting downtown. Someone passing through town wanted to discuss a possible photo project. They were to meet at the Hyatt Hotel on Wacker Drive. She did what she could with make-up to disguise the puffiness around her eyes from weeping. Then, without saying a word to me, she left and drove downtown.

Several hours later, she returned. She was transfigured. Luminous with perception. I was working at my desk. She came into my study and spoke to me in a way she had not for months: full of urgent lucidity, needing to report what she had seen and felt, needing for me to listen.

A canny parker, she had found a place for the car on Lower Wacker Drive. Running parallel to the Chicago River as it snakes through the city, Wacker has two levels. The lower level provides access to loading docks for hotels and office buildings. She was able to park within a block of the Hyatt. Stairs ascended directly from Lower Wacker into the Hyatt lobby.

"The Hyatt was full of people visiting the city. It's a completely artificial environment. There's a buzz, a canned atmosphere, a strange quality of light. It's so secure and comfortable. A safe place. So familiar. It could be anywhere. At the same time, it's completely alien. I felt as if I was from another planet.

"After the meeting, I climbed back down the stairs to Lower Wacker. About halfway down I realized that because it was Sunday, there wasn't the usual hustle and bustle of trucks coming and going. It was deserted. I panicked. The car seemed impossibly far away. I felt so vulnerable. It was as if I was moving through the underside of a dead city. I felt unbearably isolated and exposed. If someone were to attack me, nobody would ever know."

As if traversing a sea of fire, she made it to the car, climbed in, and locked the doors. Trembling, she drove south on Lake Shore Drive. She exited at Thirty-ninth Street and drove to the Ida B. Wells public housing development to drop off some photos at the police station.

"It seemed like no distance at all between the Hyatt and Wells. With no traffic on a Sunday morning, it only took me a few minutes. Both are on Lake Shore Drive. They're about the same distance from the Lake. It was like pulling off the Drive and going to India. Wells is so dirty and rundown—a Third World shantytown. At the same time, the streets are full of life. People dressed up for church passing winos on the sidewalk. The young men out at their stations selling drugs. Children everywhere. A real place. But a place that no one at the Hyatt would ever know was there. The distance between the two places is *huge*—it's like different solar systems—but in fact they're so close. Almost no distance at all."

As Patsy talked, I was flooded by relief and love. Having left in despair, she had returned with a gift. She recovered something we knew but had for a time lost sight of: the demanding, necessary perspective that our private fates are embedded in larger patterns in which we are implicated and from which we suffer. She brought the world back into the conversation.

THIRTY-EIGHT

Vermont, too, is a world of borders. Cultivated areas are edged by dense woods. Everywhere one hears the sound of mowers and chain saws: it takes constant effort to maintain a clearing against the irrepressible vitality of the returning wild. Unattended meadows quickly revert to goldenrod, asters, Queen Anne's lace, and raspberry bushes— a rough, nonchalant sort of beauty. Rolls of hay, arrayed on freshly cut fields—gold against the green—look like pieces in a board game played by giants.

Wallace Stegner draws a contrast between the West, "fragile and unforgiving" of human violations, and Vermont. "Vermont," he writes, "is a rugged country with a violent climate, but it *heals*. Clear-cut it, and it goes patiently and inevitably back to raspberry bushes and browse, then to Christmas trees and dense stands of maple, ash, beech, birch, and poplar seedlings, and then, when one is not looking, to woods."

The thought pleases me. This place where Patsy comes to heal is forever restoring itself. Perhaps that is part of the reason she finds it so consoling. She sets out for Vermont each July with high hopes and expectations. She is eager to see her parents and to have a vacation: to *vacate* her life in Chicago for a while. Above all, she hungers for the place itself—to drink it in through her senses.

Our time in Vermont is shaped by routines and rituals, from the moment when Patsy slips into the pond, soft and velvety at first light, to the moment before we go to bed when we sit on the porch and look up at the night sky dense with stars. These rhythms carry her from day to day; they comfort and sustain her. They represent for her the possibility of *rest*, the possibility of *feeling better*. But there have also been moments each summer when this lovely, carefully constructed world wobbles on its axis, moments when, precisely because she is wrapped in the comforts of this healing place, the question of whether she will ever fully heal tears at her. This summer those questions don't lie in wait for her. She brought them with her. When I arrived in Vermont, I found her emotionally spent and reflective.

"I never thought in my wildest dreams that my life would be organized around these thoughts and fears and feelings," she said as we lay in bed one morning. "What I fear most is the depression. I can see now that the threat is *inside* as well as out in the world."

After all her efforts to remap the world in light of what she has come to know about violence, after all the moment-to-moment efforts at risk assessment, it's a stunning perception: The threat is also inside her as truly as if men with hard eyes and rough hands lurked there. An accidental knock on the head, a professional setback, the deaths of friends—at any moment a triggering event can plunge her out of her life and into the condition of feeling homeless, worthless, unmoored, utterly alone.

When that happens, it's as if she had been recaptured by the man who raped her. She ceases to be the subject of her own story and again becomes the powerless object in his story—a story that ends with her annihilation. To survive, to have her life, she must struggle against that narrative trajectory. This is, we now know, necessarily a lifelong struggle. For beneath her identity, beneath the bonds of love and affection that hold her in the world, is the terrible knowledge of herself reduced under a rapist's hands to "a prey of death." That knowledge is an unending vulnerability.

"Anyone who has been tortured remains tortured," wrote Jean Améry. In 1978, more than thirty years after Auschwitz, Améry killed himself. A decade later, more than forty years after Auschwitz, Primo Levi, who wrote of Améry with such sympathy and understanding and who responded to atrocity with such sustained narrative energy, committed suicide. Both suicides are mysteries. I don't claim to know why these men killed themselves. But we can't discount the possibility that, after years of struggling against it, they finally completed their tormentors' work by taking their own lives. Nor if another reason is given—illness, say, or professional problems—can we assume that this apparently precipitating circumstance was not akin to the accidental blow to the head that brings back with terrifying immediacy other blows intended to humiliate and destroy. How many victims of rape and kindred cruelties have killed themselves years or decades later? The question cannot be definitively answered, but it must be asked.

And what of those who never take their lives but never recover them either? (A former death camp inmate: "One can be alive after Sobibor without having survived Sobibor.")

"It's not that you've fallen into the black hole," Patsy observed one afternoon as we walked in the woods. "It's that you know it's there. You've looked into it."

We walked in silence for a while.

"Those aren't all dead people in the black hole. There are living people in there."

OUR RUNS and bike rides take us through varied terrain. Up and down hills. Along burbling brooks. Into the woods. On the mountain, we run under canopies of sugar maple and red maple, varieties of birch, beech, spruce, and ash. Ferns form a cool green carpet on the forest floor. Down on the flats, exposed to the sun, we run on the shoulder beside the highway. The carnage on the road is diverse: raccoon, skunk, frog, porcupine, chipmunk, rabbit, red squirrel; once we saw the carcass of a coyote.

Many eyes watch us pass. We negotiate safe passage with territorial dogs that rush at us from yards and front porches. The lovely liquid eyes of cows—Jerseys, Holsteins, Ayrshires, Charolais—fix on us with mild interest. Barn swallows on a telephone pole, agitated by our passing, take flight. Several times in the woods we have heard the improbably loud clatter of partridge wings taking to the air. I associate the sound with India, the only place I have ever hunted; it brings back the taste of *titar* curry. Once Patsy, running alone, was startled by a crashing noise in the woods and found herself face-to-face with an equally alarmed deer; each feared the other was a predator.

We run past clapboarded farmhouses with weathered shingles and sagging barns. Pickup trucks and tractors. Household vegetable gardens and flower gardens. Shacks and trailers dwarfed by the satellite dishes beside them. Simple dwellings with Adirondack chairs on the porch oriented toward a mountain view.

In recent years, many old farmhouses have been bought and rehabbed by young professionals and urban refugees. You can tell who lives there by the vehicles parked outside—the Saab or BMW or sport utility vehicle. There is also much new construction. Meadows are consumed by subdivisions. On exquisite plots of land, individual houses, neocolonial in style, in sharp contrast to the weathered, cobbled-together homesteads so particular to their place and inhabitants, look like they were ordered out of mail-order catalogs.

This year I notice many "For Sale" signs, each with the emblem of a particular realtor like a tribal totem. They hint at turbulence beneath the placid surface of the Vermont countryside. The signs no doubt reflect IBM layoffs in Burlington. They also represent many failed marriages, I suspect. One summer, as we pass, a couple is working together on the house; a year or two later, no one is in sight and there is a "For Sale" sign. The farmhouse is renovated; the marriage, I imagine, in disrepair.

It's possible in this land of ruins overgrown with green to take the long view. The old stone fences you come upon in the woods are reassuring. They support the hope that the subdivisions encroaching on meadow and farm are temporary arrangements that will be outlived by the land they disfigure.

I sit on the porch of the cottage and watch Josh. He is down in the meadow flying a vivid black-purple-yellow kite. Approaching his thirteenth birthday, he is suspended in that moment of adolescent flowering when boys sometimes seem more delicate than girls. I marvel at his poise; an odd word to use in describing a teenager, yet in his case it fits. There can't be much string left on the spool, for the kite has reached a great elevation. It animates the landscape like a circling hawk. This is the perfect activity for patient, precise, graceful Josh. A study in elegance at both ends of the string.

Vermont provides a space, a quality of light, in which I can see Patsy and the children more clearly. My greatest pleasure is simply to look at them, to watch them move through the world. Each knows my ardent, inquiring gaze. If they catch me looking on, they seek to deflect my eye. Betsy protests, "Come *on*, Dad." Josh jokingly puts his fingers over his face as if warding off paparazzi. And Patsy is forever turning away from me. Yet when they are not aware of me, and sometimes when they are, my eyes feast on them.

THIS SUMMER there are more hummingbirds darting through Dot's garden than I ever recall seeing in the past. The sight triggers an odd association. After my sophomore year in college, I was a member of a mountaineering expedition on Mount Logan in the Yukon Territory. At 19,850 feet, Logan is the second-highest mountain in North America—several hundred feet lower than Mount McKinley in Alaska. Far more remote than McKinley, it is located deep in the Saint Elias mountain range—a world from which the glaciers have not yet receded. It is also a world, during the summer months, of endless light; there are only a few dusky hours out of twenty-four. When we descended after a month on the mountain and were flown out by bush pilots, I was thrilled by the sight of green and then, as night fell, by the enveloping darkness.

A few years earlier, another group of climbers making a first ascent of a knife-edged ridge on the southern flank of Logan, had seen a hummingbird at 9,000 feet and had been moved to name the ridge Hummingbird Ridge. The hummingbird must have been caught in an updraft and carried to that remote world of rock and ice. The image of the grizzled climbers practicing their perilous art encountering the hummingbird so far from the nearest flower has stayed with me over the years as an emblem of the glories and dangers of opening your life to forces stronger than you are—air currents, passions, themes—that might carry you farther than you ever intended to go from home.

WHEN HOME is a mountain, you can see it from afar. This sharpens anticipation as you approach and regret as you depart. On the ferry, looking back at Mount Mansfield, Patsy released silent tears.

I wonder if her parents know how much they have given her during these hard years. It's been difficult for Dot and Lew to talk about the rape. I don't know how, from the perspective of their Vermont mountainside, they make sense of what their daughter has been going through. She can be exasperated by what she takes to be their lack of comprehension. Yet it's hard to imagine what this period would have been like without their love and generosity—represented above all by the porch of the cottage, the place in the world where Patsy feels most deeply at home.

What does she feel as we drive toward Chicago? Does she feel she is returning to an alien, hostile place? She has sometimes said that the children and I have a home there but she doesn't. This confuses and pains me. Yet I recognize the truth in her words. And the loss. Améry's words resonate in my mind: "Whoever has succumbed to torture can no longer feel at home in the world."

T H I R T Y · N I N E

THE SEASONS have turned and turned. Five years have passed. And still we struggle for perspective. Again and again, we circle back to the question, "What happened?" Are we any closer to an answer now than we were in the moments after the assault when Patsy, with her eyes swollen shut, spoke with stunned lucidity of being dragged to the edge of the black hole into which victims of terror are disappeared? Something very large happened that day. Within a few minutes, Patsy experienced death at cruel hands and rebirth into the shining world. Absolute darkness followed by radiant light. Terror followed by rapture. Some experiences can't be absorbed all at once; you must spend your life working to make them yours. Shipwrecked in the midst of everyday life, she has struggled to accommodate the knowledge and questions inflicted on her by a violent man. This has been a *narrative* effort—in dreams, in photographs, in conversation. Husband, listener, writer, I have been the narrative companion: I have accompanied her. In so doing, I have assumed a responsibility not named in my wedding vows.

We were married sixteen years ago under a quaking birch in the garden in front of Patsy's parents' house. A judge officiated. The ceremony was brief. We didn't, in the fashion of the times, compose our wedding vows, but I did presume to edit the language prescribed in the

Book of Common Prayer by excising all references to God. Those deletions made the words that remained—in prosperity and in adversity, in sickness and in health—seem all the more demanding. The vows by which we entered into marriage were so realistic; they embraced so much of life's prospects and chance. Yet they didn't, at least not explicitly, include the responsibility of being entrusted with one another's stories. Now it seems that is the essence of the promises we exchanged.

THE FIFTH anniversary of the assault. A wet, misty day. At noon we went out to the attack site so Patsy could take some photographs. She was wearing a green coat and blue jeans. I sat in the car, working on this manuscript, looking up every so often to check on her. At one point, I looked up and didn't see her. After a few anxious moments, I located her standing still with her camera to her eye in the middle of the small grove of trees where the rapist had dragged her. I had mistaken her for a tree.

"It's the longest day of the year," Patsy said that night as we got ready for bed. "All day I felt that at any moment I might cry, but I didn't."

The next day she was at the kitchen sink. She was washing basil she had just picked.

"I really like this time of the year. I like the weather. I like the food."

"Do you realize," I asked, "what you just said?"

I LOVE waking to find her beside me in early morning light. Her long, strong limbs. The curve of her hip as she lies on her side with her back to me. (Is there any line in nature more beautiful?) Her dear banged-up feet. Her sun-fragrant skin. Her stubborn integrity. Beneath all her doubts and fears, there is something—preserved perhaps by her habits of resistance (not least, to me)—that is wonderfully alive and unspoiled.

I hold her close in silence. I stroke her with my hand. Entering her, I enter the world. How many times have I drunk at this spring? Returning again and again, my thirst is as keen as ever. This sensation of always being at the verge of loveliness—will I take it to the grave? We've traveled so far together. Yet the more deeply known, the more mysterious she has become. She takes me into her body with welcoming hospitality. She doesn't recoil; there is no hint of trespass. She is, I know, still "resting," and I am careful. Embracing her, moving within her, I listen deeply with my body. The passion that has sometimes bewildered us and brought us grief is a blessing upon us now: a broad current, carrying us across the years of our braided fate, to deliver us to these moments when our bodies complete the rhyme that marriage promises.

Sunlight floods the room and flows over our bodies. It's one of those golden September days when one recalls that the world is, among other things, utterly beautiful. The sort of day when a woman, finding herself with an hour before picking up her children at school, might go out for a run on the lakefront. I see her stepping out into the world. Like a cat released into the backyard, she pauses and drinks in the day. Then she begins to run, slowly at first, for the mile or so it takes to reach the Lake. Once on the lakefront, her pace quickens. I see her strong stride and erect carriage. Her economy of effort. Her dignity and grace. At the edge of the city, with the traffic speeding by on Lake Shore Drive, she is at once immersed in her body and open to the world, as if deep in the woods or high on a mountain. After a few miles, she settles into a rhythm; she locates the point at which rest and effort are one. I see a strong woman, exercising her freedom, on common ground. The day beckons. She runs among trees. Beneath a sheltering canopy of branches. Hidden in the radiant green, a man waits. In hate-blinded hands, darkness waits.